UNFINISHED BUSINESS

ALWAYS A GIFT • NEVER FOR SALE
Little Free Library
Wind Gap, PA
Charter #151205
Read it • Love it • Share it!!

Unfinished Business

Copyright © 2024 by Sam Carrodo and Ed Rabinowitz

All rights reserved under the Pan-American and International Copyright Conventions. This book may not be reproduced in whole or in part, except for brief quotations embodied in critical articles or reviews, in any form or by any means, electronic or mechanical, including photocopying, recording, or by any information storage and retrieval system now known or hereinafter invented, without written permission of the publisher.

ISBN Paperback: 978-1-963271-37-9
ISBN Ebook 978-1-963271-38-6

ARMINLEAR

Published by Armin Lear Press, Inc.
215 W Riverside Drive, #4362
Estes Park, CO 80517

■ADVANCED READER COPY

SAM CARRODO AND ED RABINOWITZ

ARMINLEAR

For Ellen, who is always the sunshine in my life.

To my wife, Christina, my children Sammy, Tony, Nicholas and Devan; and to my coaches and players who made this dream a reality.

PROLOGUE

Sam Carrodo held the microphone gently but securely in his right hand. He looked out across the Spartan Center gymnasium at the faces of the fans, parents and members of the media who had just witnessed history.

It was Sunday, April 1, 2007, but there was no fooling around on this day. The Northampton Community College women's softball team, the Spartans, had just defeated Montgomery College of Rockville, Maryland, 10-0. That win, the Spartans ninety-third in a row, came on a cold and damp spring afternoon with dozens of spectators lining the foul lines and established a new national collegiate record for consecutive games won.

Sam, the Spartan's head coach, sat at a table alongside the team's co-captains, Roxanne Schisler and Jenna Turner, the remaining players and coaches—including several players from prior year's teams—standing behind them, and attempted to take in the magnitude of what the school's softball program had just accomplished.

It was difficult to fathom, and for a rare moment he found himself lost for words.

Members of the press broke the ice with questions for the coach and his players, and then Sam introduced everyone associated with the program, from athletic director Bill Bearse to the players and coaches. All the while, he was formulating the right words for an official statement—a key sound bite that the media could run with; that might be heard on the evening's ten o'clock news or read in the next day's newspapers.

And they had to be the right words, for they would forever be linked with the historic occasion. Maybe not on the same scale as, "One small step for man, one giant leap for mankind," but something on that order.

Finally, he knew what he wanted to say. He took a deep breath.

"This started on a warm and sunny day in Myrtle Beach, South Carolina, and culminated on a cold and rainy day at Northampton Community College," Sam said. "But I can't think of any place I'd rather be right now than here."

Almost as soon as the words had left his lips, Sam knew he was wrong, technically speaking, of course. Winning streaks—at least in terms of counting up all the wins—start with winning that first game. That was certainly true of the 93 consecutive games the NCC Spartans had won over two-and-one-half seasons. But the genesis of that streak, the event or events that propelled the team on such an historic run, actually happened months before the first pitch in that first winning game was thrown.

Sam knew it. It was too late to take back his words, but he knew he had misspoken.

And in the aftermath of the press conference—after all the photographs were taken and the interviews were given, after cutting and serving the cake that formed the team's current record of 93-0, and after sharing warm embraces and a few tears of joy with his family, players and coaching staff—after all the lights in the gymnasium were turned off and he sat alone in his office, Sam thought back to that painful day at Lehigh Carbon Community College almost three years ago.

That was where the streak had truly begun.

ONE

April 30, 2004

It was a majestic day. The sun floated in a cloudless sky like a beach ball in a pool. The grass that carpeted the field at Lehigh-Carbon Community College (LCCC) smelled crisp and clean, and the infield dirt made that warm, crunching sound as players' cleats pierced the soft surface. It was the kind of day that prompted Ernie Banks, the Chicago Cubs' Hall of Fame baseball star, to say, "Let's play two."

The challenge for the Northampton Community College women's softball team that day was a much simpler one. The Spartans of NCC didn't have to play two games; they only had to beat LCCC once to advance to the Eastern Pennsylvania Collegiate Conference (EPCC) championship game. It wasn't a daunting task, considering the Spartans had won both ends of a doubleheader, 7-2 and 7-3, just one week earlier.

The Spartans also had ample motivation. In the week leading up to the game, the LCCC coach had repeatedly bad-mouthed the team and its head coach, Sam Carrodo, in the local newspapers. There were also abusive phone calls placed to the NCC girls. By game day, the Spartans didn't just want to win, they wanted to embarrass LCCC. Not because of the players on that team, but because of the coach, who most certainly was responsible for pouring fuel on the fire.

Those antics continued during the game, as the LCCC coach verbally taunted and abused the NCC players. Vulgar references were not uncommon.

But that was not Sam Carrodo's game.

Sam Carrodo took over the womens' softball head coaching position at NCC in 1998. He was a local product, born and bred in eastern Pennsylvania's Lehigh Valley. He attended Bethlehem Catholic High School and later was an assistant coach on the varsity football team and head coach of the junior varsity softball team. Coach Sam, as his players called him, had already won a state title with the Spartans the previous year, his first ever as a head coach, and had his players primed to repeat.

But they would win, or lose, the championship his way.

"I will not allow a team of mine to play those childish games," Sam told his players in the days leading up to the confrontation with LCCC. "Win or lose, we do it with class and fair play. I will not embarrass Northampton Community College, or blemish this game that we love so much by acting in a similar fashion."

Sam, of course, was far from perfect. He had his flaws, and he knew them well. He worried incessantly. He worried before a game. He worried during a game. He worried if his team had a 10-0 lead in the fifth inning; it was just his style.

Sam's obsession with guiding his team to a championship also impacted his health. A large man—Sam stood 5-foot10 and tipped the scales at 386-pounds—he had high blood pressure, sleep apnea, and was on heart medication.

But Coach Sam never yelled. No one on his coaching staff ever yelled. If a player made an error or a mistake in judgment on the field, Sam would simply take the player aside between innings and talk calmly about how the play should have been handled. In return, his players often looked at him as a father figure, and even dubbed him "the Godfather." Appropriately, his cell phone played the theme from the box office hit whenever he received a call.

So, it wasn't surprising that he would not allow his players to submit to the distractions surrounding the game.

Besides, Sam wasn't worried. Well, maybe just a little. After all, this was still Sam Carrodo. But he reasoned that the Spartans should be able to get past LCCC, and would then have been in position to play Penn State-Berks for the championship. Earlier in the season, NCC split a doubleheader with Berks, losing 2-1 before rebounding in the second game 25-2. Sam and his players were confident they'd get past Berks and move on to the state tournament.

But they weren't looking past anybody, and the early innings showed as much.

Heading into the fifth inning, everything was going according to plan. Missy Bachert, one of NCC's power-hitting outfielders, led off the second inning with a solo home run. In the fourth inning, NCC pitcher Jenn Davis walked, and Bachert hit her second home run of the game for a 3-0 lead. A two-run single by NCC second baseman Sheena Recker later that same inning helped build a 5-0 lead.

Meanwhile, Jenn was pitching a no hitter, and Sam kept reminding the girls to stay focused.

Then came the fateful fifth inning.

With one out and a runner on second base, an LCCC batter lifted a high pop up in between the pitcher's mound and second base. The ball was hit so high it seemed to hang in mid air, suspended in time. And when it moved, it seemed to do so in slow motion. When it came down, however, no one was there to catch it.

After the game, Cortnei Comstock, one of NCC's three captains, would say, "I've never in my entire life, maybe in t-ball, seen a ball that easy to catch fall untouched in the infield. It was so silent. We saw the ball go up, watched it come back down, and nobody moved."

What should have been the second out turned into a one-out, first-and-third situation. And when the next batter grounded into a fielder's choice, it should have been the final out of the inning. Instead, the runner on third scored, making the score 5-1, and LCCC was still batting.

Sam called time and went out to the pitcher's mound to talk to the team. Jenn, the team's pitcher, told her coach that he should take her out. Sam told the team's number one pitcher, Melissa Pirre, to warm up, but before he could get her into the game, the Spartans continued to implode. As Sam paced in the dugout, imploring Pirre to warm up faster, everything began to unravel.

An error by shortstop Michelle Panik, a walk, a single, another walk, another error at shortstop and an error in right field completed the carnage. Seven runs, all unearned, had crossed the plate before Pirre came on to get the final out of the inning. A 5-0 lead was now a 7-5 deficit, despite the fact that not one ball was hit hard enough to tear through a wet paper bag. The Spartans were stunned.

It was now the top of the sixth inning. Sam and his assistant coaches told the girls to remember that the team still had two at-bats left.

"If we could score five runs on them so far, we could certainly score some more," the coach reasoned.

But his words fell on deaf ears. The girls had that deep, faraway look in their eyes, and Sam couldn't have reached them if he had a ten-foot pole.

It was the first time that year that the girls couldn't get their heads back in the game. The Spartans had been down before in games, but Sam and his coaches would have a little motivational talk with the girls, and they would bounce back. This time, they just couldn't turn it back on. They would come to bat and swing so hard, trying to hit the ball as far as they could. But they were trying *too* hard, and would just pop the ball up.

The taunting continued, far stronger than earlier in the game, and now—trailing for the first time in the game—the Spartans didn't handle it well.

"In the beginning of the game we handled it, we laughed at them, and we taunted back," Cortnei would later recall. "When they taunted us late in the game, instead of getting even, we got angry. Every person tried to be the big hero, hit the big home run. Instead of one team we became nine separate players."

Players on the bench began to separate themselves, believing that they could do better, and wanting to know why they weren't in the game. In months to come, some of those players who returned for the 2005 season would confirm that they were rooting for some of the starters to fail. The frictions that Sam knew were always an undercurrent with his team were rising to the surface and dividing them. They became their own greatest opponents.

LCCC scored two more runs in the sixth inning and won the game 9-5. They celebrated while the Spartans mourned. And now the NCC players had to walk the line and congratulate their players and coaches.

"It was probably the hardest hand-slapping I've ever encountered," Cortnei acknowledged. "All I wanted to do was get my stuff and walk away from the game."

It was easy to congratulate the players; the other coaches were another story. But Sam reminded the girls that they were representing NCC, so they bit their tongues, offered congratulations, and left it at that.

Unfortunately, the LCCC coach wasn't as professional. She approached one of NCC's players, tri-captain Colleen McGouldrick, and suggested that since the girl couldn't win with her current team, she might want to transfer to LCCC and join them as a coach. Colleen's response was predictable, and she verbally lit into the coach. Hearing the commotion, Colleen's father came over, and when told why his daughter was so angry, he too went off on the coach.

But Sam would later acknowledge that the day was not about LCCC, or its coach, or its players. It was about the Northampton Community College Spartans, and the fact that they caved in at such an inopportune time.

"Why did we collapse?" the coach would ask himself many times in the hours and days following the game. "Why weren't we able to pick ourselves up and respond to adversity?"

There were almost as many opinions as there were players on the team. Some players pointed to the errors made by shortstop Michelle Panik as fueling LCCC's rally. Some blamed pitcher Jenn Davis for not catching the infield pop up that started the unraveling. Others said the friction on the team was its eventual undoing.

"Off the field, there were a lot of problems, a lot of drama," recalled Cortnei. "On the field, it was amazing how all of us could come together and play as a team. You would never have known that one girl hates another for having their spot. But I think that's what made it harder to pull things back together, because suddenly everyone only wanted to do well for themselves."

Sam had his own opinion. He knew his team was composed of a fantastic bunch of girls, but they were always bickering. There were girls on the team that if they got down or ticked off, they were done. The coach would have to look to somebody else to pick up the rest of the team. Usually, NCC was so far ahead that if the girls got their heads in the tank it wasn't a big deal. But in this game, they just weren't able to survive that let down.

Nevertheless, the girls were hurting following the loss.

"After the game my mom and relatives came up to me and said 'Good game,' but I just stood there," co-captain Carissa

Molchan recalled. "I couldn't say thank you, because I knew it wasn't a good game. We were horrible. You can't pinpoint it to one person, because there was no one person to blame. There was just one play that started a huge cascade of errors."

Many of the girls came to Sam and apologized for letting him down. They felt they had disappointed him and the other coaches which, of course, wasn't the case. NCC's team record that season was 28-4, certainly nothing to be disappointed about. The girls played their hearts out; it was just one bad inning. But their biggest concern was that they let the coaches down.

The coaches, in turn, were hurting for the girls, because they knew that had they won that game, the next step was the state tournament. In the days and weeks to come, Sam and his brother Michael, an assistant coach on the team, would sit outside in the evening and talk about that game.

The loss was harder for some players, particularly those who would not be returning to NCC the following year. For two of the team's three captains, Cortnei and Carissa, the haunting memories would not quickly dissipate.

"I don't think I will ever accept that loss," Cortnei would later announce. "That was the last game that I've played."

Carissa played the next year at Penn State-Berks, but admits that it wasn't the same. Her heart just wasn't in it.

The drive back to the college following the game was unbearable. Driving into the parking lot, dropping the girls off, and taking the equipment in for the last time was one of the hardest things Sam ever had to do. He saw the school's athletic director, Bill Bearse, and the disappointment in his heart, to have to tell him that the team lost . . . that was really tough.

The following week, the Pennsylvania Collegiate Athletic Association state championship game was held at LCCC. Sam took the girls to the game to see what they could have been playing for. For the girls who would be returning, being there seemed to fill their hearts with more motivation. Sam felt at the time that it would be a learning experience for them. Only time would tell.

For now, however, there was only pain and disappointment.

* * * *

With the end of every softball season comes the ritual of uniform collection. Most of the time the girls return their uniforms to a gym attendant; occasionally someone will bring their uniform directly to Sam.

One of the girls, a two-year member of the team who was graduating that spring, gave her uniform to Cortnei. Inspecting the uniform before turning it in, she found a letter stuffed into one of the pockets. She read it.

The letter was addressed to Sam, and its contents were not complementary.

Cortnei shared the letter with Missy, Michelle and Jenn. At first they all agreed not to show it to their coach, knowing it would hurt his feelings. Then, fearing that he might somehow learn about the letter and be hurt even more by their secrecy, they decided to show it to him.

The girls went to Sam's home and let his wife, Chris, read it first. As she read, she began to cry. When she finished, she handed it to her husband.

The letter was from one of the players. It accused Sam of maintaining a double standard on the team, and blamed him for the team coming up short in its quest for a state championship. In part, it stated:

> *"It was disgusting how you handled this team; there was no team chemistry at all because of you. You let so many girls walk all over you while having the girls, who played by every rule you set down, sit on the bench. What kind of coach does that? What kind of coach sits a bunch of girls who are good enough to play and have done nothing wrong throughout the whole season? You did that coach. You made girls wish that the season would be over quickly . . . You had a player on the team that almost all of the other players disliked. Yet you couldn't see it. Is it the rest of the team that is wrong? No, you were so whipped by this girl that you turned your head from the rest of the team, and for that we lost the championship. This season felt like a waste of my time and the rest of the team's time because of your poor judgment."*

The words, of course, hurt deeply. But more than anger, Sam—a huge man and equally sensitive individual—was overcome with disappointment, though he admitted he wasn't completely surprised. That season, the girl's father had been on him from the beginning.

The season's first game was barely five minutes old when the player's father came up to Sam and grabbed him by the wrist, demanding, "Just look me in the face and tell me the truth. Are you going to play my kid or not?"

The coach told him that it was only the first game of the season. "Of course she's going to play."

He responded with, "Well, if she's not good enough, just tell me."

Sam is an honest man, but he was not going to look at a father and tell him that his daughter is not good enough to play. He explained that she would play every other game like she did the previous year.

"We tell girls at the beginning of the season, just because you make the team doesn't mean you're going to get into every single game," Sam explained. "We let them know that up front, and they have the option to walk if they don't want to be here. This girl was a nice kid. But her bat was not there, she didn't have foot speed, and she didn't have a strong arm. We could have cut her the first year; there was no reason to keep her on the team. But we didn't. And we kept her on the team the second year as well."

The reaction by the girl's father was particularly disheartening to Sam because of a favor the coach had performed earlier in the year. The father wanted to get his older daughter into a particular four-year college, and asked if Sam would put in a good word. He had never seen his older daughter play, but Sam called the softball coach at the school and said, "You've got a helluva kid here," and she got $7,000 to go to that school.

The letter was a strange way to repay a favor.

After Sam's wife Chris had read the letter, she told her husband, "If they only knew how much time you put into all of this, and how little you get paid for your time. You do it all for them, and they are too selfish to understand."

The letter concluded with these comments:

> *"During this whole season you made me feel like I was not good enough to play. Well, I just thought you should know that wherever I go I am going to try out for the team and not give up. And I hope to God that the next coach I have will be nothing like you were this season."*

The girl went on to a four-year college. Periodically, Sam would check the softball team's box scores online. He noticed that one game she went 0-3 with three strikeouts. The next game she didn't play. The next game she went 0-4 at bat, and the next game she didn't play. Her new coach was playing her every other game, just as Sam had done. It became even clearer to him that it was a case of a father thinking his daughter is better than she is.

Sam never responded to the letter, and didn't speak with her after the last game against LCCC. He didn't respond for the same reasons he wouldn't allow his players to respond to the taunts of the LCCC coach and players—because he refused to sink to that level. He also knew that if he had responded, it would have been admitting he did something wrong. And Sam did nothing wrong.

Sam and his coaches also had the loss to LCCC hanging over their heads, and they were starting to think about rebuilding for the following year. They didn't need anything to drag them back down into the murk.

Still, there was a lot that the coach took with him from the loss.

"One thing I did learn from the LCCC game is that at the end of the fourth inning, I look at my pitcher, I watch that pitcher, and if she shows any kind of fatigue I get my other pitcher ready to go," Sam explained. "I won't make that mistake again. Just like when I coached Little League one year, in an all-star game, and it was a single elimination at that time. And we're beating the tar out of this team, beating them 10-0 in the second inning. So just like I do now, there's a passed ball and we have a girl at third base, I say, 'Stay here . . . we have enough runs, we're going to just relax. No stealing, no bunting, no nothing.' Then I get beat 12-10. That doesn't happen anymore. If I see somebody come back two or three runs, I turn the guns back on. Go ahead, till we get more of a lead. I don't like to embarrass people, but I'm not going to take a chance on losing."

* * * *

Immediately after LCCC won the 2004 PCCA championship there was an article in one of the local daily newspapers. The LCCC coach was going on and on, spewing out boastful clichés about how hungry the team was and how the girls knew what they had to do to win. It made Sam sick, but it also made him angry.

He clipped the article from the newspaper and posted it in his office. Underneath the article he taped a small index card with a clear message written in large, black letters.

GOAL FOR 2005:
NEVER LET THIS HAPPEN AGAIN.

And he vowed to put together a team that would not be defeated by LCCC.

TWO

The recruiting challenges faced by a two-year community college are many. First, you battle the stigma faced by many community colleges, that of being the orphaned child. There are some high school softball coaches who will not even let you near their players.

"She's not playing for you," the coach will say. "She's going to such and such college, and she doesn't want to talk to you."

That's not unusual to hear. In addition, NCC offers academic scholarships, but not athletic scholarships. Some coaches can come in and offer $10,000 toward tuition without batting an eye. Parents have stars in their eyes, but some of them reach too high.

NCC simply offers girls a good education and a place to play softball. And in Sam Carrodo's eyes, that's a pretty good thing.

When Sam and his assistant coaches recruit and talk about the softball program, the first thing they talk about is the school, because they believe that academics come first. And Sam believes the people around NCC are fantastic. The teachers bend over backwards to help these kids; they will not let them fail. That doesn't mean they let them slide; they work with them to help them bring up their grades, because they know the importance of academics. NCC is an academic institution, not an athletic institution, so that's what Sam puts forth first.

Sam knew he had a good core of six players returning: Jenn Davis, Missy Bachert, Theresa Meluskey, Chrysa Wassel, Gina Renaldi and Crystal Hopping. That wasn't a bad way to start.

Jenn Davis could play any position you wanted her to play, she was that good. For NCC, she mostly pitched and played third base. She's also a California girl, and her approach to, and attitude about, the game rubbed people the wrong way during her first season with the team.

In California, girls practice softball six hours a day. Jenn was used to taking batting practice for two hours by herself, and having 200 ground balls hit to her every day. She would take a round at third base, jump over to shortstop and take a round, jump over to second base for a round, and then hop back to third and repeat the cycle.

On the East Coast, girls are used to standing at one position and taking a round of ground balls. Then they wait while coaches work around the infield before coming back to them. But Jenn would work at such a high level that she would jump in front of the other girls to take ground balls. Many of the girls felt she was showing off, but she really just wanted to make herself that much better.

Jenn was also very vocal. She would say, "I want to hear you scream for the team. If we're out there playing and you're on the bench, you scream for us. If we're on the bench, we'll scream for you."

But not everyone can be a cheerleader on the bench. It doesn't mean they're not proud to be part of the team, or that they lack a passion for the game. It's just not in them to be demonstrative in that manner. And that's where conflicts arose.

Chrysa Wassel was not a cheerleader; she didn't yell or scream. Most of the time, Chrysa wore a stone face, and you couldn't tell if she was happy or sad. But Chrysa was so intense—a junkyard dog, is the way Sam described her—that people used to think she was pissed off every minute of the day. She didn't say a lot, but when she got to the point where she'd had enough, she didn't keep it in.

On the team's trip down to Myrtle Beach for a spring tournament prior to the start of the 2004 season, Jenn and Chrysa had a confrontation in the dugout. The two of them were like oil and water. Sam knew there was so much in Jenn as an athlete and a leader, but she wasn't bringing those qualities out in a constructive manner. At one point, Chrysa threatened to walk off the team, and Sam and his coaches had to chase her down and talk her into staying.

In the past, Sam had not hesitated to cut a player who may have been an excellent athlete, but whose personality was a detriment to the chemistry on the team. But some kids have that burning passion for the game, and that was the case with both Jenn and Chrysa. There was no way he could get rid of either of them, so he took a chance.

"With some kids you see that passion just radiate out of them, and some who are great athletes don't have that passion," the coach explained. "Chrysa had that burning passion for the game, so there was no way I could get rid of her."

As Sam began to assemble the 2005 version of the NCC Spartans, Jenn came to practices wanting to be a team captain in the worst way. And with that desire came a major change in her approach to the game, and to her teammates. She took on a coach's style and personality. During her first year on the team, when she would try to talk to people it would be "in your face" yelling and screaming, and the other girls just backed away from that. But now she understood how to take her passion and motivate the other girls in an appropriate manner.

Sam made Jenn a co-captain, and the other girls, seeing how she had changed, were all for it. And Chrysa and Jenn got along great in 2005. Jenn just had to recognize that there had to be a compromise, and the rest of the team had to understand her situation and background a little more.

With that hopeful beginning, Sam began a war against negativity. He sat with the coaches and told them there would be some changes. One of the biggest changes was that there will be no negative talk whatsoever. The coaches in turn told each girl that there will be no negative talk. They sat them down and told the players that if they heard any kind of negative talk, the girls would run the steps in the gymnasium stands for fifteen minutes. Sam also told the coaches that if they had anything negative to say, they would be docked pay. And if they didn't like those arrangements, then they did not have to remain part of the team.

"Sometimes, building team chemistry and blending person-alities is like making mashed potatoes," Sam would explain. "You have to keep whipping that stuff until the lumps come out."

He was determined to eliminate any and all lumps.

Missy Bachert was the team's other co-captain for the 2005 season. In 2004, Missy played rightfield. But in 2005 she lost twenty pounds and moved a lot quicker, so Sam moved her to centerfield.

What Missy *didn't* lose was her power. When she hit the ball it jumped; it literally exploded off her bat. When she swung, by the time the bat reached her shoulder on the follow through, the ball was already in left-center field. That's how hard she hit the ball. Missy also liked hitting high pitches. Normally, a player's hands come through the hitting zone at their waist, but Missy's came through around chest level. She just would just catch the ball and drive it. And by extending her arms, she could hit the ball out of any part of the field.

Sam recalled warming up for a road game at Penn State, and the men's baseball team was practicing on a field nearby.

"We were soft-tossing to Missy, and there was a tree line about three-hundred feet out from home plate," the coach said. "She hit about seven balls into the trees. The baseball team stopped practicing and came over to watch. They started yelling, 'Do it again,' every time she'd hit one into the trees. And when she finished, they applauded.

"Now, keep in mind that this was the fourteenth game of the season, so the softballs she's hitting in practice are really soft, like marshmallows being hit," the coach clarified. "With soft-toss you have to generate your own power, and Missy was still drilling shots three-hundred feet. I had to tell her to stop because we were running out of balls."

She also had a cannon for an arm, and some of the assistant coaches would back away from her throws during practice.

Missy was also the team mom. She watched out for everybody, and she tried to be everybody's friend at the same time. That's hard, because in an altercation someone is usually right and someone is wrong. You can be friends with both people, but you have to understand that one of your friends might be wrong. For Missy, that was difficult to understand. She always wanted everyone to get along.

Gina Renaldi could play both infield and outfield, but she mostly played the outfield for the Spartans. The best way to describe Gina is that she's just a sweet person, inside and out. Sam didn't know if he'd ever seen her angry. She always had a smile on her face. It was her nature to calm people, to get them laughing. And that, the coach noted, came from her parents. She did a lot for the team without even knowing it.

Gina came out for the team in 2004 a little late, but Sam said, "Okay, we'll give you a week and see what you can do." That threw her. For the first two or three days she was just a bundle of nerves. She was scared; you could see it in her eyes and on her face. But the coaching staff kept working with her, and as she became more comfortable her play improved tremendously. The way Sam saw it was, she wouldn't allow him to cut her because she became valuable to the team. He knew she wouldn't be a starter for the team in 2004, but she'd get a lot of experience and build on that for the following season.

Gina came back for the 2005 season and it was clear she had worked her tail off during the off-season, and was ready to be one of the starters. Her hitting and throwing improved, but her personality never changed. Sam still thought of her as one of the most lovable girls you'd ever come across.

Interestingly, Gina and Chrysa, who had never known each other before joining the team, became inseparable during the 2004 season. Their personalities are at opposite ends of the spectrum, but they believe that's the reason they get along so well.

"Gina's prissy . . . a lot more prissy than I am," Chrysa would say.

"I'm peppy," Gina corrected. "I'm always smiling, and I never get pissed about anything. Chrysa's very stubborn. But we've always had each other's back, and we'd do anything for each other."

Needless to say, they developed a unique relationship.

Crystal Hopping was the team's catcher, but everyone called her Hoppy. She was also one incredibly tough young lady.

Two weeks prior to the end of the 2004 season, she took a foul tip to her left shoulder—her non-throwing arm—and suffered a slight separation. She was in bad pain, but continued to play. Then, before the playoff game against LCCC, she asked to take batting practice.

"Absolutely not," Sam told her. "I don't want you anywhere near the batting cage."

"Coach, one swing is all I want," Hoppy pleaded.

The coach relented. "Okay, but you're not going to swing. Let's just see if you can bunt."

So she attempted to bunt, and the ball came off the bat and hit her right in the face, breaking her nose.

"That's it," Sam told her, "get off the field."

He was prepared to have one of the other girls catch, but Hoppy wouldn't hear of it.

"That's my position," she said. "I'm playing back there."

And she did. She rarely missed a game. Even when Sam had two other catchers, Hoppy was the one he would count on.

Hoppy was fearless; she would step in front of anything. Some big kids would come racing down the line toward home and she would step in front to block the plate. She might get knocked over, but she never dropped the ball. At the same time, she was an umpire's favorite catcher. She would have a smile on her face the whole game, and the umpire would, too.

Before coming to NCC, Hoppy had never called pitches in a game. But by working with the coaches and putting in the time and effort she learned how to call pitches, how to control and work with the pitchers, and developed into a very good player. She didn't have a lot of self-confidence, but she was internally driven and always felt she could do better.

Theresa "Toot" Meluskey played the infield for the Spartans, mostly first base. Her course of study at the college was Fine Arts, but it should have been Political Science. Toot was capable of debating and discussing any topic imaginable, and whenever a problem arose, she would be the mediator. Toot Kissinger – after former United States Secretary of State Henry Kissinger – is how her teammates often referred to her.

One day, Cortnei Comstock had been in a hitting slump. So before she went up to bat, Sam went over to her and told her a funny – and untrue – story about one of the team's assistant coaches. She cracked up, it helped her relax and stop thinking about the slump, and she started hitting again. Ever since then, Cortnei and some of the other girls became fascinated with little people. So when the team was down in Myrtle Beach last spring for a tournament, a group of the girls went out to play miniature golf. One of the girls was Toot. They were at the tenth hole, and they saw a male midget at the third hole. A large bridge stood between the two holds, so the girls all sprinted across the bridge to watch the little person golf. He saw the girls staring and starting chasing them, swinging his golf club at them and screaming, "Why are you staring at me? There's no reason to stare." And the girls took off with him running after them.

All of a sudden, Toot stopped running and started talking to him, and the rest of the girls started walking away. Then Toot rejoined her teammates and announced that everything was okay. Later on, the little person came up to the girls and apologized for going off on them. That's Toot, she just talks to you, calms you down and negotiates the situation.

Sam believed that the key with Toot was that she had a huge heart, and an incredibly soothing voice. Not a regular voice; almost like a Snow White voice. She would talk with her coach when he was driving her to or from practices and she would say, "Coach, don't worry, things are going to be fine." She had a very laid back, calm interior, and seemed to be able to handle any situation there was. Sam often said to her, "You're going to make such a great mother one of these days," because she had so much inside her.

When the team was down in Myrtle Beach for a tournament last season, Toot was the one who would come to Sam and try to get the girls' curfews extended. She would say, "Coach, I really don't think this is right. We're on spring break. I think we should have more time outside to relax." She just had a way about her.

Of course, Sam ended up extending curfew by an hour.

Toot was a good athlete, but she was also a naturally beautiful girl. She needed no makeup, her hair could be messy, and she was still beautiful. She had "it," whatever it is, and everybody saw that.

So, despite ending the last season on a bad note, Sam's confidence level for the coming year was very high because he figured all six of the girls would be starters. They already knew the system, and they were comfortable with it. He was that much ahead of the game. Now he just had to build a team around them.

THREE

Recruiting is a long, and sometimes frustrating, process, particularly for a two-year college. Word travels about a player through word of mouth, sometimes from former players.

"Coach, there's a girl on a particular team, you've got to go see her," is the familiar refrain. "I don't think she's decided on a college yet."

Sam Carrodo was well acquainted with the process. As word would come in, he would schedule time with one or two of his assistant coaches and go watch the girl play. But often it was the same story. Sam would tell the girl that he was from NCC, and immediately her nose would go up in the air and she would announce that she plans to go elsewhere. The tendency was to look down on a two-year college.

Sam always took it in stride. His well-practiced response was, "I hope everything goes well for you. But if it doesn't work out, our door is always open."

But it gets tough facing that every year. And what happens is, over time, Sam learned not to count on anything until he saw the girl with a glove on her hand, walking onto the field during spring semester. In the fall, a girl may say that she wants to play, but all of a sudden, either for academic reasons or because she's homesick, she's gone. So when girls did agree to play, Sam and his assistant coaches would try to make them feel as comfortable at NCC as possible.

The trips to see prospects play aside, Sam usually began the recruiting process by sending out query letters to high school coaches, asking if they have any players who might want to come play for NCC. Included was information about NCC's academic and softball programs. If the coaches send back a list of players, Sam responded with personalized letters to those girls along with a Candidates Interest Form so they could provide information about themselves and the position they preferred to play. Then he'd go talk to them and watch them play.

And make no mistake about it, Sam always knew what he was looking for.

"Personally, I want girls who are a little hard-nosed; girls who won't accept second place for anything," Sam once told a local newspaper reporter. "You can kind of see that in their demeanor, in the way they play the game. But, I also want them to be good kids. I don't want anyone bringing the team down with their attitude. I've already cut girls who were great athletes but their attitudes were terrible. For me, personality is huge."

The first girl Sam went to see that spring was Nikki Jenson, of Nazareth Area High School. Jenson was definitely one of the top three pitchers in the Lehigh Valley. She was also an excellent hitter. But the word was that she wanted to attend beauty school rather than play college softball, so Sam didn't think he had a chance of getting her. Still, he knew she played for the Waves, a summer league/travel team, so he went to see one of their games.

If Billy the Kid was one of the fastest draws in the West, Sam Carrodo is unquestionably among the fastest in the East—pulling out his NCC softball business card and handing it to coaches and prospective players, a status he doesn't dispute. But the truth is that unless Sam knew that a girl was dead set on coming to play for him, he did not approach her with a hard sell.

So, Sam went to the Waves game, and Carissa Molchan, one of his three captains from last season at NCC, also played for the Waves. She asked if Sam wanted to talk to Nikki, and he said, "Well, just introduce me." The two spoke briefly, but Nikki told Sam that she wasn't interested in playing college ball; that she wanted to go to beauty school. Sam understood. He told her that the door was always open if she changed her mind and wanted to come to NCC to learn and play ball.

Later in June, Sam received a phone call from Jill Lichty, the NCC volleyball coach who knew Nikki, and she told him that Nikki—who also loved the sport of volleyball—was thinking of coming to NCC. She was considering coming to NCC for two years to get a business degree, which would help her down the road opening her own beauty parlor. Sam was floored. He went to another summer league game and watched Nikki pitch a one-hitter. She was amazing.

But he didn't approach her a second time because he didn't want to pressure her or scare her away.

Then, as the school year approached, a rumor began circulating that Nikki *wasn't* coming to NCC. Sam asked Jill to find out what was going on, and to tell Nikki that he was too old and fat to worry this much; that he had a pacemaker and it would go off every time he heard that she wasn't coming to NCC.

One day while Sam was watching a men's basketball game at NCC, a girl wearing an army green sweater and blue jeans walked up to him. She leaned over and said, "Don't worry about your pacemaker. I'll be playing for you this year."

It was Nikki.

Sam beamed, then told her, "We're going to put a team behind you that will score ten-to-fifteen runs a game, I promise."

Then, with a week left in the volleyball season, the volleyball coach called Sam and told him that Nikki had broken her leg during a game. The coach went nuts.

What good does it do having her if I can't use her, he thought.

Ten minutes later Nikki called Sam and asked, "Did you hear the news?"

"Yeah, are you okay?"

"Sure," she said, and laughed. "I didn't break my leg."

Sam took a deep breath. It was a good thing he really didn't have a pacemaker.

* * * *

One day while sitting in his office at NCC, Sam received a phone call from a high school recruiting firm—the kind that charge high school students several hundred dollars and promise to find them a college.

"I have a girl for you," the caller told Sam.

"Why NCC and not some other school?" the coach asked.

"This girl wants to be a mortician," the caller explained. "There's only two schools in the state of Pennsylvania that offer

Mortuary Sciences. One is in Erie, and NCC is the other. But the one in Erie doesn't have a softball team, so you're getting her."

Signed, sealed and delivered—almost.

The girl's name was Janess Lyle, a shortstop from Bald Eagle Area High School, near State College, Pennsylvania. Within a few days Sam received a videotape from the recruiter of Janess in game conditions, and he salivated as he watched. When she hit the ball it looked like it was coming out of a cannon. The ball just exploded off her bat.

Sam was familiar with that area of the state from watching the Christmas City wrestling tournament in Bethlehem each year. Bald Eagle Area High School had a tremendous wrestling team, and a good football team, too. So he knew the school had reputable sports programs.

The first thing he did was call the school's softball coach, a gentleman named Dave Breon. Sam's policy was to talk to the coaches first to make sure it was okay to come to the school and talk to the girls. He also told the coach not to tell Janess that he was coming because then she might get nervous. And if it's an important game and she doesn't play well and the team loses, then Sam would feel like it was his fault.

So, Sam and his brother Pic (His real name is Michael, but he has always been known as Pic, though no one knows why), who is one of the team's assistant coaches, made the three-hour drive to State College, and they took Cortnei Comstock with them so she could talk to Janess about what it was like playing for NCC. They sat in the bleachers in right field and watched Janess play, and were even more impressed with her than they were watching her on videotape.

After the game, Sam had dinner with Janess, Cortnei and Pic. Janess recommended the restaurant, and ordered a buffalo chicken Stromboli.

"It's breaded buffalo chicken and cheese, and it's the greatest thing ever," she explained.

It was also huge, but Janess ate the whole thing without batting an eye. She and Cortnei were talking and joking around, and Sam could see right away that she would fit right in. He decided early on that Ness, as her family and friends called her, was just top of the line.

On the drive home, Pic turned to his brother and said, "If this girl actually comes to NCC, and we get Nikki, we're going undefeated this year." That was back in May 2004.

Sam made a return trip to Bald Eagle Area High School a few weeks later because his two other assistant coaches, Keith Greene and Robbie Robinson, also wanted to see Ness play. This time they took Missy and Hoppy, since they were girls that Ness would be playing with. The NCC entourage watched Ness play shortstop, and at one point during the game, a batter hit a wicked ground ball at her. Ness went into a split, keeping her entire body in front of the ground ball. Sam's jaw dropped. How is she going to throw from that position, he thought. But Ness threw the runner out by two strides, and Sam knew he had something special.

Meanwhile, word had spread that college coaches were there scouting Ness. And as Sam and company were watching the game, an elderly gentleman walked up to the group, tapped the coach on the shoulder, and said, "You take care of our girl."

That's all he said, and then he just walked on by. No relation to Ness, just an old timer who liked to watch the games.

While Ness would never admit it, it became clear to Sam that he was recruiting a local legend.

Sam and Pic made one more trip up to Bald Eagle when Ness' team was playing a district playoff game. It might as well have been the World Series, the place was packed. There had to be about 2,000-to-3,000 people at the game. Ness' parents and grandparents came over to talk, and everyone was very friendly, yelling out, "Hey coaches, how are you?"

"That's what made what we were doing so special," Sam would later recall. "We were giving a girl from their hometown a chance to do what she loved to do. We're just a two-year college, but the folks there treated us like we were from UCLA. It made me feel very proud."

* * * *

There is, of course, another side to all of this. A price to be paid, so to speak.

Sam had two children with his wife Chris: nine-year-old twins Devan and Nicholas. His coaching and recruiting schedule meant spending a lot of time away from them. They missed their father, and they—and Sam's wife, Chris—did not hold back in letting Sam know that he was coming up short in his parental responsibilities.

Sam also had two older sons from his first marriage. At the time of the recruiting trips to Bald Eagle High School, Sammy was twenty-four, Anthony was twenty-two. Those recruiting trips quickly became a sore subject.

Anthony had been at Penn State for four years, and Sam never went to visit him. But while he was recruiting for softball, he went to see Ness three times in two months. Bald Eagle is just twelve miles from Penn State.

Anthony was pissed, and Sam understood. He always acknowledged that he was better with other people's kids than his own. Regrettably, he didn't know if that would ever change.

* * * *

So now the team was starting to take shape. Nikki, in addition to being an excellent pitcher, was also a very good shortstop. But with Ness, considered the top-ranked shortstop in Pennsylvania in Class AA high school softball, at short, the pleasant problem—but a problem regardless—of too much talent reared it's ugly head.

Nikki's attitude, however, snuffed out any potential problems.

"Coach," she told Sam, "you put me on the field, I don't care where you play me, I'll give you one hundred and twenty percent."

That was Nikki. In her senior year in high school she pitched every game of the season, pitched batting practice every other day, it's amazing her arm didn't fall off. So, Sam told her she wouldn't have to pitch every game, because he had two other girls—Jenn Davis, the team's returning co-captain, and Robyn Carey from Saucon Valley High School—who would share the pitching duties. That relaxed Nikki a lot.

Last season, when Jenn wasn't pitching, she played third base. So Sam figured he could flip-flop her and Nikki between third and the pitcher's circle. Robyn was a big pick-up because

Sam knew she could be the team's third pitcher, and she also played first base, another position that needed to be filled.

Next, a girl named Jamye Mease, out of Central Dauphin High School, signed on. Sam had spoken with her coach and some people from her hometown, and they all said she was a great kid coming from a great family. And when she walked through the door, Sam could see she was an athlete. He thought, wow, that's my second baseman. So now the infield was set, with Jenn and Nikki alternating between pitcher and third base, Ness at short, Jamye at second and Robyn—whose nickname Sam learned was 'Dirty'—at first base.

The year before, Sam had cut a young lady named Alexis Walker from the 2004 team. She was cut because of her attitude. The coaches would ask her to try something, and she'd refuse. This year she came back with an entirely different attitude, so they kept her. She would become part of the team's left-field rotation, and one of its leading hitters.

Sam's recruiting philosophy was simple. When he would go around and talk to high school softball coaches, they'd say, "Sam, we have a girl for you. She's not a great hitter, but she can bunt. And if you get her on base, she just flies." Sam would give that girl a shot. Maybe she'll play great defense, and if she hits, that's a bonus, he would reason. Or maybe she's a great hitter but can't catch the ball. Well, now the team has a DH. If a girl came to play and showed she had a lot of heart, a lot of passion, Sam would not cut her. He would much rather keep someone who has passion, and has a great attitude, but might not be the greatest ball player, than keep someone with all the talent in the world who has a terrible attitude. Sound stupid? Maybe, but that's what Sam did.

Along those lines, he had a girl come out for the team named Kyle Lozier. She didn't do very well in tryouts, and she came out late because she attended NCC's Monroe County campus and didn't even know NCC had a women's softball team. But she showed a great attitude.

The coach called her into his office and said, "I'm not going to use you; I'm not going to be able to keep you."

She said, "I just want to be part of the team, coach. You don't have to play me at all, as long as I'm part of this team."

Sam said, "Okay, you look me in the eye and tell me that you're not going to bitch if you don't play any innings. Because the first time you bitch, you're gone. If you don't have a problem with not playing, and me getting you in whenever I can, then you can stay."

"I don't have a problem with it," she answered. "This means a lot to me. I just want to be part of this team."

So, he kept her. She never complained, and she wound up playing more than he thought she would.

* * * *

Sam was sitting in his office at NCC one morning when a young woman came to his door. She introduced herself as Kristy Kroll, a first-year student at NCC, who hadn't played softball in a few years but wanted to try out.

He had never heard of her, but told her to get her glove.

Kroll was a gem. She could pitch and play centerfield, she could hit and she could run. And she had just fallen into his lap. He was ecstatic.

In the coming weeks, the bulk of the team would travel to Maryland for a fall exhibition tournament. It took a few innings for the girls to warm up, but Kroll and her teammates lit up the place with their hitting. NCC played two games and won both, 11-2 and 24-6. Pitching-wise, Kroll flat-out shut down the opposition. Sam was impressed; he knew he had something special. Between Jenn, Nikki, Dirty and now Kristy, he had four dominant pitchers he could rotate to keep everyone fresh.

But then the US Government stepped in.

Kristy was a National Guard specialist in the Charley Company 228, FSB (forward support battalion) unit—a medical company made up of medics, and lab, x-ray and dental technicians. In November, she received word that her company was to report to Camp Shelby in Mississippi in January for six months of training, to be followed by a one-year stint in Iraq.

"I hated to lose her," the coach recalled, "but I couldn't stop the US Government."

Kristy took a glove and ball with her, said she would practice as much as she could, and in two years would be back to resume her education and play for the Spartans.

Sam just hoped she would come home in good health.

* * * *

Nothing in life is certain except death and taxes. That's why Sam often said that—as far as a girl playing for NCC—nothing is certain until he sees her walk onto the softball field in the spring with a glove on her hand. He'd been in the game for a long time, and he knew that if he phoned a girl and she didn't phone back, it meant she wasn't coming. She just didn't want to tell him.

That was the case with Ness. But Sam also knew that Ness was a special player. So, after leaving several messages for her and not getting a return phone call, he said, "The heck with this," and drove the three hours to see her.

"I'm kind of scared," Ness admitted when the coach arrived in Bald Eagle. "I don't know if I can do this. I've never been away from home."

Sam suggested she come down for a weekend, stay with one of the girls from last year's team, and see what it's like. Ness agreed, and drove down for a day. She came to Sam's house for dinner, sat and talked with all the girls on the team. Then, as she was walking out the door, she gave the coach a hug and said, "I'll be back in the fall. Don't worry about it."

But Sam was still a wreck, because he really wanted Ness to come to NCC.

Finally, the fall semester began and Ness was on campus and in class. But for the first two weeks she was homesick and crying, and she didn't like her roommate. And Ness was the kind of girl who didn't cry about anything, but she was upset over being away from home.

"As soon as I got to NCC I went through a week of orientation, which was okay because you're around lots of people," Ness recalled. "Then classes started. I'd go to class, come back to the dorm, and cry. I'd call my mom, and she would start crying, so I felt bad and didn't call her anymore. This went on for a week. Then Sam would call. He felt bad because I was crying, and he asked if I wanted to go out for cake and coffee. At first I said no because I didn't want to be a nuisance, and I thought my feelings would pass. But I finally said yes because I couldn't take it anymore. If I could have turned around and gone back home, I most certainly would have."

Jamye Mease was also staying in the dorm, and she was feeling homesick as well. So Sam drove over with his kids—nine-year-old twins Devan and Nicholas—and went with Ness and Jamye for coffee and cake. Ness was sitting outside in front of the dorms when he arrived, and it absolutely broke his heart to see her sitting there crying. All he could tell her was that things would get better, but Ness didn't know that. Her heart was aching.

The group went out for cake, Ness and Jamye got to know each other, and they both felt more comfortable. And in the fall the team scheduled some practices and conducted several fundraisers, so between those activities and school, the girls were too busy to worry about anything else.

Sam always tells the girls, and he tells their parents as well, that when they come to NCC, he's going to treat them like they're his daughters. He tells them that the girls are going to be protected, that nobody is going to hurt them, and that he's five minutes away if something happens. If they need to get away, they can always come to his house for dinner or just to watch TV with him and his family.

Sam and his coaching staff help the girls through the academic process as well. They help them register for classes, and they stay on them about academics, because they know that's the most important thing. There are privacy laws at school, so

Sam is unable to see their records, and he trusts that the girls are telling him what's going on. But he stays on them to focus on their academics.

Leaning back in the chair in his NCC office, Sam knew that recruiting could be a trying experience, but that didn't change the fact that the process was also so much fun. He got to meet a lot of people. He would go to a game to watch one girl, and soon he'd be watching the whole team, girls that he never would have known about.

He smiled and nodded to himself. He wouldn't trade it for anything.

FOUR

Cabin fever—it's a condition that produces restlessness and irritability caused from being in a confined space. The actual word is a slang term for a claustrophobic reaction that takes place when people are isolated and/or shut in together for an extended period of time.

According to Wikipedia, the online encyclopedia, the term possibly originated in the United States at the time when settlers would be snowed in at their log cabins and had to wait for the spring thaw in order to travel to town. Another possible source for this phrase could be that during an outbreak of some disease, people who had a fever were confined to a cabin as a quarantine. Most likely, the phrase may be associated with ocean-crossing sailing ships in which passengers had to endure weeks and months of slow travel while living in cramped cabins below deck.

Whichever definition or origin you subscribe to, cabin fever was the dominant affliction that engulfed the NCC women's softball team early in 2005.

The spring semester at the college began on January 16; indoor softball practices in the NCC gymnasium began that day as well. The school's new Spartan Center and large, state-of-the-art gymnasium would not open for another five months. That meant working out in the old gym, which was small and poorly lit. And because it was one level below the first floor of the College Center building, the girls felt like they were practicing in a hole in the ground.

The gym was also open to view from the first floor via a walkway that bordered three of the four sides of the sunken court. Spectators and passersby would often gather to watch portions of the team's practice. They were also a disruptive force. Male students entering or exiting the nearby fitness center would stop and whistle or shower the girls with cat-calls, dividing their attention and prompting Coach Sam to temporarily halt practice until the offensive individuals left.

Set-up time would often eat away at practice time, because it took a minimum of twenty minutes to set up the batting cage. Then, for the first ninety minutes of practice time, the softball team shared the facility with the tennis team. That significantly limited what Sam and his coaches could do in practice, especially with the outfielders, given the confined quarters. On several occasions, despite the cold weather, the coaches took the outfielders outside just to be able to hit some fly balls to them.

But it was home, and Sam knew from past experience that the challenge at hand was two-fold: getting the girls in softball shape to start the season, and keeping them from going stir crazy—a.k.a., developing cabin fever.

After a few weeks of practice, Sam began setting aside time for the girls to play wiffle ball. That helped them work on hand-eye coordination, but it also kept things loose and enabled the girls to have fun. And having fun, Sam knew, was the best medicine to combat cabin fever.

"We joked around and tried to make things as much fun as possible," Sam recalled. "My assistant coaches would pick on me endlessly. So I would walk around all ticked off and the girls would start laughing. Everybody is happy except me, because they're laughing at me."

He also held contests. The most popular was setting up a garbage can at the far corner of the gym. The objective was to throw a total of ten balls into the garbage can. Each girl got three chances to add to the collective total, so it became a group function, working toward a common goal. And the motivation was a pizza dinner if they achieved their goal.

"It brought them together as a team because they were cheering for each other," Sam recalled. "They were also doing something great, because getting the ball anywhere near the garbage can is a very good throw. So now they're working on their throwing and they don't even realize they're practicing. They were just hungry and wanted to eat."

Each time they reached their goal, Sam would raise the bar at the next practice, gradually increasing the number of balls that needed to fill the garbage can. He was building team unity, no doubt, but eventually the game became tedious and the allure of pizza became old hat.

Jenn Davis and Missy Bachert, the team's co-captains, worked hard to keep the bickering to a minimum and the cliques from forming. That had been a problem the previous year, and they were determined not to let tensions and disagreements fracture the team again.

"If there was a problem on the gym floor, we had a meeting afterwards," Jenn explained. "We told the girls, we're not going home until we fix this problem."

One day, the girls seemed to be getting on each other's nerves more than usual, and actually started to go after and pick on one another. It was simple stuff, like who had to listen to and take orders from whom, or who they had to respect.

Sam noticed. He called timeout, sent his coaches back to his office, and took all the girls into the nearby racquetball room where he delivered a pointed message.

"We have six coaches, and that's who you listen to," Sam said. His voice never rose above normal speaking volume, but the tone and the message were clear. He was ticked off, big time, and the girls were going to understand that. "You listen to what we say, what we tell you to do, and that's it. You have a couple of captains here who can express their feelings to you, but they don't tell you what to do. Neither does the girl next to you. We tell you what to do."

The team's trip to Myrtle Beach, South Carolina, to participate in the annual Snowbird Softball Tournament, was right around the corner. The year before, the trip south had been a nightmare. Every day Sam would receive a phone call in his room from one of the girls complaining about one thing or another, and every day he would have to call a team meeting in an attempt to clear the air. The meetings often turned into bitch sessions, accomplishing very little, and Sam had no intentions of reliving that experience.

"Whether you know it or not, you ladies have the potential to be the greatest team ever at this school," Sam told the team. "The other coaches are talking like you could go undefeated this season."

Sam's eyes surveyed the room, stopping briefly to look into the face of every girl on the team. He had their attention.

"There's a possibility that could happen . . . but it's a long season," he cautioned. "And if you continue to bitch and moan and go back and forth at one another, you can forget about going undefeated. You can forget about winning a state title. That's not going to happen."

Sam paused. He seldom got upset, but this was one of those rare occasions. He took it upon himself to address the situation. Even his assistant coaches, whom he had ushered off to his office, did not know the intent or content of his team meeting. But he was determined that the March trip to Myrtle Beach—that the entire season, for that matter—would be a much calmer, much less drama-filled season. He was sick of drama. He remembered how it ripped apart last year's team, and he was not going to let it happen again.

"Whatever problems you have, you'd better leave them in this room," the coach admonished, his voice echoing off the four walls of the empty racquetball room. "Leave that garbage in here with the echoes. Don't take it with you. Don't bring it to practice, and don't bring it back on the field."

Sam scanned the faces of his team one last time to make sure he still had their attention. No one even dared to blink.

"The coaches and I are going to be pretty easy-going," he said. "We're going to be fun to be around. But if you cross over the line that I don't want you to cross, you're going to know that you shouldn't have. Now, I'm going to give you fifteen minutes to talk among yourselves, and then I want you back out onto the court. It's over, and I don't want to hear about this again."

Sam paused a moment, the silence providing ample opportunity for his final words to sink in. Then he turned and walked out of the racquetball room.

The silence remained after Sam closed the door behind him. It was a deafening silence that seemed to last a good deal longer than its actual ten second duration. Then team co-captain Jenn Davis turned to address the team.

"Okay, if anybody has anything on their mind, get it off now because we're going to handle this," Jenn announced to her teammates. "Get it off your chest right here, or else go home."

Missy followed suit.

"We're not going to be at each other's throats like last year," she said. "We're fixing this now."

Their passion was clear. All the talent in the world meant nothing if friction ripped the team apart. Gradually, their teammates opened up, and spent the next several minutes talking. No major drama, just clearing the air.

"I really don't think there was that much friction between anybody," Missy would later recall. "There weren't little cliques. I think it was just that everyone needed to get to know each other a little better."

Mission accomplished. And Sam would later acknowledge that while the start of the season was still several weeks away and his team meeting was only meant to foster team unity, it would ultimately prove to be the turning point in one incredible run to a state title.

* * * *

Preparing for the trip to Myrtle Beach for the Snowbird Softball Tournament is two-fold. Working out in the gym, fielding ground ball after ground ball, and taking hundreds of swings in the batting cage is only one half of the equation. Raising the funds to play in the weeklong tournament and provide room and board for fifteen players and six coaches is the more challenging aspect.

Compared to other events, the Snowbird Softball Tournament wasn't that expensive. The cost was $285 per person for the week. Players' parents who made the trip—and quite a few did, given that you could do a lot worse than spend a week vacationing in Myrtle Beach in mid-March—did so at their own expense.

Transportation was provided by NCC in the form of three vans that were well stocked with snacks and beverages for the ten-and-one-half-hour drive. Sam drove one van, while assistant coaches Pic and Robbie drove the two others. Robbie always drove the lead van. That was just one of Sam's superstitions.

Despite the reasonable costs, the dollars still had to be accounted for. Sam viewed the fundraisers as good team-bonding activities.

"We're fighting together for a common goal, to raise the amount of money we need to make the trip to Myrtle Beach," the coach explained. "And we have some fun."

The previous year, the team held a car wash, but it almost got them in hot water. They set up shop near a well-traveled section of Broad Street in downtown Bethlehem, but were getting few takers. In an attempt to attract more customers, Colleen McGouldrick walked out into the middle of Broad Street in shorts and a bikini top and began to flag down passersby.

It might have worked, but a police car arrived and admonished her to stay out of the street.

"Coach, I'll wear whatever it takes to bring some money in," she told Sam when he was made aware of the incident. Undeterred, Colleen finished the afternoon standing in the bed of a truck and yelling for people to come get their cars washed.

More recently, the car washes were coming up dry, so the team resorted to arranging comedy nights and basket bingo events. Those proved to be highly successful, raising enough money to transport the team to Myrtle Beach.

* * * *

With the monies raised to fund the trip to Myrtle Beach, Sam set about preparing for the tournament. The goal was the same as the previous year—to win the tournament and go undefeated in the process, something that had never been done in the twenty-five-year history of the tournament.

Those odds didn't phase Sam. Last year's Spartans team had gone 7-1 in the eight-game tournament, the lone blemish being a one-run loss, 9-8, using the international tie-breaker rule. Under that rule, if the score of the game is tied after completion of seven innings, the offensive team begins its turn at bat in each half inning of subsequent innings with the player who is scheduled to bat ninth in that respective half inning being placed at second base. So, if the number five batter is scheduled to lead off, the number four batter in the batting order will be placed on second base at the start of the inning. The rule is used to increase the chances of a team scoring and bring about a quicker resolve to the score—not unlike college football where teams begin play in the overtime periods at the twenty-yard line.

That ruling, Sam believed, was the only thing that kept last year's team from running the tournament table.

The schedule of games was announced in advance, so Sam was well prepared.

"I knew who we were playing and on what days we were playing, so I researched everybody," the coach explained. "What they do for this tournament is they'll tell you there's this many teams down there, and you'll write back saying I want to play this team and this team. But they write back saying that team doesn't want to play you. This is who you're going to play. We're a two-year community college. We get the same kind of feelings from schools down there as we do up here. The Division I and the II schools that play in the tournament feel the same way. They don't want to play a two-year community college because it does nothing good for them. So, we get to play all the community colleges."

Sam knew which teams were tough and which weren't based on the level of play he'd seen at last year's tournament. Of course, those schools and coaches recruited new players just as he did, so there were some unknown quantities that made precise scouting reports impossible. But based on the information he had and what he'd seen in his own team practices, he set his lineup and pitching rotation—Nikki, Jenn and Robyn—and was ready to go.

The goal of going undefeated aside, Sam and his assistant coaches still wanted to see how the players handled game situations. Until the Myrtle Beach tournament, they'd been limited to practices in the school gym, and had not yet sent a full squad onto a regulation softball field. How the players fielded their respective positions and how they gelled as a team were the key questions that needed to be answered.

FIVE

The Myrtle Beach area of South Carolina is considered by many to be a year-round vacationers' paradise. Its sun-drenched shores and wide sandy beaches stretch sixty miles along the Atlantic coastline.

Beyond the sun and surf, Myrtle Beach is home to championship golf courses, live entertainment theaters, amusement parks, historical sights, and a wide array of shopping and dining experiences.

But during spring break week every March, it becomes home to female athletes from dozens of colleges across the country when it hosts the annual Snowbird Softball Tournament.

The drive down had been uneventful for the three NCC vans, until hitting a rest stop in Maryland. The hub of the rest stop was a large, indoor food court that also housed a few novelty and gift shops. In one shop, Sam and his assistant coaches found an assortment of photo machines—the kind that offered up several backgrounds. People could pop their heads into cut-outs in the scene, thus positioning their heads on someone else's body.

"We were way ahead of schedule," Sam recalled.

The four coaches spent forty-five minutes taking photographs and laughing at themselves. Meanwhile, the girls sat in the vans wondering why the coaches were taking so long in the rest rooms.

Sam laughed as he recalled the scene. "The photos are classics."

The NCC softball team arrived late in the afternoon on Saturday, March 19, and Sam and his coaches knew the drill well. They checked everyone into the Bermuda Sands Hotel, the same resort they'd stayed at in prior years, which sits about one-hundred yards yards in from the ocean. The girls buddy up, staying in double-bed rooms, and Sam and his coaches occupy the penthouse suite, which conveniently has a full kitchen with a refrigerator, and a balcony that faces the ocean.

"I want a place for the parents to hang out, so we get the suite," the coach rationalized.

After unpacking, the coaches attended a meeting where they were given pamphlets on events at Myrtle Beach, important phone numbers, breakfast schedules for the team, and practice times. The tournament organizers also supply each team with tee-shirts and a bag of softballs to use during the week. It's all very well organized and handled in a professional manner.

Each team plays two games on Monday, Tuesday, Wednesday and Thursday—eight games in total. Friday is set aside to make up any games postponed due to rain, and then teams head home on Saturday.

Sunday is set aside for practice, but teams also have the option of setting up scrimmages or exhibition games. The games don't count against a team's record, but for teams from the northern states, it's a good way to get players into their first on-field game conditions of the season.

Sam opted for the exhibitions, and scheduled games against two teams: Dominican University, a Division III program out of Illinois that was ranked 11th in the nation at the time; and Gettysburg College, a strong Division III program from western Pennsylvania.

"I think those schools wanted to play us because they wanted to shine against us," Sam said. "They wanted to build up their girls."

The Spartans squared off first against the Dominican University team, known as the Stars. NCC took an early 1-0 lead, but the Stars came back to put five runs on the board in the fourth inning. The Spartans added a run in the sixth, but fell short and lost the game 5-2.

After the game, the Dominican players and coaches were commenting to the NCC players that "we can't believe you're a community college," an indication that once the girls started hitting, they might just be as good as Sam and his assistant coaches thought they were.

Next up were the Gettysburg Bullets, whom Sam called the tougher of the two teams NCC would play that day. The Bullets jumped ahead 2-0 before the Spartans rallied and took a 3-2 lead into the seventh inning. But in the bottom of the seventh, the Bullets tied the score 3-3, putting the international tiebreaker rule into play starting in the eighth inning. For the Spartans, that meant starting the top of the eighth inning with a runner on second base and Missy—the team's cleanup hitter—at the plate.

"You have to advance that runner to third, and then there are several ways to get that runner home," Sam explained. "A passed ball, an error, a single, a sacrifice fly. So I had Missy bunt."

It was a perfect sacrifice bunt, moving the runner to third with one out. But the next two batters failed to plate the run, grounding out to short and flying out to left field. And when the Bullets scored in the bottom half of the inning, the Spartans were on the short end of a 4-3 game. It also called into question Sam's decision to have his cleanup hitter bunt.

"When he put the bunt on, I thought, it's Missy," said Pic, Sam's brother and assistant coach. "The way things worked out, it made him look goofy in everybody's eyes. But it was absolutely the right call to make. You've got to do that."

Not everyone agreed. And as Sam and his coaches were leaving the playing field, he was ambushed by a parent of one of the players.

"You're stupid, you're stupid," the parent repeated several times. "You don't know how to coach softball."

Sam thought the man was joking, so he laughed and just kept on walking. But the man was relentless, and continued to step in front of Sam and berate him in front of all the other parents.

"You're stupid," he continued to yell. "You don't take the bat out of the number four hitter's hands. It's not good baseball."

Sam attempted to put things in perspective.

"It doesn't mean anything," the coach explained. "The tournament hasn't even started yet."

The father wouldn't listen, and continued his tirade until assistant coach Keith Greene stepped in between the two men, allowing Sam to leave the premises.

Sam returned to the hotel room and began to pack his suitcase.

"I'm going home, I'm done," he told his assistant coaches as he began throwing things together. "I cannot have someone talk to me like that in front of the parents, doubting what I want to do, and creating all kinds of negativity."

The coaches let Sam blow off some steam, then worked to calm him down. Cooling off but still determined to leave, Sam called Bill Bearse, NCC's athletic director, to inform him of the incident. Bearse asked if Sam had touched the man or vice versa, and Sam said that no physical contact had been made.

"Don't leave," Bearse told him, and together, he and the assistant coaches convinced Sam to stay.

Everything blew over, and Sam felt better a few days later when the father apologized for what he had said and the way he acted. But being the constant worrier that he is, Sam asked coaches from several other teams if they thought he had employed the proper strategy during the game.

"I don't care who comes up to bat, you bunt the runner over," was their collective response. "That's just the way it is."

But still Sam worried.

Sitting in the hotel suite late Sunday night with his assistant coaches, Sam assessed the two exhibition games his team had played earlier that day. The pitching had been good, and the defense was ready. The hitters just needed to start hitting, and Pic was convinced they would.

"In the two exhibition games, the girls knew that they didn't play to their potential, and it pissed them off," Pic said. "You could see the fire in their eyes, and that had us smiling from ear to ear. And we thought, wow, we actually have the team that we thought we had. We knew, but Sam didn't, that as soon as they started hitting, it was over."

But Sam should have known. He set a curfew for the girls of 11:30 p.m., and every night they were in their rooms by 10 p.m. There would be no fooling around. They had come to play softball.

* * * *

The tournament began on Monday morning, with the Spartans scheduled to play two games against Columbia-Greene Community College, a junior college out of Hudson, N.Y., that competed in the Mountain Valley Conference at the Division III level. Sam had researched them from the year before, but because players are only eligible to play at the community college level for, at most, two years, rosters turned over frequently and it was difficult to know the exact make up of the current team.

So Sam continued to research. His assistant coaches worked with the girls during warm-ups, handling soft-toss, infield and outfield drills. Sam watched the players on the Columbia-Greene Twins to see if they could hit, if they had any good gloves. And when the Twins took infield practice, Sam had his girls sit on the bench and watch as well, so they were prepared. Very little was left to chance.

The Spartans were the home team for the first game, with Nikki in the pitching circle. The Twins broke on top 1-0 in the first inning, and the Spartans answered with an RBI single from Missy in their half. A run-scoring double by Mease in the third inning helped the Spartans open a 3-1 lead, but the Twins strung three consecutive doubles together in the top of the fifth inning for a 3-3 tie.

Then the Spartan bats came to life. A walk, two doubles and a triple plated three runs in the bottom of the fifth for a 6-3 advantage. Then back-to-back doubles in the sixth, followed by three consecutive singles and a three-run homer by Ness plated six runs and ended the game on the 10-run mercy rule, 13-3.

The second game wasn't much different. Jenn started in the pitching circle, and the Spartans had build a 5-1 lead by the fourth inning. Seeing that he had the game fairly under control, Sam switched pitchers.

"We put Robyn Carey ("Dirty") in to pitch and she self-destructed," Sam recalled. "She just started walking people, so we put Jenn back in to pitch."

The walks helped the Twins cut the deficit to 5-2, but the Spartan bats went back to work. Missy, who hadn't started the second game, came off the bench to club two home runs and a double in three at-bats, and the Spartans cruised to another mercy-rule shortened win, 14-2, in six innings.

"The girls proved to us they could hit," Sam said. "After that, the biggest problem was, do we go out to eat on the way back to the hotel, or wait and eat out at night?"

The money from fundraising events was sufficient to cover one large meal per day. Breakfast was covered in the cost of the hotel, but since most of the girls skipped breakfast, they were starving by the end of the second game. The team opted to go out for a late lunch, and Sam's restaurant of choice was All-American Steak and Seafood Buffet.

"That was the night Ness ate four steaks," the coach recalled. "Four big steaks."

It wasn't the last buffet the girls would see that week.

* * * *

When players hit the way the Spartan girls did the first two games of the tournament, people take notice. So it didn't take long before college coaches paid a visit to Sam's hotel room to ask if, following Tuesday's games, they could take one or two of the girls out to lunch, or put some of the players through a private workout.

Sam checked with the players and their parents, and all parties were receptive.

"It's awesome," said Sam of the recognition the girls were receiving. "It's great. And the thing that was neat about these guys is that there's a mutual respect around the coaching ranks. One of them will say, 'Coach, I only want to know about your second-year players. I don't want to know anything about your freshmen. I'm not here to take people away from you,' which is cool."

A coach from Emanuel College, in Franklin Springs, Georgia, was very excited about meeting with Jenn. It's a very Christian-oriented school, where students and faculty attend church together every Friday. And Sam knew that this was in-your-face Jenn the coach wanted to meet.

"That school would have changed the first semester she was down there," Sam thought.

So he gave his player some words of advice.

"Before she met with the people from the school, I told her, 'Jenn, don't ask them to pass the effin' potatoes. And don't say, Jesus, this is great food. Just be nice.' She went and got along great with everyone."

But Jenn is Jenn, and during her warm-ups with the coaches from Emmanuel College watching, her second pitch was wild and in the dirt, bouncing away from the catcher. Jenn stood on the mound and said, "Aw shit . . . oops," then just laughed like crazy.

Second-year players Jenn and Missy were the main objects of coaches' desires. A coach from West Virginia State University offered both players the same deal—just about everything would be covered, including books. All the girls had to pay for were the meals. But neither wanted to be that far from home. They eventually ended up with a good deal from the women's softball coach at Bloomsburg University who laughed and, half jokingly, told Sam she'd like to package the entire team and take them with her. Sam, of course, couldn't have been happier for Jenn and Missy.

* * * *

Day two arrived, and the Spartans were scheduled to play two games against the Panthers of Tompkins Cortland Community College, a Dryden, New York-based school that played in the Mid-State Athletic Conference. Sam's research led him to believe this would be the toughest team they would face all week, so of course, he's on edge all morning.

Nikki took the edge off quickly. She threw a one-hitter at the Panthers and the Spartans won their third straight game of the tournament, 10-0, in another mercy-rule game shortened to four-and-one-half innings.

Now the girls are starting to gel, and they started talking about wanting to go back and re-play the two exhibition games they lost on Sunday.

Sam was just content that the trip, thus far, had been a pleasant one.

"The year before, there were problems Saturday night, problems Sunday night, problems Monday night—every day there were problems," the coach recalled. "I was sick of it. I wanted to pack up and leave. But this trip was so enjoyable, not to mention we were beating the heck out of everyone."

By the second game, even the parents were getting into mid-season form. The incident from the exhibition games was a distant memory and any remaining tension had subsided. That was clear every time Missy came to bat.

"Jamye Mease's father is a card, and he's always getting people going," Sam recalled. "Every time Missy would come up to bat he would scream, 'Bunt her, bunt her.' And then she would hit a massive home run, and he would yell, 'You should have bunted her.'"

There was very little bunting in the second game against Tompkins Cortland. With Jenn in control in the pitching circle, the Spartans scored five runs in the first inning, four in the second, two in the third and four more in the fourth. Jenn and Jamye each homered, and Missy hit two more as the Spartans routed the Panthers 15-3 in a four-inning, mercy-rule shortened game.

After the game, the Panthers' coaching staff approached Sam.

"Can you please help us?" they asked. "Tell us what drills you use so that our team can hit like your team. We've never seen anyone hit like your team before, ever."

One of the coaches even commented that he couldn't hit a ball as far as some of Missy's moon shots.

"After that second game, I knew we were special," Sam recalled. "But I still didn't think we'd go undefeated. There's no way I thought that, but my assistant coaches wouldn't stop talking about it."

That's because it was raining hits in Myrtle Beach—twenty-three of them over the two games played on Tuesday, and a total run differential of 25-3.

But the real storm was just around the corner.

SIX

Tuesday night, the storm of the season descended on the Myrtle Beach area. Sitting on the balcony, Sam and his assistant coaches could see the wind coming across the ocean. They could see the storm brewing, but they had no idea just how powerful this storm was.

No one did, because people were still riding the ferris wheel at the amusement park down the street from the Bermuda Sands Hotel as the storm hit. And when the power went out, they had to ride out the storm atop the ferris wheel.

That was not a pleasant experience given the wind that whipped across Myrtle Beach.

"The wind picked up one of the balcony chairs, and it wasn't a lightweight chair, and threw it against the wall," Sam recalled. "The chair just stuck there. And it didn't stick there with its back against the wall, the legs of the chair were against the wall. The wind was holding the chair in place. It was humming."

The power went out, came back on again briefly, then went out again. Sparks flew from the transformers up and down the street. Police were out in force, doing their best to maintain calm and order in the midst of the storm.

In the suite at the top of the Bermuda Sands Hotel, Sam, his assistant coaches and many of the players' parents were enjoying themselves despite the foul weather. The atmosphere was festive, the laughter abundant, and the softball team was the dominant topic of conversation.

"This team really plays together."

"They're really good."

"Do you think they can win the tournament?"

Sam was trying to keep things realistic, pointing out that there were still four games to be played, when everyone in the suite was struck by a force, a presence.

The door to the suite was always left open to allow the players' parents to come and go at their leisure. The door opened into a long hallway, maybe twenty to twenty-five-feet long, that led to the kitchen and living room areas. The hallway was pitch black, but now, out of that blackness, a single white light moved slowly down the hallway.

"It was like God was coming," Sam said. "All you could see was this white light, nothing else."

Then Shelby, a large black man, one of the Snowbird Tournament directors, opened his eyes and smiled. Everyone burst out laughing.

"I had to keep my eyes and mouth closed because I wanted to scare you," said Shelby, who was wearing a miner's hat with the light turned on.

He had succeeded.

* * * *

The trip to Myrtle Beach was more than a one-week tournament. For Sam, it was the time when the team came together. In his words, it was the greatest bonding experience.

"You drive together for eleven hours in a van, you get to talk, and when you get down to Myrtle Beach you go out together as a team and get to know each other better," Sam explained. "And in the heat of the games, you get to see what somebody has inside them that you didn't think they had."

With blow-out wins in their first four games of the tournament, the Spartans were proving Sam right; that they indeed could be one of the best teams ever at NCC. The players, the parents and even Sam were upbeat.

But Sam's brother Pic was not.

The trip to Myrtle Beach was a difficult time for Sam's younger brother. Pic had been married to his wife for thirteen years; they had been together for more than twenty years. Each year they went on vacation, and when their daughter Marissa came along, those vacations were usually to the beach or to Disney World. Each morning, Pic and his daughter would go for a walk.

But not on this vacation. Pic and his wife had recently divorced, and Sam's younger brother felt like his world had come apart. Pic and his daughter, who was ten-years old at the time of the divorce, were inseparable, and he often referred to those ten years with her as "the best thing that ever happened to me."

The divorce was changing those feelings, and that was tearing him apart.

Pic had watched his brother and sister go through divorce, and in his mind he did not want to be a weekend father. In his head, he felt it would be much better if he were out of her life completely than to only be there on weekends.

But then something happened.

The first night at Myrtle Beach, Sam announced the schedule of games for the week, the majority of which began early each morning. That was going to be a problem for Chrysa, who explained that she had trouble waking up right before a game and playing. She said that she had problems in high school on road trips because she would sleep on the bus, and when teammates woke her right before the game she'd be grouchy and cranky.

Pic made the offer of joining him for a walk in the morning. Actually, he challenged her, telling Chrysa that he didn't think she could wake up early enough, say 5:30 a.m., to walk with him.

"And if you tell me I can't do something, then I'll do it," Chrysa said.

So on Sunday morning, bright and early, Chrysa was waiting for Pic by the door to her room, lacing up her sneakers as he arrived.

Then they walked. They walked the beach every morning that week, talking about softball, initially. But then Pic, a shy person by nature, opened up about how he wished his daughter was there; how much he missed her and his wife. Chrysa would listen, then say things that made Pic think; helped him make sense of things again. Helped him get through each day of the trip.

"I had been putting up a front," Pic said, of trying to smile and act like nothing was wrong. "But those little walks every morning reminded me that I was with my daughter. My daughter and Chrysa are so much alike; she's like Chrysa's mini-me, and it helped get me through the day."

Each evening, Pic called Marissa and spoke with her. By the end of the week in Myrtle Beach, he and his wife were on better terms, and eventually wound up "being better friends than when we were married."

Pic became more than just a weekend dad. In addition to spending every weekend together, Pic began taking Marissa to school each morning. It meant the world to him to be part of her life.

"To this day," Pic recalled following the team's 2005 season, "Chrysa has no clue what she did for me, but she got me through that entire episode with my wife. There aren't many people I can sit down and just talk to, and I was able to talk to her about anything. She's just a special kid."

The walks were good for Chrysa, too.

"They helped me relax before a game, because, seriously, I'm always nervous before games," she admitted. "And then if I made an error, I'd get mad."

Chrysa benefited from the walks in another respect. There were family problems at home. Her father lost his job earlier that year, and had recently signed a five-year contract for a work assignment in Kuwait. The family tensions at home carried over to school, and Chrysa was having trouble with some of her classes. She dropped one class, and was worried that she might not have enough credits to allow her to play softball.

And softball was important.

"I used softball as a getaway," Chrysa explained. "It was like, okay, I'll deal with all that other stuff at home. But when I came to the games I came to play softball and relax. I would come to the games and feel better. The coaches and my teammates would give me a hug and make me feel better. It was still there, but you just push it out of your mind."

The morning walks also brought to the surface Chrysa's deep dislike for seagulls, and led to her adopting one of the many nicknames she acquired while playing for the Spartans.

"One morning we were out for a walk and I found this stick, and it looked like a piece from a picket fence," Chrysa recalled. "I picked it up and tried to throw it at the seagulls because I think they're annoying. They always come up to you and try to take food from you."

Chrysa took the piece of fencing back to her room, stole a black Sharpie marker from Sam's room, and wrote across the would-be sword, The Seagull Hunter. She took it with her on every walk after that.

* * * *

The heavy rains from Tuesday night's storm left the fields at Myrtle Beach unplayable, so Wednesday's games were postponed until Friday so as not to interfere with Thursday's set schedule. That day, the Spartans had two games on tap against the Mohawk Valley Community College Hawks out of Rome, New York.

Jenn pitched the first game for the Spartans, an easy, 12-1 win in a five-inning, mercy-rule shortened game. She allowed only three hits, two of which came in the first inning and accounted for the Hawks' lone run in the game. Missy connected on two more home runs, giving her seven in the first five games of the tournament.

Game one, however, was the calm before the storm; a storm that, in some ways, made Tuesday night's downpour seem mild.

Nikki took the pitching circle in the second game and had a 2-0 lead before the Hawks tied the score 2-2 with two unearned runs in the bottom of the second. A two-run homer from Ness in the top of the fourth gave the Spartans a 4-2 lead.

The Hawks got a run back in the bottom of the fifth, making the score 4-3, and had runners on first and second with two out when a Hawk batter hit a ground ball to Jamye Mease at second. The Hawk runner going from first to second appeared to interfere with Jamye's fielding of the ball, but she still made a true throw to first base and nabbed the batter by a step and a half.

Third out of the inning—or was it?

The Spartans began jogging off the field, leaving the softball in the pitching circle for the start of the next inning. But the umpire at first base never made a call. The Hawk runners on second and third came around to score, and the batter went all the way to second base before the umpire signaled "safe." Half the Spartan players were already in their dugout.

All hell broke loose. Sam and his coaches hit the field and began arguing with both the first base and home plate umpires. Robbie, one of Sam's assistant coaches, is also a softball umpire when he's not coaching. He's also black. He told the umpire that he was wrong; that he's been an umpire for many years and he knows the rules.

"I wouldn't expect anything less out of somebody like you," the umpire replied.

Sam went nuts. "What did you say?"

"You heard what I said," the umpire answered.

Then Robbie blew up. The arguing got louder and angrier. Even the parents were climbing against the backstop and screaming. It took several minutes for things to settle down. Once they did, the Spartans had to return to the field, but now they trailed 5-4. The team was shaken. Nikki was crying hysterically.

Sam approached his pitcher and told her to compose herself.

"Go out there and prove to me that you're the ballplayer I know you are," he told her.

Nikki still had tears in her eyes when she returned to the pitching circle, and co-captain Jenn called the infielders together for a meeting at the mound. The umpire who had called the runner safe said that the Spartans were not allowed to meet on the mound. Earlier in the game, the same umpire would not let members of the Mohawk Valley team hold a mound meeting, so tempers with that umpiring crew had been brewing early, and had the Spartans and Hawks coaching staffs working as allies to stay calm in the face of poor umpiring.

Jenn pulled the team together anyway.

"Screw him," she told her teammates. "This is allowed. Don't listen to him."

Nikki's focus returned and she retired the next batter for the final out of the inning. The Spartans came in to bat for the top of the sixth, and Sam had a message for his players.

"If the umpires are not going to help us, we'll do it ourselves," the coach said, emphatically. "We'll get them back with our bats."

Missy issued a directive.

"Everyone up," she told her teammates. "No one is sitting down until we get runs on the board and we're ahead."

As one, the Spartans moved to the dugout fence and began cheering, stomping their feet and kicking the fence in support of their teammates.

"I never saw anything like that in my entire life," Missy would later recall. "It was awesome."

Sam saw the look in his players' faces.

"They looked like they were going to rip somebody to shreds," he said. "They were mad. No, they were incensed."

Alexis Walker led off with a single, and a fielder's choice left a runner on first with one out. Back-to-back walks followed, and with each walk the cheering and stomping from the Spartans' dugout grew louder. The bases were loaded with one out for Nikki. She struck out looking for the second out. Sam paced in the third base coaching box, his mind racing.

What kind of team do we have, he wondered. Are we going to be the same kind of team that folded against LCCC last year? When we get down, will we just quit and not fight our way back, or will we rise to the occasion?

With the second out of the inning, the cheering quickly subsided. Jenn was the next batter. She was nervous, but she was also angry.

"I don't think I've ever felt so angry at something in my life," Jenn said, describing her feelings after the on-field incident. "I was so angry at those umpires. But I told everyone that if we lose, it's because of a lack of runs, not because the umpiring was bad. We just had to be the better team."

She shook off her nervousness, turned to her teammates and implored them to continue making noise.

"I can't hear you," she yelled. "And if I can't hear you cheer I'm not going up to the plate. I've gotta hear you."

The cheering began to build once more, and all of Sam's questions were answered quickly. Jenn crushed one of the first pitches she saw over the centerfield fence for a grand slam and an 8-5 Spartan lead.

"The stands erupted, our dugout erupted, and the coaches were all screaming," Sam recalled. "I swear to you, if it wasn't bolted to the ground, that dugout would have come up. And that was the second time in my life I ever slapped a girl on the butt when she came by me at third base, because you can't do that kind of stuff. But Jenn deserved that one."

Then the floodgates opened, and the Spartans' emotions poured onto the field in the form of hits and runs. Jamye, Missy and Ness strung together hits, two more runs scored, and the Spartans were up 10-5. With each hit, the girls screamed louder and louder, grabbed each other, stomped the ground and kicked the fence.

"We're doing this," they yelled in unison.

Nikki went back to the mound and shut the door the rest of the way, adding a solo home run in the seventh inning to complete the 11-5 win.

"That was a big FU to the umpires," said Missy. "We just said, 'We don't need the umpires. Let's play our game. Let's play softball. Let's go back to the roots.' And we did."

And Sam knew his team was going to be all right.

"Looking back on things, that was the turning point, because the girls could have put the game in the dumper right there, and who knows what would have happened the rest of the season," Sam recalled. "Now we know this team is strong enough to come back against anybody, because that was a good team we played. Now we know that we have a team that, whether they're up or down, they're going to fight and they're going to claw. And the parents were already talking about a state championship game in Pittsburgh, and we're still in Myrtle Beach. It was very exciting."

And the tournament wasn't over.

SEVEN

Winning softball teams have to eat. And when the Spartans ate, the restaurant of choice was a buffet—any restaurant that had a buffet, actually.

"Buffets all the time," Gina Renaldi lamented.

It didn't matter if the restaurant was the All-American Steak and Seafood Buffet or Grandma's Kitchen, if a buffet was available, the Spartans could be found chowing down.

The thrill of eating all you wanted for just $12.95 may not have been a hit with every player on the team, but there was rationale to the madness for always choosing a buffet.

"If you asked the girls what they wanted to eat, each girl would say she wanted something different," Pic said. "One wants pizza, one wants Italian, one wants a salad. So, if we went to a buffet they could pick whatever they wanted. It didn't matter if they ate their money's worth or not. Everybody got what they wanted."

Gina was one of the girls for whom the all-you-can-eat approach didn't matter.

"I don't eat a lot," she explained. "When it comes to dinner time I eat little platters. All the places we went to were good, but I didn't really get my money's worth."

Others in the group were divided in their opinions.

"The freakin' buffets," said Nikki, rolling her eyes. "I had to go out to dinner with my parents just to get away from the damn buffets. I couldn't take it. And even if I have to cook, we are not going to buffets next year."

"Oh, but weren't those steaks great?" asked Ness, who single-handedly downed four one night.

Sam made it a point to tease Nikki about the buffets. "I can't wait for such and such buffet," he would say, in mock-excited tone. "It has everything, and it's so cheap. I don't know if the food is a good quality, but we can eat all we want."

Nikki would just roll her eyes again and walk away.

Then, there was the monetary consideration. Sam recalled the team's post-game celebration after winning the state title that year. The restaurant was Applebee's.

"No buffet," Sam remembered. "The girls wouldn't let me go to a buffet. And it usually costs around $220 for a buffet for the whole team and the coaches. Applebee's came to $600. So I said to the girls, now do you understand why I go to buffets?"

It still didn't make the food go down any easier.

* * * *

Friday came and it was time to make up Wednesday's rained out games. To that point, the Spartans had played doubleheaders against each of their opponents. The three softball fields used during the Myrtle Beach tournament were set off from each other in a sort of triangle shape with a common walkway running between them. Teams would finish their first game, walk from field A to field B, for example, take a fifteen-minute break, and then play game two. On Friday, however, the Spartans played separate games against two Ohio teams: the Clark State Community College Eagles, out of Springfield, and the Columbus State Community College Cougars, from Columbus.

Sam knew, and the girls did too, that the Spartans were just two wins away from becoming the first team to ever go through the Myrtle Beach Snowbird Softball Tournament undefeated. And both games offered their share of unusual circumstances.

The Clark State game was first, and prior to the game, Pic noticed that the Eagles team and many of the parents were sitting together on the bleachers and holding a large photograph of a girl in uniform. He wondered, did something happen to this girl that she couldn't be with the team? Had she, God forbid, died? He had to find out, so he approached a father of one of the players.

"Who is that a picture of?" Pic inquired.

"That's not our pitcher, our pitcher is over there warming up."

"No, I mean the eight-by-ten picture."

"No, she's just four-foot-eleven."

Pic shook his head, turned and walked away. When he reached Sam and the other assistant coaches, he shook his head again, then told them, "You guys are not going to believe the conversation I just had."

The bizarre pre-game happenings continued. It seemed that Clark State and Columbus State played each other regularly during their season. Normally, if that's the case, the tournament organizers will not schedule a game between those two teams. But as it turned out, the two teams were scheduled to play each other later that day. And the Clark State coach did not want to play them. In short, she did not like their coach.

She approached Sam with an unusual request.

"Could you hurt one of our girls so we don't have to play this next game?"

Sam was stunned. "I don't want to hurt any of your girls."

"Just tell your pitcher to throw it at her and let it hit her somewhere," the coach instructed. "We really don't want to play them."

Sam turned and headed back to the Spartans' dugout. "Oh man, I can't do that," he mumbled to himself.

Ironically, early in the game, Nikki threw a pitch in the dirt that bounced up and hit one of Clark State's players. The girl was not hurt, but the coach began pointing toward her and yelling, "Go down. Go down," but the girl never got the message.

The Spartans then made short work of the Eagles. Three runs in the first and another four in the second opened up a quick 7-0 lead that took any fight there was out of Clark State. Nikki pitched a two-hitter, and the Spartans inched closer to history with a six-inning, 12-2 win.

Next came Columbus State, and Sam had been briefed on the antics of the head coach.

"He likes to intimidate players and get inside their heads," he told his team. "He'll scream and yell and curse at his players like you've never seen before. And it doesn't matter if he's up by ten runs or down by ten runs, all he's going to do is bunt, so be prepared for that."

They were. Jenn was pitching and Nikki was at third, ready to pounce on any bunt attempt. And the Cougars' coach made it easy for them. Early in the game, he rubbed his face to signal for a player to bunt. Jenn looked toward her coaches.

"Well, that was a tough sign to pick up, wasn't it?"

After that, every time the Cougars' coach rubbed his face and the batter began to slide her hands up on the bat in bunting position, the entire Spartan infield moved in several steps. Between them, Nikki and Jenn recorded eight assists thwarting bunt attempts.

"The girls were on a mission to go undefeated in the tournament," Sam would later recall, "and they didn't want to leave any doubt on the field."

The Spartans left no doubt at the plate, either. They scored three runs in the first inning, two more in the second, four in the third and six in the fourth en route to a mercy-rule shortened, six-inning 15-4 win. All the while, the Clark State coach had her team sitting in the bleachers, watching and cheering for the Spartans. It made for a long game for the Cougars' head coach, who just sat on a bucket near first base and yelled at his team.

But the Clark State players weren't the only spectators cheering for NCC. The Spartans had a sizeable fan base present for the tournament, despite being some 650 miles from home. Teams located just an hour from Myrtle Beach had fewer spectators at the games. Some local teams from North and South Carolina may have had two people in the stands cheering them on; the Spartans had about twenty parents on hand.

"It was nice to see all of that orange," said Pic, referring to the T-shirts the parents wore bearing the school colors. "They took up an entire section of the bleachers."

After the game, the NCC players congratulated each other, then simply packed up their bats and gloves and got ready to move on. Winning the tournament was nice, but they were focused on the bigger picture. They had some unfinished business to tend to. Their goal was to win a state title.

* * * *

That night after dinner, several of the girls took a walk along the streets of Myrtle Beach, unwinding and quietly enjoying what they had just accomplished. Most of the girls were window-shopping, but Caitlyn McGouldrick, Colleen's younger sister, had other ideas.

"She was trying to flirt with guys," Gina recalled. "A group of guys drove by slowly in a car and she turned around and yelled 'Hi,' and just kept on walking. She walked right into a tree, then fell to the ground."

The rest of the girls were laughing hysterically. Caitlyn, of course, got up quickly and pretended that nothing had happened, but she knew otherwise.

"She wouldn't allow us to walk back along the same street because we would then pass the guys in the car and she didn't want them to see her," Gina said. "Our nickname for her is graceful. She trips over her own feet."

Fortunately for Caitlyn, they never did run into the boys again.

* * * *

The truck stop off I-95 near Fredericksburg, Virginia, was no different than hundreds of other truck stops across America. But that changed on Saturday, March 26.

Driving home from the Myrtle Beach tournament, the NCC softball team pulled off the highway so the girls could make a pit stop and the coaches could fill up on coffee—unleaded, of course, for the long drive.

As assistant coach Robbie Robinson steered the lead van along the highway off-ramp, a scene was unfolding like something out of a movie. A short distance from the off-ramp, a large tractor-trailer was laying on its side, wheels still spinning rapidly, from a rollover that happened just seconds earlier. Hundreds of heads of cabbage, the trailer's contents, were sent spiraling across the blacktop.

Without hesitation, the three NCC vans drove straight for the overturned trailer. Another car, one with New Jersey plates, also pulled up. Sam jumped out, then told Robbie to take the girls up to the service station. Then he, Pic, Keith, Jenn and Chrysa, descended upon and climbed on top of the trailer's cab where they found the driver pinned underneath a crumpled dash board and steering wheel.

"The poor guy was just laying there with the steering wheel bend down over his legs," Sam recalled. "We could see he was in pain."

Pic maneuvered his way around large shards of glass, the remains of the front windshield that had been smashed when the trailer tipped over, and entered the cab.

"Sam, you've gotta get in here," Pic yelled after surveying the scene.

Sam climbed in after his brother, the two of them squeezing into the small confines of the compressed cab as much as they could, and began pulling on the steering column, but it wouldn't budge. They were also afraid that any movement might further injure the driver, who was already grimacing in severe pain.

Meanwhile, diesel fuel was pouring out of the trailer and the engine was still running.

"How do you turn this thing off?" Sam yelled.

The driver motioned toward the dashboard, or what remained of it. Jenn climbed on top of the cab as it lay on its side and entered from the passenger side window, searching for a key or a switch to turn off the engine. Pic and Sam continued pulling at the steering column while Keith worked underneath in an attempt to free the driver's pinned legs.

People at the truck stop began gathering and shouting.

"You've got to get out of there," they were yelling, but Sam and company continued working to rescue the driver.

"We were putting everything we had into moving that steering wheel," Sam recalled. "We didn't realize it was danger-ous; we weren't thinking that the diesel fuel might ignite. I don't think we realized it until everything was over. At that moment, it was the furthest thought from our minds."

At one point, Sam was able to move one of the driver's legs out from under the steering wheel, but one foot remained pinned under the crumpled dash. Freeing one leg, however, seemed to ease some of the driver's pain.

Jenn finally found the button to turn off the engine. The roar of the diesel came to an abrupt halt, and the sound of the music the driver had playing in his cab could be heard. It was opera, which added yet another surreal quality to the scene.

Diesel fuel continued to flow from the trailer.

Sam felt someone pulling on his shoulder and yelling at him.

"Knock it off," he yelled back. "We're trying to get this guy out."

Then he turned and saw who was behind him.

"We're paramedics," the man responded. "Now get out of here."

Sam and Pic began to climb out of the cab.

"Don't you understand how dangerous it is?" a female member of the paramedic team asked, not waiting for an answer. "There's diesel fuel all over this thing."

Sam could only shrug his shoulders. "Lady, we're just trying to help."

"Help by vacating the premises," she said.

Sam and the others began walking away, looking back over their shoulders as they did. It was a frustrating feeling because the driver of the trailer was still pinned under part of the dashboard.

"The look on that guy's face," Sam later recalled, "he was petrified, and in so much pain. And we felt helpless because we couldn't do anything."

Robbie and the rest of the team were waiting at the far end of the truck stop in front of a convenience store when Sam, Pic, Keith, Jenn and Chrysa drove up. They went inside the convenience store for coffee, told the girls what had happened, and it was then that they realized how dangerous the situation had been.

Sam looked down and saw that he was bleeding from the side of his leg. Probably cut it on part of the windshield, he thought, and didn't even notice it until all the commotion had calmed down.

He sipped his coffee and looked back across the truck stop in the direction of the overturned tractor-trailer. Slowly, he shook his head from side to side.

"That was something," was all he could say.

EIGHT

When teams experience a big win or a major accomplishment, as the NCC Spartans did by becoming the first team to ever run the table at the Myrtle Beach Snowbird Softball Tournament, it's not surprising if—emotionally, at least—they experience a let down in the games that follow.

Given Sam's penchant for worrying, he could be expected to be fret over how his team might start the regular season following their return from Myrtle Beach. Would they be overconfident? Would the lay off of a few days get them out of sync? Legitimate questions, but that wasn't what was on the coach's mind.

"My biggest worry at that point was the weather," Sam explained, recalling how much colder it was back in Pennsylvania following the team's one-week stay along the South Carolina coast. "I wasn't sure how they were going to perform in cold weather. And it was cold. The girls couldn't hold the bat properly, and their hands were stinging every time they hit the ball."

In previous years, the girls wore hoodies—sweatshirts with hoods—in order to stay warm on cold days. But the 2005 Lady

Spartans were tough. All they wore on the upper part of their bodies was under armor and their uniform shirts. They even wore shorts, despite the bitter cold of late March in the Lehigh Valley, having long ago discarded the sweat pants that were available to keep their legs warm.

"The girls hadn't worn sweat pants in three years," said Sam. "The pant material was too heavy, and the waist bands didn't stretch. The girls hated them, and they never wore them. No matter how cold it was, they just wore shorts. They adjusted well."

That was evident once the games began. Not only were the Spartans hot at the plate, but Jenn and Nikki were shutting down opposing batters on a regular basis. Through the first eight games of the season, all wins, the Spartans outscored their opponents by a total of eighty to one. It didn't take a degree in rocket science to figure out that the Spartans were averaging ten runs a game, which brought back memories of Sam's promise to Nikki to put a team around her that would score fifteen runs per game.

"I thought he was full of crap," said Nikki, recalling her coach's promise of substantial run support. "But it was like, okay, whatever you say. Then, once we got on a roll, oh man, I was just awed seeing how far Ness and Jamye could hit the ball."

Sam, of course, was happy with the way the Spartans were playing, but he took no pleasure in running up scores or embarrassing opposing teams. That much was evident during the Spartans' opening day wins, 9-0 and 12-0, over Lincoln University.

"This was Lincoln's first year as a team, and they had nothing," Sam recalled. "Each player used the same bat, and the girls had no cleats. The coach and I talked before the game, and I said I would try to get some equipment for them, help with game balls and other stuff we had that we weren't using. It was very disappointing to watch their level of play."

The Spartans, however, were another story, clicking on all cylinders. Before the season began, Sam spoke of how the top seven players in the lineup would be counted on to produce a lot of runs. Anything the bottom of the lineup produced would be icing on the cake.

There was icing galore in an early season doubleheader against Montgomery County Community College. The Spartans won easily, 13-0 and 9-0, and the bottom third of the lineup stood out. During the two games, Jamye and Toot scored four runs, Gina scored two and Chrysa scored one.

The following day against Cecil Community College of Maryland, Sam gave Nikki and Jenn a rest and started Robyn "Dirty" Carey in the first game—the first start since her meltdown in Myrtle Beach. She didn't disappoint.

"She looked good in practice, then she went out and shut everybody down," said Sam.

Dirty threw a one-hitter with five strikeouts as the Spartans prevailed 9-0 in the first game of the doubleheader. The Spartans were hot, even if the weather wasn't.

Cecil Community College had only nine players on its squad, giving it a decided disadvantage from the start. That disadvantage grew in the second game of the doubleheader when a Cecil player gave her coach a little too much lip. The coach admonished the player for not hustling on and off the field, and the player responded with, "You can't win without me. I'm your best player."

"See you later," the coach replied, pointing to the bench. "We'll play with eight."

Sam stood in his team's dugout, watching and listening to the exchange. He marveled at how the coach handled the situation.

"If I only have nine players, I don't know if I'm going to do that or not," he later reflected. "You have to, but I don't know if I would. Maybe wait until the next game and sit the girl. But the coach had the class to just say the heck with you. She wasn't going to have it affect the rest of the team, and she played with eight. I told her after the game, I gained a lot of respect for her when that happened."

The Spartans prevailed in game two, 11-1.

* * * *

If the on-field excitement wasn't enough, the beginning of the season also brought an off-the-field development, as Sam and Pic found out. Toot sought out the two coaches one day prior to practice.

"I'm going to be a mommy," Toot announced.

"Get out of here," Pic said, but then he saw how serious Toot was. And how frightened.

"I was scared at first, like any teenager is going to be," Toot explained. "It's a bittersweet thing. It's the best thing that could happen to you, but it's at the worst time, because it's during softball season."

Sam and Pic didn't pepper Toot with twenty questions. They were happy and excited for her, and comforting at the same time. They were also glad to know that there was a reason for Toot's recent out-of-character behavior.

"I was at that stage where I was really moody, and at games I was getting so mean to everybody," Toot said. "I went from this happy girl, just being mellow, to going around and telling everyone to shut up. I was freaking the girls out, and they were all saying, 'What's going on with Toot?'"

Sam's first concern was for Toot's safety, and the safety of the child she was carrying. He thought about fitting her with a football-type flack jacket or rib pads to protect her. But Toot's doctor said that wouldn't be necessary and gave her clearance to continue playing, providing she didn't do any sliding or diving, so Sam played her at first base.

But Toot didn't want to tell her teammates the news—at least not yet. She hadn't even spoken with her parents at this early stage. She wanted to wait until after her first ultrasound, to make sure everything was fine with the baby. Sam and Pic agreed to keep things quiet, but knew that the ultrasound appointment couldn't come soon enough. Especially as far as Toot's teammates were concerned.

"There would be an obvious situation where I had to slide into a base, and I wouldn't, and the girls would yell, 'Come on . . . why aren't you doing anything?'" Toot explained. "And I didn't care about hurting myself, but I was worried about hurting the baby."

Toot also became a little paranoid. She worried that she might get hit in the stomach with a pitch. In one game, a girl on the opposing team ran into her, so Toot went to her doctor the next day to make sure everything was okay, which it was. The only impact that the pregnancy had on her during games was that she would tire more easily by the end of the first game of the doubleheaders.

"I would notice by the second game that she was tired, but she would say, 'Let me play, let me play,'" Sam recalled.

Road games were interesting. Toot would always sit up front in one of the vans with Sam, munching on crackers and snacks because her stomach was turning. Bathroom stops also happened a great deal more frequently.

"I couldn't believe the other girls didn't pick up on things," Sam said.

Toot did reveal her secret to Hoppy and Nikki, but that was it. Neither of them felt it was their place to tell the other girls, but that didn't make it easier to keep things quiet.

"Some of the girls were getting really frustrated because Toot would be really short and snippy," Nikki explained. "And I would just say, 'Let it go. It's just Toot,' or, 'She's just having a rough time right now. Be the bigger person in this and just get over it.' It was hard because they didn't understand why we were defending her, but for the most part we all kept our emotions under control."

Sam, however, saw Toot's pregnancy as yet another omen—a good one. It was one of the many things were happening that caused him to flash back to 2003 when the Spartans won the state championship. Early in that season, the Spartans traveled to Montgomery County Community College for a doubleheader. During the games, outfielder Colleen McGouldrick slid into second base, sprained her ankle, and missed most of the regular season.

This year, when the team visited Montgomery early in the season, outfielder Alexis Walker slid into third base, sprained her ankle, and didn't play the remainder of the year.

Back in 2003, shortstop Michelle Panik was pregnant during the season. This year, it was Toot. For a coach like Sam who was incredibly superstitious to begin with, the omens were downright scary.

"I believe that everything happens for a reason," Sam explained. "But all these things that were happening, I didn't think they were just a coincidence."

Sam made the mistake of sharing these omens with his coaching staff, and they immediately found laughs at his expense.

"We'd pick up a soda and say, hey, we drank this soda back in 2003," Pic said. "We turned it into a big joke."

Laughter was a powerful elixir for the Spartans. One day prior to a practice, Sam sat the team down and told them that Pic had a medical problem that started several months ago. Of course, Pic had no idea of the story his brother was about to tell. Sam explained that one day, Pic woke up and found that his penis had turned orange. The doctor put him through multiple blood tests, cat scans, all sorts of tests, but still couldn't figure out the problem. Finally, the doctor asked Pic to take him through his daily routine. Pic told the doctor that he gets up at six every morning, showers and shaves, gets to work by seven, and gets home around five. Oh, but first he stops at a 7-11 to pick up a porno movie and a bag of cheetos, then he goes home.

The story brought roars of laughter from the girls, and made Pic's life miserable.

"I must have gotten three cases of Cheetos by the end of that season," Pic recalled. "Every day at practice, somebody else was bringing in a bag of Cheetos. To this day, I'll see girls and they'll hand me a bag of Cheetos."

* * * *

Meanwhile, the Spartans were having their share of laughers on the softball field, though it wasn't always humorous to their opponents. And in some respects, it was beginning to affect the girls, who were openly looking for more challenging competition than they had seen.

"Is this what it's going to be like all the time?" they asked.

Sam explained that, "These are the teams in our league, we have to play them. And anybody else we play, if coaches don't go out and recruit, you're going to see more of what you've been seeing. There's nothing I can do about it."

He also wasn't disappointed the way the season was playing out. It's a long season, he reasoned, and the fact that the Spartans were winning by large margins enabled him to rest some of his players periodically so they would be strong at the end of the season, come playoff time.

Sam was also glad to see his players were hungry for more competitive games; games that didn't end after five innings because of the mercy rule. And he knew those games would come soon enough.

After back-to-back shutouts of Penn State University – Abington, the Spartans had a doubleheader against Cedar

Crest College. Sam knew the Division III Falcons were usually better skilled than the teams NCC had played so far.

But they were still no match for the Spartans.

In the first game, Nikki hurled a two-hitter and went three-for-three at the plate. Jamye clubbed a solo home run, and the Spartans blanked the Falcons 8-0. Dirty pitched the second game, and the second pitch she threw was launched for a home run. One-zip, Spartans in the hole.

"I thought, 'Oh shit, let's see how Dirty reacts now,'" Sam said. "Because when something bad happens to Dirty, she'll sink down and you really have to pull hard to get her back out of the hole in which she puts herself."

No excavation was necessary this day. Dirty settled down, giving up just one hit the rest of the way, and the Spartans cruised to an 8-2 win. More importantly, Sam saw the fire return to their eyes for the first time since leaving Myrtle Beach.

"They never stopped believing in themselves, but now they had some competition," Sam said. "Now we were back to where the girls were excited. They were ready to play, and we saw what they could do."

What the Spartans could do was never more evident than in a weekend road doubleheader against Penn State University – Mont Alto. The school is located about 45 minutes south of Harrisburg, near Chambersburg National Park, almost to the Maryland border, a long ride for the players and coaches. And with a noon starting time, that meant hitting the road early.

The travel vans pulled out of the NCC parking lot around 8:30 a.m., barely reaching the highway before one of the girls had to use the bathroom. After pulling into a nearby service station,

Sam and the coaches went inside to get coffee, and by now the entire team had to use the bathroom. There was only one stall, so the bathroom break took longer than anticipated.

Finally back on the road, someone noticed that all of the batting helmets were left back at the school. The vans turned around and drove back for the helmets.

By now, Sam was starting to flip out. It was 9:20 a.m. before the vans were back on the road again, and he knew they had a two-hour drive ahead of them. He wanted to be at Mont Alto by 11—a full hour before game time to give the girls a chance to stretch, warm up and take batting practice. With the delays, that wouldn't happen.

"I was fuming," Sam recalled, "but I'm trying to keep this frustration to myself. I'm thinking, who the hell's in charge of the helmets? Why weren't they here? Why does everyone have to take a piss at the same time?"

The vans arrived at Mont Alto at 11:15 a.m., and Sam, angry that the girls wouldn't have a chance to take batting practice, instructed them to take infield practice. And that's when it happened.

"It was like the girls turned on the switch, just going to this other level," Sam recalled. "Pic and I were watching, and it was like they morphed right in front of us. I had never seen that before."

Pic said, "They're ready."

"Yeah, I can see that."

Others saw, too. Without any batting practice, the Lady Spartans clubbed six home runs in a double-header sweep of Penn State University – Mont Alto. After the two convincing wins, the Spartans were 22-0 on April 9. As Sam walked off the field one day, he was stopped by John Sweeny, NCC's men's baseball coach.

"What's your record now, Sam?" Sweeny asked.

"We're 22-0."

"Man, that's fantastic. How many games do you have left?"

"We should have around forty or so by the end of the season."

"Run the table."

Sam reflected a moment. "I don't know, John. That's tough to do with twenty more games to go."

"You run the table," Sweeny insisted. "That would be pretty special." Then he wished Sam good luck, turned and walked away.

Sam fought the urge to get caught up in the excitement. His coaches were talking about an undefeated season, his players' parents were already making hotel reservations for a trip to Pittsburgh and the state championship game, and now other coaches at NCC were jumping on the bandwagon.

Still, Sam was holding back. And with good reason.

"Every time I phoned in results of our games to the daily papers, they'd take the information and say, "Okay, thanks for phoning in the scores. Talk to you later,'" Sam explained. "It didn't matter that we were 18-0 or something like that at the time. We weren't getting any recognition for what we were doing. The papers would just run a small box score the next day. Nobody was saying anything, so that's why I kept it in my mind that what was happening was no big deal."

But it was. And time would tell.

NINE

Despite his obsession with worrying, Sam knew the 2005 NCC Spartans had the ability to make the season a memorable one.

He'd had the same feeling two years earlier, when he coached the 2003 Spartans to a Pennsylvania state championship. At the start of that season, he surveyed the girls to see if they knew someone who could follow the team, videotape the games, and put together a highlight film with music when the season was over. One of the girls volunteered her boyfriend.

"He did a great job," Sam recalled. "It was fantastic."

When combined with video taken by one of the parents of the playoff and state championship games, it made for a wonderful memento.

Sam wanted to chronicle the 2005 season the same way, so early in the season he set about to catch lightning in a bottle one more time. Instead, he got the shock of his life. He got zapped.

The girls didn't know anyone they could recommend, so Sam checked with the school's radio and television department. Did they have anyone who might want to take on this project for their portfolio? Sam was told they did. Her name was Tamara, and she would meet Sam and the team one day at practice to discuss how she would handle the project.

The next evening, Tamara made her way to the softball field, and Sam, his coaching staff and the players could not believe their eyes.

"She was a big girl," Sam recalled. "She was built like an Amazon; like a Samoan wrestler. She had a shock of black, curly hair growing up and out from her head that was thick enough and wide enough to block out the sun."

Tamara looked to make an immediate impression. She began by detailing she techniques she was going to employ as she videotaped the Spartans' games. Then she switched gears and recalled her days as a high school softball player in Connecticut. A "tremendous player" was the expression she used, and asked if she could take a turn in batting practice to "see if I still have it."

With the girls laughing behind her back, Sam gave her the go-ahead.

"She had vintage Ty Cobb form," Sam recalled, "never putting her hands together when she hit."

The bat and ball didn't come together too often, either, prompting Sam to comment to his coaches that, "I think she lost *it* somewhere between here and Connecticut."

Subsequent exchanges and videotaping sessions went even less smooth. Tamara lived in Allentown but did not drive. Sam had to pick her up before every home game and then bring her back when the games were over. Other than the time lost from his day to chauffeur his videographer, the trips were uneventful until one evening when Pic went along for the ride.

"Oh," Tamara said to Sam, "so this is your son?"

"That's my brother," Sam corrected. "There's only a four-year difference between us."

Pic, of course, enjoyed the comment, however inaccurate it was. But Tamara was quickly grating on Sam's nerves. To make matters worse, she would walk out onto the field during games while Sam was coaching third base to discuss camera angles.

"I'm going to take the camera to center field and turn it this way, and then I'll move it over to right field and turn it that way, so we can get some different angles," Tamara explained.

Sam was incredulous. "Whatever you want to do, just go ahead and do it, but you can't keep walking onto the field."

It came to a head late in the season during the semifinals of the Eastern Pennsylvania state playoffs. Tamara ventured onto the field to have her usual chat with Sam about camera angles. Seeing her approach, Sam turned to assistant coach Keith Greene and asked him to, "Get her away from me, now."

Keith has a way about him. He screams, flies off the handle, and people have no idea what he's saying. *He* knows what he's saying, but there are no real words coming out of his mouth. On this day, Keith turned in one of his best performances and lit into Tamara. She left the game, and was not heard from again until she phoned Sam prior to the state championship game in Pittsburgh.

"I want to go out to Pittsburgh with the team," she said. "I've gotta have this film and I need to finish it."

"I can't buy you a room, and the school can't buy you a room," Sam told Tamara, who could not afford a room on her own.

"Then I'll sleep on the bus."

"The bus company won't let you sleep on the bus."

"But I have to be there when you win the championship."

"I understand, but my hands are tied. There's nothing I can do."

Sam hung up the phone, and he never heard from Tamara again. The only tape he received was from an early season game that focused solely on the pitcher and catcher and never changed camera angles. It was shot from center field. No zoom. The pitcher and catcher looked like ants. It was not something for the archives.

* * * *

Players and coaches are human. They check the schedule in the beginning of the season and mark the calendar for key games against familiar adversaries. They may be looking forward to playing against an old friend, or exacting revenge against an opponent who has beaten them in the past.

For Sam, it was the latter. The date was Wednesday, April 13, and the opponent was Penn State University – Hazleton.

"I want to beat this team almost as much as I want to beat LCCC," Sam would explain, and with good reason.

During Sam's first five years of coaching softball at NCC, the Lady Spartans always fielded good teams. Perhaps not of the caliber that was currently ripping opposing pitchers to shreds, but solid softball players. Each year the Spartans would make it to the Eastern Pennsylvania finals, and each year they would lose to PSU - Hazleton. The PSU players, however, were not the object of Sam's animosity. It was the PSU coach.

The PSU coach had a reputation for being an egomaniac; a reputation that he apparently earned through his actions. He could be beating teams 44-0 and he would still have his players bunt and steal bases. He was cocky and obnoxious, and further irritated opponents by wearing yellow socks adorned with happy faces. And because his team always won its division, the Eastern finals were held on PSU's field. Prior to the games, he was presented with the coach of the year award, and he would dance around home plate with the trophy.

Soon, rumors began circulating around the league that the coach was paying players to attend the college. The word was that his wife had a lot of money, so he transformed a large barn on his property into a multi-purpose facility. There were batting cages and pitching circles on the lower level, and apartments for players upstairs. He would train players year-round, and give them menial jobs on campus with disproportionate salaries.

"One year I was recruiting a girl from Tamaqua, a catcher, who was going to come down and play for us," Sam recalled. "I phoned one day and the girl's mother told me that her daughter was going somewhere else, to Penn State – Hazleton."

"He's giving us money," the mother explained.

"Oh, really, that's great," Sam responded, playing dumb.

"Yes, he's giving my daughter a job on campus and paying her $1,500 a semester."

"Really? What kind of job?"

"Well, it's a fake job. All she really has to do is go in and turn on the lights in the gym each morning, and she gets $1,500."

"Wow, that's a great deal," said Sam, his congenial voice belying his anger. "Congratulations. I hope your daughter does well."

The obnoxious PSU coach retired, suddenly, after the 2002 season, but that didn't erase the memory of many painful, one-sided losses. Or the images of him dancing around home plate, his smile socks flashing mocking grins at opposing teams. And the new coach who took over had to bear the brunt of his predecessor's sins. His team was pounded on regularly, and he knew it was payback for all the times the previous coach would run up the scores.

Sam and the Spartans showed little sympathy that day. They jumped all over the PSU pitcher for six runs in the first inning and five more in the second—an 11-0 lead before the Lady Lions knew what hit them. Ness crushed a three-run homer, Missy clubbed two round-trippers and Jamye tacked on another. The game was stopped after five innings with the Spartans on top 19-0. But long before the onslaught was halted, the PSU fans began ripping into the Lions' coach.

"Why can't you get girls like this guy has?"

"Why can't you play ball like this?"

"You suck as a coach."

"You're terrible . . . you have to leave."

By the start of the second game, the PSU fans began directing their frustrations at the Spartan players. In particular, three male students seated in the bleachers just behind the third base coaching box were needling Sam and every player who came to bat.

Then Nikki, who pitched the first game, walked to the plate. The jeers and cat-calls continued. Nikki fouled off a couple of pitches behind home plate, and the jeers got louder.

"The field is that way," the hecklers yelled, pointing in the opposite direction of the backstop.

Nikki stepped out of the batter's box. She looked down at Sam, who was standing in the third base coaching box, glanced briefly at the three men seated in the bleachers, then looked back to Sam.

"She just moved me with her eyes," Sam recalled. "It was like she was saying coach, take two steps to your left."

Sam took those two steps. Nikki stepped back into the batter's box and ripped a one-hopper to Sam's right. The ball was hit so hard Sam heard it sizzle as it went past him. It bounced up into the bleachers where it caught one of the hecklers on the leg. Nikki flashed Sam a smile.

"Okay," Nikki said softly to herself, "now I can hit."

The hecklers were never heard from again.

But the hitting barrage on the field continued. In the second game, the Lady Spartans clubbed five home runs and ran off ten runs in the second inning on their way to a 24-1 rout. At one point, Ness pounded a pitch deep to center field, and the center fielder just dropped her glove to the ground and stood there, refusing to chase the ball.

"What's that all about?" said Sam, who was then coaching first base, to no one in particular. But the Lions' third baseman responded.

"You're making a mockery of the game," she answered.

"How are we making a mockery?" Sam returned. "We're just hitting the ball. If you can't stop us from hitting the ball, that's your fault, not ours. And I'm not going to have my girls change their swing just because you can't stop us."

The Spartans dropped forty-three runs on the PSU Lady Lions that afternoon; forty-three paybacks for the embarrassments of years gone by, but not forgotten.

The NCC vans bypassed a Friendly's Restaurant on the way home, the girls were just too tired to stop and get out of the car to eat. So they pulled up to a McDonald's drive through and took their dinner on the run. Twenty-three Big Macs to go, please.

* * * *

The ride home from PSU – Hazleton was a quiet one, and it gave Sam a chance to think. The Spartans were more than half way through the season, and had pounded every team they had played. Few games went the full seven innings. So Sam, ever the planner and worrier, was thinking ahead. If the Spartans won their division, they would have home field advantage in the playoffs, and the Eastern Pennsylvania championships would be played on their field.

That was the good news. The bad news was that the eastern championships were scheduled for Saturday, May 1, the same day that his twins, Nicholas and Devan, were to receive their first Holy Communion. The games were slated to begin at 10 a.m., the holy communion at 10:30. And there was very little room to negotiate when it came to those starting times.

Sam felt trapped. He had a responsibility to the team, but he also had a responsibility to his children. Of course, there were those who would tell him he really had no decision to make, but that wasn't Sam. He had a great deal of loyalty to the softball team, maybe too much, but that's who he was. And he had been worrying about this potential conflict ever since the season's schedule had been announced.

Am I a father, or am I just a coach, he thought to himself. Don't I care about my family and my children?

Sam's wife, Chris, looked to simplify things for him.

"You know what decision you'd better make," she told him.

Sam knew as well, but that didn't stop the voice in the back of his head from calling out: "I want to be at that game. I don't want to miss that game."

The agonizing decision-making process continued well beyond the trip home from Hazleton that day.

* * * *

Jenn and Missy were co-captains on the Spartans' 2005 team. They led by example and, when necessary, vocally. But theirs weren't the only voices that helped keep the Spartans working as a finely tuned machine.

One of those voices belonged to Nikki. Not only would she encourage those players on the bench to cheer for their team-mates, she would put a bug in a coach's ear to "get the girls to scream louder." That was often the case with girls who played in the first game of a doubleheader and sat out the second game, or vice versa. Nikki would make sure that even though the girls weren't in the game, they were still *in* the game.

On a Sunday afternoon against Penn College, Nikki took that 'encouragement' to another level. Several of the girls who were not playing in the first game were sitting together when one of their cell phones went off.

Next, it was Nikki's turn to go off.

"I told them it was very inappropriate that they would be talking on cell phones or text messaging during the game," Nikki recalled. "It shows that their heads are not in the game; that they're not part of the team."

Nikki took the opportunity to issue a clear directive.

"I don't ever again want to see you with your phones on the bench or during practice," she said. "You should be up against the fence cheering on your teammates. Because when you get your playing time, that's what everyone else does. And you're disrespecting your teammates by not staying in the game."

Everyone on the bench heard the exchange, including Sam.

"She handled the situation beautifully," he said. "It was the last time I ever saw cell phones during a practice or during a game."

The trip home that day from Penn College, following the Spartans' 10-1 and 17-2 doubleheader sweep, included a stop in Williamsport, site of the Little League World Series every August since 1947. Looking out over the field from beyond the right field fence, Sam said he was blown away.

"It was an awesome sight," the coach recalled.

On the hill beyond the stadium's left field wall was a huge bronze statue of Casey at the Bat. The girls took turns posing with the statue while their teammates snapped away with their cameras, and then everyone gathered for a team photo.

For a rare moment, Sam was relaxed. It had been a beautiful day.

TEN

When you hit the ball and score runs at the rate that the 2005 Lady Spartans did, people are going to talk. Some of that talk will not be complimentary.

The most frequent accusation Sam heard that year was that the girls were using illegal bats. After all, no one could hit the ball as hard and as far as they were—or at least that's what some opposing teams reasoned.

Those accusations came to a head during a doubleheader at Penn State University – Schuylkill. A section of the outfield, in deep left-center, inclined up to a fence. In almost straightaway centerfield, about three-hundred-twenty feet away, there was a soccer goal. In a pre-game meeting at home plate to review the ground rules, Sam asked what the rule was if a ball was hit up and over the fence, or if it got entangled in the soccer goal. He was told by the umpires and the Schuylkill coach that, "It will never happen; don't even think about it."

Sam looked at the umpires. He didn't want to be difficult, or seem to brag, but he knew the way his team was pounding the ball. And even if the chance of a ball being hit that far was slim, shouldn't everyone know what the ground rule was in advance? Sam thought so.

"Guys, right now, we're crushing the ball," Sam tried to explain. "We're going to hit that fence."

One of the umpires shook his head. "I'm telling you, it's never going to happen," he said, ending the conversation.

Sam shrugged his shoulders, walked back to the dugout, and waited. It didn't take long. Nikki was the first batter of the game, and on the third pitch, she launched a rocket that landed right up against the fence. She easily rounded the bases for a home run.

Missy, Jenn and Lex, as teammates had begun calling Alexis Walker, also drove pitches up the incline and against the fence during the course of the first game that ended in an 8-0 Spartan win. Missy even clubbed a triple that almost landed in the soccer net.

In the stands, the Schuylkill pitcher's father was outraged. He had never seen his daughter pounded in this manner, and he was beside himself. He offered up an explanation in the form of illegal bats.

"There's something wrong," he said to his daughter between innings. "Check the bats; this isn't right. They shouldn't be hitting you like this."

But the Lady Spartans were, and that prompted the umpires—if for no other reason than to appease the Schuylkill coaches and the people in the stands—to check one of the NCC bats; the one that made a slightly different sound when the hitter made contact. Pic gladly walked it over to the home plate umpire.

"I know your bats are legal," the umpire told Pic. "Just put up with me because they want me to look it over."

The umpire scanned the bat, then handed it back to Pic.

"Everything's fine here," he said, then turned and walked away.

Sam even loaned the bat to some of the Schuylkill players for soft toss practice in between games of the doubleheader. It didn't change anything, except perhaps making the Spartan players angry. Their hitting ability was being called into question, and a bat was given credit for their success. So, they exacted their revenge at the plate, pounding Schuylkill 30-0 in the second game.

Throughout the games, the Schuylkill third baseman, a short and stocky girl who was as pleasant as could be, kept up a running dialogue with Sam when he was coaching third base while the Spartans were batting. The ongoing chatter did not sit well with much of the home crowd, which began shouting, "Stop talking to the coach."

The girl had been telling Sam that he and several of the NCC girls looked familiar, but that she couldn't quite place them from the previous season. But after a few innings, and after the Spartans had launched a few rockets up against the fence in left-center field, the girl had total recall.

"Now I remember you," she told Sam. "You're the team that beat the shit out of us last year."

Sam could only laugh.

* * * *

By this point the Spartans' record for the season stood at 32-0. The parents were asking if they should make reservations for the state championship game in Pittsburgh, and Sam was busy running playoff scenarios through his head. The top two teams from each division get into the playoffs automatically. The second- and third-place teams in each division play each other with the winner qualifying for the playoffs, a system that gives the third-place team some added incentive. The two teams that win the pre-playoff game join the two teams with the best records in their division as the four teams that qualify for the Eastern Pennsylvania Collegiate Conference Championships; all the games are played on the same day at the field of the No. 1 seeded team. The team with the best record plays the team with the fourth-best record, then the second- and third-seeded teams square off. The two winners play for the EPCC championship and the right to play the western winner for the state title.

The Spartans were currently the No. 1 seed, so if they held serve, the EPCC championships would be played at NCC. And unless the wheels came completely off the bus, the Spartans were not about to have a letdown.

That much was clear in doubleheaders against Delaware and Montgomery community colleges on April 19 and 21, respectively. The Spartans pounded Delaware 22-0 and 14-0, with Nikki pitching a no-hitter in the first game. She also reached base four times and scored three runs. But it was her base running in one of the two Montgomery games—both lopsided wins for the Lady Spartans—that reinforced in Sam's mind what a gem of an athlete she was and how knowledgeable she was of the way the game should be played.

Nikki was on first and Gina was on third. A ground ball was hit to the second baseman, who decided to try to tag Nikki rather than throw to the shortstop covering second base for the force out. Nikki stopped in her tracks and began backing away from the second baseman, all the while motioning for Gina to head for home plate. Nikki stayed in the rundown long enough for Gina to score the run. Then she just walked over to the second baseman and said, "Okay, you can tag me now." It wasn't an all-important run in an 18-2 blowout, but it demonstrated Nikki's knowledge of the game.

"She's way ahead of the game," Sam would later explain. "Her parents are hard core, one in softball and the other in volleyball. And when I say hard core, I mean it in a good way. They are so knowledgeable, they know every facet of the game. That has transcended down through their three children. And I always say, if you have tremendous kids, then the parents must be special people."

But Sam's adoration of Nikki didn't stop him from being nervous. In the second game against Montgomery, the Spartans were winning 10-2 when Sam sent Pic out to take his place coaching third base late in the game. With the sizeable lead, Pic felt no need to flash any signals to the hitters. That didn't sit well with Sam.

"He saw that I wasn't giving any signals and the next inning he pulled me from coaching third," Pic recalled. "I asked, 'Why are you pulling me?' And he said, 'Because you're not flashing signals. We have to score because these guys are coming back.'"

Pic laughed when recalling the scene. "Yep, he pulled me. It was 10-2, and he was all nervous because I wasn't doing anything to help us score runs."

The game, of course, was never in doubt, and Sam would later admit that, "I shouldn't be worrying."

Especially after what happened as the girls were leaving the field following the doubleheader win at Montgomery Community College. Several of the Montgomery players' parents stopped Sam and his coaches and told them that, "This is the best team we've ever seen play the game of softball." They added that not only was it the best, but one of the nicest as well, with very well-mannered girls.

"That made me feel good," Sam recalled. "It was a nice thing to hear."

But that didn't stop him from worrying.

* * * *

Somehow the Spartans had made it through thirty-six games and—other than the select few who knew—Toot's pregnancy was still a secret being kept from much of the team. A recent ultrasound, however, had revealed that the baby was fine, and everything was going smooth with the pregnancy. Sam approached Toot.

"It's time," he told her. "It's time to tell the team what's been going on. Some of the girls have noticed the way you've acted and it's bothering them. I don't want this to tear us apart at this point in the year. Let's tell them." Toot agreed.

Prior to practice one day, Sam called the girls in from the field after stretching for a team meeting. He had decided that he would position Toot's pregnancy as one of the many omens he had noticed during the course of the season.

"I want to point out some things that have been going on throughout the season that have paralleled the 2003 season when we won a state title," the coach explained. "Let's call them omens. Two years ago, we had a girl slide into third base and twist her ankle. This year, Lex slides into third base and twists her ankle. That's one omen. Two years ago, a kid I coached football with at Bethlehem Catholic, perfect health, died in his sleep the day after we won the state championship. About a week ago, I got an email that a girl I went to high school with died while teaching her daughter how to drive. That's two omens."

Now, Sam had the girls' undivided attention. Some bought into the omen theory, other's thought their coach was nuts. But whether they believed in his omens or not didn't matter. He knew they were listening.

"And the third omen is, two years ago, Michelle Panik, the shortstop on our team, was pregnant and played the entire season pregnant," Sam continued. "And this year..."

The girls all began looking around. "Who's pregnant?" they asked.

"Toot's pregnant," Sam announced. "That's why she's been acting so weird lately."

Immediately the girls began hugging and congratulating Toot, and it was easy to see that it was a relief to have the pregnancy out in the open.

"Is it safe for her to play?" the girls asked.

"From day one, we got clearance from everyone, so she's fine to play," Sam explained.

"Great," they said. "Let's just keep going from here."

"It was a huge weight off my shoulders," Toot recalled. "And by the time I told the girls, my parents already knew, so it was out in the open and I was more willing to talk about it."

Toot informed her teammates that she was having a girl, and everyone wanted to know if she had picked out a name. She hadn't. Was she trying to come up with a name that related to softball or the team?

"It's weird because you can suggest so many different names to someone, but when it's your child that you're naming you think, no, that's not good enough," Toot said. "People will just abbreviate it and call her that, and it might be an ugly nickname. I'm just trying to come up with the perfect name."

Then, with reference to her coach, "But not once have I thought about Samantha or anything like that."

Even Sam had to laugh at that.

* * * *

The NCC Spartans were scheduled to play a doubleheader against Lehigh Carbon Community College on Saturday afternoon, April 23. It was the first scheduled meeting between the two teams since the Spartans' painful loss to LCCC a year earlier in the EPCC semifinals. The date had been marked on Sam's calendar since the games were originally scheduled, long before the current season began.

He was anxious for payback.

Then Saturday came and it rained. The games were postponed, and NCC athletic director Bill Bearse wanted to reschedule them for that Monday. But LCCC was in third place in their division, which meant they had to play Penn State University – Mont Alto, the second-place team, to see which team would qualify for the playoffs.

That game was scheduled for Tuesday.

"The LCCC coaches said that they had to play their game on Tuesday," Sam recalled. "And if they played us on Monday, their girls and their pitcher would be tired."

Bearse suggested that NCC and LCCC make up their games on Thursday, and the LCCC coaches agreed. But Bearse was skeptical.

"Look, if you lose to Mont Alto and you're knocked out of the playoffs, you're still going to play us, right?" Bearse asked.

Yes, they said, they would play NCC on Thursday.

Now the Spartan players were doubtful.

"They're running away coach," the girls told Sam. "If they lose, they're not going to play us."

Sam tried to keep everything positive.

"Relax, they're going to play us," he told his team. "Bill has done all he can."

But in private with his assistant coaches, Sam knew better.

"They're going to find any excuse not to play us," Sam told them. "And if they lose, they definitely won't play us."

Sam was right. LCCC lost to Mont Alto, failed to qualify for the playoffs, and then told Bearse that they wouldn't have enough players to play NCC. The games were cancelled. It was a blow to most of the players, Toot in particular, since her high school softball coach was now the head coach at LCCC.

"I was so psyched the whole season, just waiting to play LCCC and to beat them," Toot said. "We wanted to beat them really bad. We were out for all of them. To have the games cancelled, it's like waking up on Christmas morning, seeing your presents and not being able to open them. To have them on the schedule and then not be able to play them, it was such a downer."

What made matters worse was that the season-ending games against Luzerne Community College and Penn State University – Scranton, were also cancelled. The latter was to have been the team's Senior Night celebration.

"In our by-laws, we can count those games as forfeits," Sam explained. "If you try to reschedule the games and the other team refuses to play, you can count the forfeits as wins on your schedule. But we don't do that."

The cancelled games meant that the Spartans went through the regular season undefeated, and would be the No. 1 seed in EPCC Championships. It also meant Sam's team would have a ten-day layoff until the championship tournament, a long layoff for a team on a roll.

But the coach was preoccupied with an even more pressing issue.

* * * *

The EPCC Championship Tournament was scheduled for Saturday, April 30. NCC was pitted against PSU – Schuylkill in the first game, followed by PSU – Mont Alto against Luzerne in the second game. The two winning teams would then square off that same day for the EPCC title.

But Sam's son and daughter, twins Nicholas and Devan, were to receive first communion that same morning. The coach recalled wondering, "What the heck am I going to do?"

"I knew it was a huge day for my children," Sam explained. "But I don't want to miss the games."

He decided that since he had the option of deciding what time the first game would start, the one NCC would play in, at either 10 or 11 a.m., and the communion was scheduled to begin at 10:30 a.m., he'd schedule the start of the NCC- Schuylkill game for 11. That way, he reasoned, he could go to the communion, see his kids receive, and then leave quickly and get to the game.

"People were saying to me, 'Are you nuts thinking you should be at the game?'" Sam recalled. "I told them that I had a responsibility to be there, and they'd say, 'But this is your family.' You can't imagine the battle that was going on inside me."

On the outside, Sam felt that by going to the start of the communion and then leaving in time to be at the game, he'd be "in the clear" with his wife and kids. Inside, he knew his family still wouldn't be happy with his decision.

When Saturday morning came, the heavens opened and heavy rains forced the tournament to be postponed until Sunday. Sam was safe. And if there ever was an omen that somebody upstairs liked him, Saturday morning's downpour was it.

ELEVEN

How do you motivate an undefeated team? Do you *need* to motivate a team that just ran roughshod over every team it played, en route to a 36-0 regular season record? Sam thought he needed to. And anyone who tried to argue with him was quickly reminded of the Spartans' EPCC semifinal loss to LCCC just one year ago.

"You can't take anything for granted," Sam reasoned. "You step off a curb to walk across the street, you'd better be looking both ways, because you don't know what's going to happen. That game against LCCC taught me a lesson in life, and I don't take anything for granted any more. That's why I felt I needed to keep motivating the girls."

Adding fuel to Sam's cause was the fact that the Lady Spartans' opponent in the first round of the EPCC playoffs was PSU – Schuylkill, a team they had just clobbered 8-0 and 30-0 a few weeks earlier. He didn't want the troops being lackadaisical.

"I don't want to take the chance of the girls coming in and thinking this is nothing; that they're going to kick the crap out of them," Sam said.

In addition, the Spartans hadn't played in about a week, prompting Chrysa Wassel to proclaim to Sam in the days leading up to the playoffs, "We're going to scare the crap out of you in the first game, and then we're going to blow them out in the second game."

But Sam knew he had pretty much used every cliché in the book during the course of the regular season. So he turned to Tony Cocca, a good friend who coached softball and football at nearby Whitehall High School, whom Sam referred to as "probably one of the greatest motivating speakers I know."

Cocca's response?

"Sam, they're 36-0. What motivation do you need to give them that you haven't given them already?" Cocca asked.

"I just need to light a fire under them so they don't go out there flat."

Cocca relented and gave Sam the matches he'd need to light that fire. Then, on the morning of the playoffs, Sunday, May 1, after the Spartans took infield and soft toss practice, Sam called the team into the gymnasium, sat them down on the bleachers, and spoke.

"At this point now, you're not the hunters anymore, you're the hunted," Sam began. "You're the people they're coming after right now, and if you don't get back into that mindset of being the hunters, if you sit back and just be defensive instead of being aggressive, you're going to get eaten up. So you have to get back that mindset where you want to be the hunter."

Sam paused momentarily. The gymnasium was as silent as a tomb. Nobody said a word, they all just sat there. He wasn't certain if that was good or bad, if he had their attention or his words were going right over their heads. Regardless, he continued.

"You can go to the banquet table, but if you don't eat you're going to leave hungry," Sam cautioned. "Just like if you go to these playoffs now and you don't play to your potential, you're going to walk away unfulfilled, and that's going to be in the back of your head for the rest of your life. The what if, I should have, I could have, all those questions. If you can look in the mirror after this is all over, and say you gave every single thing you had and not question yourself once, then that's all we can ask. But, this is your time to make your mark. We're a few games away from being the greatest team ever here at Northampton. It's our next step on the ladder, so now it's time to take your next two steps and get us to Pittsburgh. Don't sit back. Be aggressive, and let's go get these people."

Again, the girls didn't say a word, nothing. Sam hoped it was just the way they were, taking their business-as-usual approach.

* * * *

The Spartans, the home team, took the field for their semifinal match against PSU – Schuylkill precisely at 11 a.m. It was then that Sam noticed that the Schuylkill team, which had vigorously complained during the teams' previous meetings that the Spartans were using an illegal bat, were now using the same bat. It was as though they were convinced that the bat was the key, not the players, so they went out and purchased the exact same bat.

Sam couldn't help but smile. Oh well, he thought, imitation is the most sincere form of flattery. But he wasn't smiling for long.

Nikki was in the pitching circle for the Spartans, and she uncharacteristically walked the leadoff batter. The next batter lined a ball to left field where Chrysa slipped on the wet grass and fell as the ball sailed over her head for a run-scoring double. The next batter lined a double to left centerfield, another run scored, and Schuylkill had a quick 2-0 lead.

Sam sat in the dugout and shook his head. We're in trouble, he thought. We're 36-0, and now it's going to cave in on us.

The Spartans were retired easily in the home half of the first inning. Two more hits produced another run for Schuylkill in the top of the second, and the visiting team had a 3-0 lead. The Spartans went out weakly again in the home second.

"We weren't doing anything, and there was no emotion," Sam recalled. "But then Nikki started to shut the door."

Nikki's pitching began to turn the momentum. Starting in the third inning, she struck out eleven batters in a row, finishing with fourteen for the game. Now the Spartans needed an offensive spark, and they got it from Gina Renaldi. Not known for her power, Gina led off the third inning by launching the first pitch she saw over the left field fence for a home run. The Spartans were on the board, the crowd began going beserk, and the girls came to life.

Nikki was next. She walked, stole both second and third base, then scored on a single by Jenn Davis, bringing the Spartans within a run at 3-2. Two innings later, in the bottom of the fifth, Jenn singled and came all the way around to score on a double into the right field corner by Ness. Tied game, 3-3, two innings to go—and the momentum had swung in NCC's direction.

The Spartans left runners on second and third in the sixth inning, but Nikki struck out the side in the top of the seventh. All along the third baseline, the crowd—sitting on blankets and beach chairs—roared with anticipation.

Ness flew out to center field to open the home seventh, and Missy grounded out to third. Two outs, no one on base. But Missy's grounder was a bullet that nearly knocked the third baseman's glove off. She recovered in time to throw Missy out, but she was clearly in pain as she grabbed for her thumb.

Jamye Mease singled to keep the inning alive. Toot then grounded to third, and the third baseman, with her thumb throbbing in pain, had a difficult time handling the ball. Her throw to first was off the mark, and dribbled past the first baseman. Jamye advanced to third and Toot to second with two out, the winning run now sixty feet away.

Sam was coaching third base. Jenn, standing in the dugout, called out to get her coach's attention. She met him midway between the dugout and the coaching box.

"Bunt."

"What the hell are you talking about?" Sam asked.

"I'm telling you right now, bunt down to third base," Jenn answered. "The third baseman is not going to be able to handle it. She's a wreck right now."

Sam called time. Bunt with two out and runners on second and third? It sounded crazy, and he knew the whole season came down to this one decision. He looked at Jenn.

"Bunt," she implored him.

Robbie came running down from coaching first base. "What's going on?"

Sam relayed Jenn's idea. Robbie considered it for a moment, then agreed. "Yeah, we have to bunt."

Sam relented. "Okay, let's do it."

Lex, the designated hitter, was scheduled to bat. Sam called her back and sent up Dirty to execute the crucial bunt.

Dirty stepped into the batter's box, Sam returned to the third base coaching box and flashed Dirty the bunt sign. On the first pitch, Dirty lowered her bat and bunted the ball, rolling it slowly up the third baseline. Jamye began racing for home. The third baseman charged, and as she began to grab the ball with her bare hand, her feet slipped out from under her.

Sam watched from the third base coaching box as the entire scene, which seemed to be taking place in slow motion, unfolded in front of him. When he saw the third baseman slip, he thought, "Oh my god, there's only one play she can make."

The third baseman realized that, too. Falling backwards, she did the only thing she could and flipped the ball underhand toward the catcher, who was waiting anxiously at home plate for the throw. The ball seemed to hang in mid-air as it drifted toward the catcher's outstretched mitt. The crowd, which had been roaring earlier in the inning, had grown silent.

Jamye barreled toward home, straining to beat the throw. She slid, and her foot hit the plate just as the catcher lowered her glove to make the tag. The umpire, bent over at the waist for a close look, threw his arms out to either side.

"Safe," he yelled.

It was bedlam at home plate. Jamye was mobbed by her teammates, who had been moving toward home plate from the moment the play began to unfold. Dirty, who had sprinted hard to first base, retraced her steps and joined in the celebration. The Spartans had a 4-3 win, and for one of the few times all season, the girls' emotions spilled out onto the field.

"I told the girls to go relax," Sam recalled. "Then I went over and talked to Schuylkill's team, because you know, when you play in this league and you play against the same teams year after year, you get to know the coaches and players real well. And I went over there, and started to talk to them, and said I was going to miss their senior players, because I know this is the last game we're going to play against them. I just wanted to tell them how much I appreciated the girls, and the girls who were leaving after two years, how classy they were, and how hard they fought. And how we always hated to play them because we knew how tough they were and it was going to be a great and well-played game. And I'm crying, and they're crying, and we're hugging each other, and it was just an emotional time."

And, there was still another game to be played.

* * * *

With a thrilling semifinal win in their pocket, the Spartans got to unwind for about two hours and watch as PSU – Mont Alto and Luzerne battled in the second semifinal. The Spartans would square off later that afternoon against the winner of the Mont Alto-Luzerne game for the EPCC title.

Luzerne was an unknown entity to Sam and the Spartans. A doubleheader had been scheduled between the two teams for the last week of the regular season. But with the seeding already set for the EPCC playoffs, and knowing the two teams could meet just around the corner, the Luzerne coaches decided to forfeit the games rather than let the Spartans get an advance look at their team.

The decision angered Sam and his players, but it became a moot point when Mont Alto knocked Luzerne out of the playoffs in the second semifinal game. Now it was NCC against Mont Alto for all the EPCC marbles. And after an exhilarating semifinal win, Sam was glad his team had a chance to rest.

"The wait is good because now you get to see who you're going to play next," he explained. "You get to watch them, and if your pitcher is really on, you can rest her for the second game. You also let the emotions settle down a little bit, and are able to get something to eat. For Mont Alto, you have to play, then warm up and play again. You don't stop."

And Mont Alto didn't stop. With Jenn on the mound for the EPCC final, Mont Alto strung together four hits and scored two runs to take a 2-0 lead in the top of the first inning. It seemed like déjà vu all over again. But in this game, the Spartans' bats were alive from the first inning on.

Run-scoring hits by Missy, Ness and Dirty put the Spartans back on top, 3-2, in the bottom of the first inning. Gina doubled home a run for a 4-2 advantage in the fourth inning. But in the top of the fifth, a single and two walks loaded the bases for Mont Alto with no outs. Sam called time, went to the mound and—as hard as it was for him to do—took the ball from Jenn.

"I know it was disappointing for her," the coach explained, "but I also know she's good for four or five innings in a pressure situation. And as soon as she gets in trouble, we pull her."

Nikki came in and struck out the next two batters, then issued a bases-loaded walk to force in a run. She struck out the next batter to limit the damage, and the Spartans took a 4-3 lead into the home half of the fifth. That's when they got down to business.

A two-run homer by Missy and a two-run double from Chrysa put the Spartans up 8-3 heading to the sixth inning. Nikki kept the Mont Alto bats silent in the top half of the inning, then led off the home half of the sixth with a walk. Jamye singled one out later, and Sam called time to talk to Missy before she stepped into the batter's box.

"End this thing now and let's go to Pittsburgh," the coach instructed.

"What are you talking about?" Missy asked.

"If you hit a home run, that's our eight-run cushion, and the game is over," Sam explained. "So end it now."

Missy grounded out to the pitcher. Two outs. Sam had the same conversation with Ness.

"Hit a home run and let's get out of here," he told his shortstop.

Ness obliged, driving a fastball over the leftfield fence for a game-ending, walk-off, three-run homer. The score was 11-3, putting the mercy rule into effect.

As Ness rounded the bases, Sam stood in the coaching box at third base and began screaming, "You did it. We're going to Pittsburgh."

The Spartans were the EPCC champs.

* * * *

As shocking as it might sound, Sam viewed going to the Pittsburgh area to play the Community College of Beaver County for the Pennsylvania Collegiate Athletic Association state championship as a bit of a vacation. After watching the Spartans blow through the season and rally to win the EPCC title with an undefeated record, hitting the road to play for the state title was like a getaway, mostly because of the attitude Sam shared with his coaches as the season unfolded.

"We would just sit around together at night and talk," Sam explained. "And I said that if we make it past the EPCCs, there's nothing that's going to stop this team. They won't let anything get in front of them. And I told these guys, 'I will be so proud to put a gold medal around your neck at the end of this season.'"

For Sam, Keith and Robbie, heading west to Monaca, Pennsylvania was like a return engagement. They were all there two years ago when the Spartans defeated the Titans for the 2003 state title. But this was the first trip for the other three assistant coaches, Pic, Jack and Mark, and Sam wanted them to know what winning a state title feels like.

He even took steps to whet Pic's appetite.

"I want you to sit down and watch this," Sam told his brother during the week the team was preparing for the EPCC tournament.

"What is it?"

"It's the state championship game from two years ago," Sam explained. "I want you to watch the last out."

So Pic watched. He watched as the last out was recorded, and saw the girls jumping, screaming and crying as they hugged one another. He saw Sam make a short speech, then introduce each of the girls as he handed out the gold medals. And as he watched, tears began to run down his cheeks.

"I want to experience that," Pic said, interrupting the taped celebration. "I want to feel what that's like, and see the girls' reactions."

And now Pic, and the other assistant coaches, had their chance.

* * * *

The six-hour bus ride to Beaver County was long but uneventful. The girls passed the time watching DVDs on the two screens that hung in the front and rear of the bus. Sam was happy just to relax after a hectic week of planning and preparation.

First, Sam called the Titans' coach and the two exchanged congratulations for winning their respective league titles. Traditionally, the two teams exchange gifts just before the best two-out-of-three championship series begins, and the host team will arrange for a large meal or picnic following the games. The visiting team travels to the site on Friday, and two games are played on Saturday. If either team wins both games, it's over. If the teams split the two games, they come back on Sunday and play one game for the championship.

"Two years ago, they put out a big spread after the games so everyone could eat," Sam recalled. "I asked the coach if they were going to do that again, or if I needed to make arrangements for my team to eat somewhere."

The Titans' coach apologized, but said that the school had a new athletic director who "was not into that stuff, so we're not going to do anything when you come out." The girls on the team didn't want to exchange gifts, either.

Sam said, "That's fine," and he let it go at that. But the new athletic director's attitude, and that of the girls on the team, bothered him. It would soon turn out to be just the tip of the iceberg.

The NCC bus arrived in Beaver County around 8 p.m. Friday night after stopping for dinner along the way. Buffet, of course.

"Got to be consistent," said Sam, true to his superstitious nature. "Can't change routines at that point."

Friday night was one to remember, or to forget, depending on your perspective. Sam's coaching staff and many of the players' parents were in the hotel lounge, joking, drinking and standing around listening to the DJ during open mike night. The choice of beverage went from soda to beer to beer shots—and anything else that was readily available. Gina Renaldi's father plunked some coins in the Karaoke machine and sang "Amore." Robbie did his best on some Barry White tunes, while Pic, Jack and Keith teamed up for "It's Raining Men."

Sam? His family had accompanied the team on the trip, so he was relegated to the hotel room to babysit his twins, Nicholas and Devan.

"I spent the evening watching The Incredibles," he moaned on Saturday morning.

By then, he wasn't the only one moaning. Pic sat at the breakfast table looking like a train wreck, his arms dangling loosely off the sides of his chair.

"I don't feel good," Pic said.

"That's your own fault," said Sam.

Keith didn't look any better. Sitting at the table with a blank stare, he looked like a body that had just been embalmed, except for the sweat that was running down his face.

"I don't feel good," Keith echoed.

Sam shook his head. "Just drink some water and get better. We have a state championship game to play."

* * * *

The games were not played on the same field that had been used in 2003. That field, Sam recalled, was almost identical in size to NCC's home field. But the Titans' coaching staff had done their homework. They had heard the stories. They knew that the Spartans had pounded out fifty-seven home runs as a team that season, and they were determined not to get beaten by the long ball.

Instead, the games were played on a field that resembled a baseball field, at least in terms of the outfield dimensions, which stretched 390 feet from home plate in every direction. It was also, as Sam recalled, a dog-awful field in terms of its condition.

"But they could have held the game in the parking lot and it wouldn't have mattered to these girls," Sam said. "They were ready to go."

At a practice prior to the EPCC championships, Sam had given each girl on the team a small plastic bag with their number on it, and instructed them to take the bags out to their respective position on the field. Once at their position, he told the infielders to grab some dirt and fill the bag, and the outfielders to do the same with a few blades of grass, then come back in from the field.

"What's this for?" they asked.

"Don't worry about it," Sam said, brushing off the activity. "It's just a way for me to remember all the players."

Sam also visited his parents' graves before the trip west, taking some grass and putting it into Missy's bag, and a handful of dirt for Jenn's bag. Neither girl knew what he had done at the time.

On Saturday morning, as the girls were preparing to take the field in Beaver County to warm up, Sam gave each girl her plastic bag, and told them to go out to their positions. When they got there, he instructed them to open the bags and dump the contents onto the ground in front of them, kicking it around a little so it blends in with the field. Then he called them back in.

"Now this is our field," Sam said as the girls gathered around. "It isn't their field any more, it's our field. We haven't lost on our field at all this year, and we aren't going to lose here."

After the games, Sam would tell Jenn and Missy about the additional contents of their plastic bags.

"That way, my parents are with me at the games as well," Sam explained.

If the plastic bags of dirt and grass weren't enough to motivate the Lady Spartans, Sam had one more message to deliver. Just before the game began he gathered the team together. He told them to look him square in the eye, and he looked back at each of the girls. Then he took a deep breath.

"They can't beat you," he said. "I've never lied to you, and I'm telling you to your face, they cannot beat you. Just go out and hammer them."

It took a few innings, but the Spartans soon brought out the hammer. Trailing 1-0 after three innings, the Spartans scored four runs in the top of the fourth, highlighted by a run-scoring double by Ness and a two-run homer from Missy. Now it was 4-1, and the Titans had their heads down as they came in from the field. Nikki, on the mound for the Spartans, induced three quick groundouts in the bottom of the fourth, and the Spartans were poised to make some more noise.

In the top of the fifth, the hits just kept on coming. Missy's two-run triple highlighted a nine-run inning as the Spartans batted around and took a 13-1 lead into the bottom half of the inning. Three outs later, and the Spartans walked off the field congratulating each other for winning the first game in their familiar, mercy rule-shortened fashion.

Just then, the Titan players trotted back out to take the field. Sam approached the home plate umpire.

"Isn't the game over?" he asked. "We have more than an eight-run lead."

The Titans coach yelled out, "We're not playing by those rules. There's no rule that says we have to end after five innings." He explained that the school's by-laws allow them to continue playing even if one team is ahead by eight runs or more.

"But there's nothing in our by-laws that says that," Sam said. "And if there's nothing in our by-laws, then it reverts to NCAA rules. And those rules state eight runs after five innings."

"I'll confer with my team and see what we want to do," the Titans' coach said as he gathered his team together.

"See what he wants to do?" Sam said to the umpires. "It's a rule."

After a brief conference, the Titans' coach announced, "Okay, we'll give it to you."

Sam shook his head as he turned and walked back to his team's dugout. "Give it to us?" he mumbled to himself. "We just spanked you."

It wasn't the last spanking the Titans would receive that day.

* * * *

The Spartans ended all suspense early in the second game. With Jenn on the mound, the Titans, now batting as the visiting team, scratched out an unearned run in the top of the first. In the bottom half, Missy followed a single by Jenn and a walk to Jamye with a three-run homer. Now the crowd, even the Beaver County faithful who were ragging on the NCC players in the first game, were applauding out of respect for someone who could hit a ball as far and as hard as Missy did.

The hits continued, and by the time the first inning was over, the Spartans had a commanding 8-1 lead. They scored two more runs in the second inning, and after the Titans added a run on a sacrifice fly in the top of the third, the Spartans plated three more runs in their half for a 13-2 lead after three innings.

Before the second game, Sam had called the team together and explained that if they had a big lead, and he could see the game was going to end shortly, he was going to make sure all the seniors were on the field when the game ended.

"So, if there's a couple of seniors sitting out the second game, and we get to that last inning, they're going in," he stated, and no one had a problem with it.

True to his word, leading 13-2 going into the fifth inning, Sam made sure he had all his seniors manning positions on the field. Mark, one of the assistant coaches, told everyone in the dugout to stand and scream until the last out was made. And when Nikki fielded a ground ball at third base and threw to first for the final out, the girls exploded onto the field in celebration. The business-as-usual attitude was gone, and all the emotion of an incredible, undefeated championship season came pouring out.

Gradually, the excitement subsided. The Spartans were preparing to line up for the medal and trophy presentations when the Titans' coach walked up to Sam and handed him a box.

"Here's the trophy," he said. "Forty-and-0, great job." Then he walked away.

Unfazed by the snub, Sam took his time handing out the medals to each of the players and coaches. One by one, he called them out by name so that they could be recognized for their accomplishment. He saved his co-captains, Jenn and Missy, for last. Then he spoke to the team.

"I told you in the beginning of the year that you could possibly be the greatest team that NCC has ever had," Sam said. "You set a goal in the beginning of the year to be here, and once you got here, you were not going to be denied. You have to have one point in your life where you set your mark for how people will remember you. And to set that mark, you have to work hard and go beyond what you feel you can do. Today, you set that mark. Today, you are officially the greatest team ever at NCC."

Later that day, back at the hotel, the corks were popped on four bottles of champagne. Glasses were raised, toasts were made, and a new Pennsylvania state champion softball team was celebrated.

* * * *

Shortly after the Spartans' crowning achievement, Sam was approached by the president of Northampton Community College. His question was simple: "The girls went undefeated and won a state title—what do you want?"

Sam thought back to a conversation he'd had with some of the girls in the van while driving back from Beaver County. He recalled Chrysa Wassel's idea.

"How about a billboard?" Sam asked.

The president didn't bat an eye. "You've got it," he said.

It didn't take long to arrange. The girls were gathered for a photography session, and shortly thereafter, their images were pasted on two billboards overlooking Rt. 22, which runs east and west through the Lehigh Valley. One billboard was in Easton and faced westbound traffic, the other was in Bethlehem and faced eastbound travelers.

The headline on the billboard was simply stated. It read, "40 and ohhh," and congratulated the NCC women's softball team on an undefeated season and a state championship.

"That billboard was huge, and it really made me feel proud," Sam said. "People wanted to know why the billboard didn't show the coaches too, and I told them that it wasn't about us. It was about the girls."

But what was even more special, the coach recalled, happened a few days later as Sam was leaving his office and walking out of the Spartan Center. An older gentleman approached him from behind.

"40 and 0, that's something incredible," the man said.

Sam stopped in his tracks and turned to face the gentleman.

"Yeah, it was a great ride," the coach responded.

"Do you know how many people you made happy by doing that?" the man asked, rhetorically. "Even people who don't go to the school. You touched a lot of people with what you guys did this year."

Sam nodded silently. The older gentleman was right. The Lady Spartans led the nation in scoring that season, their 437 runs surpassing the next highest-scoring team by 60 runs. In the process, they hit fifty-seven home runs while striking out only fifty-four times. And they pitched to an earned run average of a microscopic 0.97.

The gentleman continued.

"That's never going to be done again, you know that, don't you?"

Again Sam nodded. "I know," he answered. "But, stranger things have happened."

TWELVE

If going undefeated, winning a state title and leading the nation in scoring is paradise, then Sam Carrodo was in paradise following the Spartans' sweep to the championship against Beaver County. It made the long bus ride back to Bethlehem and the NCC campus that much easier to take.

But that was only part of Sam's life—the softball part. The other half of his life, his family side, was tattered, as Sam was torn between being a good father and being a good coach. More often than not, Sam was preoccupied with being a good coach. He knew it, his wife Chris knew it, and his 9-year-old twins, Nicholas and Devan, knew it.

Chris Carrodo had been married to Sam for nineteen years. As a coach's wife, she knew that whether it was football, softball or little league, there would always be a team in her husband's life. And because of Sam's dedication, and the fact that he was very good at what he did, she knew that she would always have to share part of him with a group of adolescents who were not his flesh and blood.

"The girls are great," Chris said of the 2005 championship team. "They're a great group, and their parents are great also. And Sam has a certain connection with the girls, especially last season."

That said, Chris acknowledged that there was still resentment, especially where the 2005 team was concerned. There was always something that Sam was putting before family. Whether it was a girl's problem with her grades, whether it be practice or traveling, trying to get baby sitters until Chris—who works a full forty-hour week—could get home when Sam was on the road, something about the team was interfering with family life.

Chris wasn't complaining, not to the extent that the situation made her angry. But there were times when the team obviously came before the family. Chris resented that, and so did Nicholas and Devan.

Part of Sam's problem was that he had all the patience in the world with other people's children, but very limited patience with his own. He had no problem teaching other people's children how to throw a ball or swing a bat, but almost expected his children would develop the skills naturally. And when that didn't happen, Sam, or his children, or both would become easily frustrated.

"Throwing a ball in the yard is like torture for the kids when Sam is there," Chris explained. "He's a great guy, and he loves them, and they try real hard. But they have a hard time seeing him out on the field talking to the girls, pumping them up, then coming home and yelling at them when they're throwing a ball against the shed. They have a problem with that. They try to please him, but I don't think he sees that. He's always running in six other directions."

The children simply wanted to spend more time with their father. Devan, who wants to play softball in school when she gets older, wished her father was home more often to teach her how to play the game, and put on a brave face even though she was hurting.

"He's really attached to the softball team," Devan explained. "And he tries to spend time with us, but sometimes he just can't. Sometimes when he's at the softball game I call him to see if he's okay. But then he's in the middle of something and has to hang up. So sometimes I feel very sad about that."

Nicholas, on the other hand, made no bones about his feelings.

"He loves the softball team more than us," he said, wiping a tear from his eye.

But the children don't tell their father how they feel for fear of hurting his feelings.

Chris explained that there are times when lines need to be drawn, clearly dividing work and family life, but she didn't think Sam knew where to draw the line, or even if he could draw a line. She knew her husband cared, and that he wanted his players to succeed, but she also felt that he gets too wrapped up in what he's doing. He could be yelling at the children one minute, then pick up the phone if a player or player's parent called and be sweet as can be the next.

"He might talk to the parent for forty-five minutes, and they love him," Chris said. Sam's patience level with his children, however, was a different matter—a problem he readily admitted.

"I want my kids to play ball, and I'll go watch them," Sam explained. "But I know I will not be able to coach them because I expect too much out of them."

Part of the problem could be traced to when Sam's first marriage failed. His wife divorced him when his sons Sammy and Anthony were eighteen-months old and six-months old, respectively. She took the children, and she left. At that point, Sam turned stone cold, shutting down emotionally because it hurt so bad to have his children taken away.

"I don't know if I have the same kind of feeling with my twins or not," Sam admitted. "That I'm trying to shut off the emotions just in case something would happen and they would leave. I just don't know."

Nicholas was a ball boy during one of the seasons Sam coached football at Bethlehem Catholic. That was good, and it enabled father and son to spend some time together, but it was hard for Devan.

"I was only able to be in the stands with my mom and cheer for him, and I really missed him," Devan said.

There was a time when Sam was home often. A back and shoulder injury forced him to stop working, and he quit coaching at Bethlehem Catholic to spend more time with his children. But Sam's lack of patience often got in the way.

"I just don't have the patience with younger kids when their attention span goes off, and you tell them something three times and they still do the wrong thing," Sam explained. "Nicholas can be in the outfield, a butterfly will go by, and he'll go off chasing the butterfly. So I say 'Forget it, we'll try this another time.' And then they go crying to mom that dad doesn't want to help them.

But I've told them that as soon as they focus and tell me they want to do something, I'll be there to help them and teach them as much as I can."

Will that time come? Will it be too late?

The problem also extended to Sam feeling self-conscious about his weight. He rarely went to school plays in which his kids appeared, perhaps just sneaking in and out quickly so he wouldn't be seen. He didn't want to be seen; he felt that the way he looked, he was an embarrassment to his children. Even when it was 90-degrees outside during the summer, Sam would wear a jacket in an attempt to cover as much of himself as he could. Quite simply, he was embarrassed and didn't want to be seen by people in public situations.

Except when he was coaching.

"When I'm coaching, there could be a million people in the stands and I wouldn't care, because I'm lost in everything else that's going on," Sam explained. "But in an individual situation, a one-on-one thing, I don't like to be seen. And it's my own fault that I'm the way I am."

Sam's weight and health issues might even have been affecting his younger children. Devan would often get out of bed, worried, if her father wasn't home by 1 a.m. She would go downstairs, turn on the television, and watch while she waited for him to come home.

"If it got to 2 a.m., I would start crying, because I really don't want him to get hurt," said Devan, fighting back the tears as she replayed the scene in her mind. "Even though I really don't like him paying all the attention to the softball team, I really, really care for him. Sometimes I think that I really don't want to grow up because I want to spend so much time with him, and I don't want anyone to die. Because I love my dad very much."

Chris recalled Sam's recent dilemma over whether to attend his children's first communion or coach the softball team in a playoff game. The fact that rain postponed the game on the day of the communion was irrelevant. Chris knew that her husband had chosen the softball game over the communion.

"And I could tolerate that," she pointed out. "I didn't like it, and I was very vocal about the whole thing. But I could tolerate it because I've dealt with it for nineteen years. I understand his dedication, his love for the game, but the kids and I would have been more appreciative if he had been a little more caring about us during that whole time."

Unaware of Chris's comments, Sam seemed to echo that sentiment.

"I don't think it's so much that Chris hurts because I pay more attention to the team," Sam said. "I think she hurts because I don't pay enough attention to the kids."

Chris had no animosity toward the girls who play on NCC's softball team. Many had been over to the house; some even called her 'mom,' like she was their second mother. Others who have graduated still came by to visit.

"That's because of Sam's dedication and his caring," Chris explained. "A lot of players would never think of coming to their coach's house. And the same thing happened when he was coaching Bethlehem Catholic football. The players would just stop over at night to watch TV. That's neat."

Chris took a deep breath and paused, relieved at unburdening herself on the subject yet stressed about the content of the conversation. Nicholas and Devan sat nearby, the looks on their faces reflecting their mother's thoughts.

"There always seems to be something about the team that comes before our needs," she emphasized. "And to a certain extent, I understand that. Girls that age are very emotional, and things can be very upsetting to them. But I don't think Sam realizes the extent to which it hurts us."

So, where does the line get drawn? Can the line be drawn?

Sam explained that even though coaching the softball team is, technically, a part-time job, it's also a year-round job if done correctly.

"I have to dedicate myself to this just like I would a regular job," Sam said. "It takes a lot of time. We only get paid for three months, but it's a year-long thing. Once the season is over, you travel a lot to recruit. When the recruiting is over, you have to watch over the kids, make sure they register and that they maintain their grades. Then you start fundraising for the trip to Myrtle Beach, and by the time that's over, the season is ready to start."

Sam paused to gather his thoughts. It was not an easy subject to get one's arms around.

I know I don't spend enough time with my younger children, and I did it to my older ones too," he continued. "My older boys said that I care more for the players I coach than I do for them; that I treat them better than I treat my own family. And that breaks my heart."

Sitting at his desk in his office at NCC, Sam leaned back and rubbed his face with his hands. It was an emotionally draining subject, and a situation for which he had no solution.

"The other day, I had the kids hitting into a little cage, and they were doing so well," he recalled. "I told them how proud I was of them. That got them excited. And then they stopped; they didn't come out the next day to hit, so I just dropped it, too."

No hits, no runs, but perhaps one big error.

* * * *

The euphoria of winning a state championship was also tempered by the knowledge that the Spartans were missing one of their own. Six months earlier, Kristy Kroll had been sent to training camp in Mississippi, preparation for an 18-month tour of duty in Iraq.

Sitting in his office inside the NCC Spartan Center, the summer well underway, Sam figured that by then, Kristy had likely been in Iraq for a month or two. And it terrified him.

"My girls are all like daughters to me, I love them dearly," Sam explained. "And now one of them was gone and might not be coming back. Inside you think, well, it's going to happen to somebody else. It's never going to happen to someone I know. But it was a very scary thing, and there was nothing I could do. It was out of my hands, and that was frustrating."

Sam took some consolation in knowing that Kristy was not alone. Her boyfriend, Sean, was a member of the same reserves unit, and they had been deployed to Iraq together. It wasn't much, but knowing both Kristy and Sean as he did, it was something to hold on to.

"Kristy is one of the sweetest kids you're ever going to meet," Sam explained. "And Sean is a terrific young man. The two of them would do anything for you. And that should be obvious, because they went to war to save our hides."

Still, Sam wanted to get in touch with Kristy; to reach out to her in some way. He scanned the Candidates Interest Form she had completed when trying out for the softball team, and found her email address. But would she have access to email? Was she pinned down in some foxhole, or was she stationed in a camp with access to computers?

Sam took a chance. He wrote out an email; he told Kristy that he was thinking about her, that he missed her, and how well the team had done that season. Then he clicked the 'Send' button.

Two months passed without a response. Sam wrote again, reiterating that he was very proud of her, and that she was missed. Now he was really worried.

A few more weeks passed. Then, just as Sam was about to burst inside, the pressure was relieved. Kristy sent back an email.

"She told me that Iraq was a very scary place to be," Sam recalled. "She could tell me what camps she was in, but she wasn't allowed to tell me the exact locations. And I don't want to know the exact locations because that will scare me even more."

Kristy had actually arrived in Kuwait on June 19, 2005, Father's Day. Her unit was stationed there for almost a month, and in July was sent up to Ramadi, Iraq.

Kristy wrote that the training in Mississippi had been stressful, but that it had to be to prepare you for what was ahead. She noted that she'll never forget what it was like being on the plane and landing in Kuwait. "And when we got off the plane, it felt like a blow dryer was just beating on you, it was so hot out there. And then you knew that you were in some other country, and have no idea what it's going to be like. There was nothing around. When you looked out the windows of the plane, there was nothing around. It was very strange."

Her email reported that as part of a mission, she had been on a transport plane going into Baghdad Airport about three weeks after U.S. troops had taken the airport. The plane had to circle the airport twice, then dive virtually straight down as rocket-propelled grenades flew past. Once on the ground, there was little time to deplane and seek shelter and safety inside the airport.

Kristy's unit was a medical company, so the mission for her was two-fold.

"I felt that my mission was to help the dentist get through, because he's the one the troops needed to see," she explained. "And I felt like it was my job to make sure he got there. So the whole time I wasn't just looking out for myself, I was making sure he was safe as well."

At NCC, Kristy had been studying to become a dental assistant. As a student, she was limited to cleaning teeth. All that changed while she was in Iraq, where she found herself extracting teeth and performing root canal.

"She was learning fast in conditions where I don't know if I could even iron a shirt," Sam explained. "I would be ironing right up my arm. I wouldn't even be looking at the shirt, that's how scared I would be over there."

But Kristy also found herself working in an emergency room environment. She was present when soldiers were brought in with their legs blown off, or with bullet holes in their heads.

"I can't take watching that in a movie, and Kristy was seeing that in real life," Sam said. "Soldiers were dying in front of her, and she had to experience that almost every day for a year-and-a-half. I could never do it, but that's why I love her so much."

Kristy was scared, that much was clear in the emails she exchanged with Sam. But repeatedly, she would write that she was proud of how well the team had done. She deflected the attention from herself, noting that living day to day in danger was pretty much a way of life in Iraq.

"You kind of become used to being on edge," Kristy noted. "And you really have to be in order to survive. You're always looking for places to take cover, because you never know what's going to happen. So you have to try to imagine as you're walking somewhere, everything that could happen at a particular moment. And you just have to think logically what would be the best thing to do, without being completely stressed out where you can't even think."

Sam was stressed enough for both of them, and he would remain that way during each three- and four-week period while he waited for another email from Kristy that said she was okay.

THIRTEEN

Re-building at the community college level is a regular occurrence. Student-athletes have only two years of eligibility, so turnover occurs every year. That's why Sam recruited a year or two in advance. He didn't just scout high school seniors, he kept his eye on promising juniors and sophomores as well, talking to them and their parents and spreading the word about NCC's athletic and academic programs. It was the only way to stay ahead of the game.

Re-building an undefeated, state championship team, however, was a tall order. And of the fifteen girls on the 2005 roster, only four would return for 2006: Janess Lyle, Alexis Walker, Nikki Jenson and Caitlyn McGouldrick. But with those four on board, in particular Ness and Nikki, both of whom were named captains for the 2006 season, Sam had a solid foundation around which to build. And if championship teams are built solid up the middle, there was no better place to start than with a dominant pitcher and an exceptional shortstop.

One of Sam's first stops on the recruiting trail was at Phillips-burg High School, just over the Delaware River in Phillipsburg, New Jersey. He had received a Candidates Interest Form from a Phillipsburg senior outfielder named Lisa Klinger, so he watched her play in a game and came away impressed.

"She was everything she was built up to be," Sam recalled. She was also the type of student-athlete Sam liked to recruit— someone who had a little bit of a chip on her shoulder. Someone with something to prove.

Lisa had been playing varsity softball at Phillipsburg since her freshman year. It was a game she had loved ever since her grandfather, Willie Morales, a major league baseball player in his youth, introduced her to the game. She had a passion for the game, and the 5-foot-1 switch-hitter displayed that passion every time she took the field. Her four-year goal at Phillipsburg was to be named captain in her senior year, but that never happened.

"In my senior year, the coach switched and did things differently," recalled Lisa, the disappointment still evident in her voice. "He let the girls chose who they wanted as captain. Right then and there my heart sank because I knew I wasn't going to get it. The day they were choosing, I didn't even want to be there."

It became a popularity vote, as can often happen in high school. Lisa played the game the same way she went about her schoolwork—with a quiet determination to get the job done. She wasn't outspoken and she wasn't giggly—and she wasn't named captain. But instead of diminishing her passion for the game, it fueled it.

"Growing up, I didn't have a lot of help from my parents, so a lot of the decisions and choices I had to make I made on my own," Lisa said. "But coach Sam came into my life when I was in high school, when I didn't have anyone to steer me in the right direction. I never thought having a little bit of guidance would make such a big difference in my life."

Lisa had to choose between attending Warren Community College, which was local, or commuting to NCC. Sam told Lisa that he wanted her to play softball for him at NCC. Warren didn't have a softball team. Warren didn't stand a chance. Sam had himself a lightning quick, switch-hitting centerfielder. And in retrospect, Lisa would have no regrets.

"I needed a team that treated everyone as if they were part of a family," Lisa explained. "In high school it was more a sense of competition, whereas here at Northampton, everyone works together and cares about one another. That made me realize how good I have it."

And how glad the NCC Spartans were to have her.

* * * *

As often happened, Sam would hear about a possible recruit through word of mouth. One day, Nikki Jenson's father told Sam about a girl who played for Phillipsburg High School that he should check out. The word was, she was another Gina Renaldi but with blonde hair. Sam adored Gina, so that was all he needed to hear.

The girl was Roxanne Schisler—Roxy to almost all who knew her. She was a catcher who also played first base and the outfield, and she could hit with power. But when Sam visited Phillipsburg to see Roxy play, he was told by her coach that she was pretty set on attending East Stroudsburg University, and Sam never pushed an athlete when she had her mind set.

"I want them to go to the bigger schools," Sam explained. "I want them to get the scholarships. So I just talk to them and leave the door open in case something happens."

And something *did* happen, because Roxy's academic grades prohibited her from going to East Stroudsburg.

"When I went to high school I didn't think that grades mattered," Roxy recalled. "I thought my pure talent was going to get my anywhere I wanted to go. The reality was that I didn't try as hard as I should have in high school."

Roxy, like Lisa, had a passion for playing softball. Her parents signed her up for a local team at the age of five when she began hitting wiffle balls over the fence in their back yard. She fell in love with the game, and by high school she was playing almost year-round.

But something was wrong. When Sam said "hello" to Roxy after the Phillipsburg softball game, she barely said two words. Normally a confident young lady with her head held high, her chin was resting on her chest and she made little eye contact. She was at a point where she had pretty much given up on everything.

"I was going to go to the local community college, which is like the 13th grade of my high school, and doesn't have a softball team," Roxy recalled. "It was senior year, and all my friends were going away to school. They had already been accepted, and I was getting rejection after rejection. I thought of myself as a failure."

Sam had a brief conversation with Roxy, then left. Two days later, while at home, he got a phone call from NCC's athletic secretary that Roxy and her mother were there at the school. And it turned out that Mrs. Schisler and the athletic secretary knew each other from childhood. Small world.

Sam drove over to the college, and after a short conversation, Roxy announced that she was coming to NCC.

"NCC was the perfect situation for me," Roxy said. "I love the school, and getting to meet Sam has been a really great experience for me."

Academically, Roxy worked her butt off. She learned to balance athletics and academics, and put more time and effort into her schoolwork than she ever had before. The result was a solid 3.0 GPA.

And, she still managed to excel on the softball field.

* * * *

A phone call from a coach Sam knew well brought in another player. Jen Horner, who coached softball at Northwestern High School, phoned with the usual flash: "I have a girl for you. She's been my best athlete the past two years. She can play infield or outfield, and she wants to come play at Northampton."

Her name was Amanda McGimpsey, and she was an athlete. Gimp, as she quickly became known, played both softball and basketball through high school, then focused on softball in college.

"I think it was because my friends and my family thought I was better at softball than basketball," Gimp explained. "I like basketball because there's more contact, it's more physical. But with softball, I like getting dirty."

Sam didn't even need to watch her play. He had a recommendation from the coach, someone he respected, so it was a done deal.

When Sam first met Gimp, he could see from how solidly she was built that she was, indeed, an athlete. And he was thankful that she had chosen NCC.

"I could have gone to LCCC, which is just ten minutes away from my house," Gimp explained. "But I wasn't sure about their criminal justice program, and NCC is known for its program. And the kids who graduate from my high school and don't go to college further away end up at LCCC, so I just wanted to meet new people."

Gimp would become a mainstay at third base for the Lady Spartans during the 2006 season.

* * * *

Sam had heard a lot of good things about Jenna Turner, a pitcher and infielder who attended Northampton High School. He watched her play in several summer softball tournaments and liked what he saw. At the time, Jenna indicated that she wasn't certain what she wanted to do after high school graduation—wasn't certain if she even wanted to attend college—so Sam backed off.

Then he spoke with Jenna's high school softball coach, Debbie Anthony, a woman whose opinion Sam held in high regard.

"She's a great athlete, and she's a great student," Sam was told. "I think you should pursue her." So he did. He watched her play in another tournament, spoke with her, and then phoned to follow up on their conversation. Then he waited.

Several days passed with no return phone call, so Sam called again.

"From what I had seen, I felt this girl should be playing ball," Sam said. "She had so much ability, and was solid academic-wise. Plus, Debbie Anthony was high on her, and I respect Debbie's opinion a lot."

So he kept at it, and eventually Jenna decided she would attend NCC. Sam felt he was being persistent; Jenna had a different take on it.

"She said that I was borderline annoying when I kept calling her," Sam explained. "She even gave an interview to Channel 10 before the 2006 state championship game, saying that I was bordering on annoying by calling her all the time."

Now Sam saw his infield rounding into shape. He had athletes who could play multiple positions. Ness was a staple at shortstop. Nikki and Jenna alternated between pitching and playing second base. Gimp could also alternate between second and third base, depending on who was pitching. And with Roxy catching or playing first base, the team was rounding into shape.

Everything was falling in line.

* * * *

Several phone calls and a trip to watch Roxy play in a summer league game would bring in the five remaining pieces to the puzzle.

Sitting in his office one day, Sam received a phone call from a senior at Easton Area High School, Kellie Connolly. She explained that she had never played high school softball, but had been playing recreation ball for Forks Township since she was twelve-years old. She had even played some baseball.

"There wasn't a softball team when I first moved to Forks in 1995," Kellie recalled, "so I started playing on a co-ed baseball team. I love sports in general, and I love the feeling of being part of something, being part of a team."

High school softball hadn't worked out for Kellie.

"I didn't get along great with the coach, but I just love playing softball," she explained, "so I just played for my township team."

Sam had heard the I've-played-a-lot-of-recreation-ball-explanation before.

"Kids will say that all the time," Sam explained. "Then they come in and they can't throw the ball from one wall to the other."

Kellie was different; Kellie could play. She was a solid infielder who could hit. She was a keeper. She was also enamored with NCC softball, courtesy of the 40 and Ohhh billboard on Rt. 22.

"The billboard was right by the exit I took to get to work, so I saw it every day," Kellie said. "I thought it was really awesome, and I thought it would be a privilege to play for the team, to be part of what they had already started. And when I finally made the team, it was a good feeling of accomplishment."

A phone call from former player Cortnei Comstock brought Tabetha Niceforo to Sam's attention. A solid outfielder who could hit, Tabetha played for Pen Argyl High School.

"But she's very shy," Cortnei told Sam. "You'll have to call her up and talk to her."

So Sam phoned. Tabetha told Sam she was going through a lot of problems at home, including her parents divorcing, and she was currently working two jobs. She also planned to enroll in the nursing program at NCC, which was very demanding on a student's time. She didn't know if she could also handle playing softball.

But, she decided to try out for the team.

"She was fine," Sam said. "She was good enough to play."

Shortly thereafter, a visit to watch Roxy play in a game for the Lehigh Valley Waves, a summer travel team, left Sam even more impressed. It also introduced him to Jen Keifer, a solid defensive outfielder with a tremendous throwing arm. At the plate, she swung and missed a lot, but when she made contact, the ball went deep.

Sam brought her into the fold.

A call from Sam's high school alma mater, Bethlehem Catholic, delivered Katie Sculley, an outfielder and designated hitter who knew how to hit.

Finally, as the fall semester was starting up, Kyle Lozier, a part-time player from the 2005 team, brought her roommate, Lana Good, to a voluntary practice. Lana, a redhead who played high school softball at Palmerton High School, wanted to try out for the team. She was welcomed to workout with the team in the fall, and tryout when the spring semester began in January.

Sam considered the group he had assembled; the girls who would compete for jobs and eventually make up the 2006 version of the NCC Lady Spartans softball team. He felt good about the cast and crew, but it was only September, and he wanted to keep everything in perspective.

"After going 40-0, I didn't think about going undefeated again," Sam reflected. "It would be ridiculous to think about something like that. Well, maybe not ridiculous, but it wasn't something I was considering. I always tell the girls that if we have three losses in a season, that's a lot for us. But, you don't think you're going to go undefeated a second time. That's not going to happen again."

Those would prove to be famous last words.

FOURTEEN

By the fall of 2005, Sam was as deep in depression as a person could be. And it was nothing that an undefeated season and state title could cure. It was beyond softball, well beyond athletics. Sam's health had deteriorated to the point where taking drastic action was no longer just a doctor's recommendation. It was a matter of life and death.

Fifteen years earlier, Sam had been a horse. He weighed 265 pounds and bench-pressed 520 pounds. He had twenty-two-inch arms, a twenty-inch neck, a sixty-four-inch chest and a forty-inch waist. He was slapped with layers of muscle.

One day, he was driving a delivery truck when he stopped to unload an order of cookies. The truck was filled to the roof, and when Sam tried to open the back of the truck, the door jammed. Undaunted, and stubborn, he climbed up onto the truck's rear ledge, grabbed the handle on the door, and stood up in an attempt to deadlift it and force it open. The door flew open, but Sam lost his footing. He fell backward off the ledge but did not let go of the door handle as it flew open.

Sam couldn't have done more damage to his upper body if he had worked at it. He tore the rotator cuff in both shoulders and blew out two discs in his back. It took seven shoulder surgeries—four on his right shoulder and three on his left—and back surgery to remove seventy-five percent of the injured discs to correct the problems.

In the aftermath, however, those problems were dwarfed by new ones. Sam was unable to work for an extended period of time. He was also unable to workout; unable to lift weights and maintain his strength and conditioning. The weight piled on, and over a ten-year period, he ballooned to more than 380 pounds. The added weight didn't do his injured back any good.

Eventually he was able to return to work, but after a few years he again tore the rotator in his right shoulder and blew out two discs in his neck. More surgeries, more inactivity, and considerably more depression.

"I was in constant pain," Sam recalled. "I really wasn't able to coach. I could go out and recruit, but I couldn't do anything except talk and teach. That's why I had several assistant coaches who did everything for me. I felt useless as a coach."

He couldn't sleep at night. So by morning, he would take his two children to school, come home, and by 9:30 a.m. he would fall asleep. He would sleep in the afternoon. For a while, that's all he was doing.

"One time I was sitting in the recliner in front of the TV and talking to my son, Sammy," Sam detailed. "We're talking, and he's standing right above me. The next thing I know, I opened my eyes and he was gone. I had fallen asleep while talking to him, and an hour had passed."

Sam went to the doctor; it was desperate times. He had tried just about every diet. He was unable to exercise because he couldn't lift weights, and when he tried walking, his back would give out. One day his son, Sammy, suggested they take a walk. They went down the block and around the corner, Sam dragging one leg as he walked, the pain surging through his back.

"Dad, stay here," Sammy finally said. "I'll get the car, come back and pick you up."

"Bullshit," Sam yelled. "I'm walking. I have to do this."

Sam made it home, but it was the last walk he would attempt to take.

Desperate and depressed, Sam was referred by his doctor to Vitaly Sawyna, from Sacred Heart Hospital in Allentown, whose specialty was bariatric surgery, otherwise known as gastric bypass. After an examination and consultation, Dr. Sawyna delivered a clear message to Sam: Have the bariatric surgery or you're going to die.

Sam had been advised to have the procedure done two years earlier; that six or seven months down the road he would be fine. But he knew it was a dangerous procedure, and he was afraid. This time, however, he was determined to see it through.

"My wife didn't want me to do it; nobody wanted me to do it," Sam recalled. "They said, 'You're going to die.' I said, 'You know what? I have a doctor telling me that if I don't do this right now I'm going to die. So, I'm either going to die fast, on the operating table, or I'm going to take five years to suffer and then die.'"

Sam opted for the here and now.

But, there's a lengthy process that bariatric surgery candidates must first endure; numerous tests that have to be conducted in order to receive insurance clearance. Even before the testing began, however, Dr. Sawyna asked Sam to write him a letter explaining why he wanted the surgery.

Sam laid it all on the line.

> *"I've tried everything and nothing works. I feel like I'm an addict for food, I can't stop. And I know with my schedule, I won't eat all the way through the day, but then I'll get home and then I eat non-stop. You can't do that. I can see it now, I don't want to die. I have four children I want to see live, and I don't want them without a father. Even though I haven't been a great father, I will become a better father, I feel, if I get through this. And live for them. And that's what I'm doing right now, is living for my children."*

Dr. Sawyna reviewed the letter, then sent it off to Sam's insurance carrier. If the insurance company wouldn't cover the bariatric surgery, there was no way Sam could afford the procedure on his own.

"I wouldn't burden my wife with that, because she's working every day, sometimes six days a week, and I'm sitting at home," Sam explained. "And that caused a lot of animosity between us. It was terrible. And if I could work, I would work. I wanted to work. I didn't want to sit back and have people give me money for nothing. I'm not working for it, and the insurance companies are sending me workers' compensation money. And she would say, 'Why do I have to get up every day and you get to sleep? Why do I have to go to work and you sit at home and do nothing.' And it would kill me, because now I'm not a man. I'm not the provider. I'm a bum. I'm worthless, I'm not a father, a husband or a man. And it would kill me, because I'm a very proud man. My father and mother raised me to be a very proud person, and at that point in time, I was not proud of myself as a father, husband and person."

Three weeks later, word came back from Sam's insurance company that the procedure would be covered. Now the testing began.

The first test Sam underwent was a sleep apnea test. Sleep apnea is a condition characterized by temporary breathing interruptions during sleep. The pauses in breathing can occur dozens or even hundreds of times a night. During the test, which is performed at night, a harness is strapped to a patient's head and chest to monitor their breathing and heart rate during sleep. A patient has an 'episode' if he or she either stops breathing or has a significant decrease in breathing rate during sleep. If the patient incurs 20 episodes in one hour, they're put on a CPAP machine, an acronym for Continuous Positive Air Pressure. This machine has a mask that fits over a patient's nose and possibly their mouth. The unit provides increased air pressure to help overcome obstructions that are associated with obstructive sleep apnea.

Sam checked into the hospital at 10 p.m., was prepped for the test, and went to sleep. Before long, a technician woke him up and told him that he would have to go on the CPAP machine. He'd had 166 episodes in the first hour alone.

"No wonder you're falling asleep during the day," the technician said. "It's like you're running a marathon at night trying to breathe and sleep."

The technician hooked Sam up to the CPAP machine. But the machine, which provides a constant intake of air, made it difficult for Sam to breathe out against the air flow. The technician switched to a BiPAP machine, or Bi-level Continuous Positive Air Pressure. This is an advanced variation of a CPAP machine, but uses different air pressures for inhalation and exhalation. It's often used when users of CPAP machines have difficulty breathing against the pressure from the machine.

The BiPAP machine worked. Sam slept, and he had no further episodes.

Next up was a nuclear stress test. Sam received an injection—a radioactive 'tracer' that allows the heart muscle to be seen on special x-rays. Probes were attached to his chest, enabling technicians to take 'pictures' of his heart while he exercised as well as during rest.

Sam mounted a treadmill and began walking. The technicians told him he had to walk for at least seven minutes in order to build the heart rate to a certain level. Sam began walking, and gradually, the technicians increased the treadmill's elevation. Ninety seconds shy of the seven-minute mark, Sam indicated that he was unable to continue.

"Push it," the technicians told him.

"I can't," he said, and stopped walking. He began coughing, and breathing became difficult for a few moments, then eased up. He had failed the test, but in Sam's case, failing was a good thing. Failing meant you 'passed' as a candidate for bariatric surgery.

A heart specialist was next, and Sam was asked to wear a halter monitor for twenty-four hours. When the physician evaluated the results, he found that Sam had experienced numerous tachycardia episodes, or a rapid beating of the heart. The episodes were occurring at night, while Sam was sleeping, likely due—in part—to his heavy breathing.

"Sam, I can't give you pills to slow your heart rate, because if it then slows down, it might go too slow," the doctor explained. "And I can't give you pills to increase your heart rate because when it speeds up, it will go too fast."

The doctor recommended that Sam have the surgery, "or your heart will just give out."

Finally, Sam had a psychiatric evaluation to make certain he was in the right mental state of mind to be making such an important decision. Sitting in the psychiatrist's waiting room, Sam spoke with patients who were considering the same procedure he was. He heard the horror stories and the success stories.

"People were telling me, 'Your family will tell you not to do this,'" Sam recalled. "'Your friends will tell you not to do this. And it's not because they don't want you to be better. It's because they don't want you to die.'"

But Sam had his mind set. "If I die on the table, I die on the table, and it's done. But I also had an opportunity to change my life, so I wasn't going to stray from the path. For the first time in my life, I was going to do something for me."

* * * *

Sam passed every test—or failed every test, depending on your perspective. Either way, he was approved for bariatric surgery. And since his $1,500 medical deductible had already been met for the year, as long as he had the procedure before the end of 2005, insurance would take care of everything.

He scheduled the procedure for November 25, the day after Thanksgiving. But his wife didn't think that was a good time, and suggested putting it off for a couple of weeks. Sam agreed, and rescheduled the surgery for December 3. Again, Chris balked, suggesting that it was too close to the Christmas holiday.

"You won't be able to help me, and you won't be able to enjoy Christmas because you'll be hurting," Chris said. "And, you're not going to be able to eat.

"Eating is what got me here," Sam said.

"But you're never going to be full, and you won't be able to eat what you used to."

"Eating what I used to is killing me," Sam answered, and he tried to explain how the procedure worked. "Right now my stomach is a football, and I have to eat tons of food to fill it. With the operation, they cut away your stomach, take the part that is most resistant to stretching, and make this small sack. The stomach stays in, because it still has to make the enzyme for digestion. But they staple the stomach shut, bypassing it, so the food you eat goes from your esophagus to the small sack and on to the large intestine. Now, my stomach is the size of an egg. So when I eat a small amount, I'm going to feel full."

It all made sense to Sam, but he gave in and looked to reschedule the procedure one more time. Now, however, it had to be moved to January 3, 2006, which meant having to put up $1,500 to cover the insurance deductible. But Sam viewed it as a small price to pay for the potential of what lay ahead.

On the morning of January 3, Sam sat in the waiting room at Sacred Heart Hospital, waiting his turn. He had been on a liquid diet for the past two days, emptying his system of anything solid. He was hungry, and he was scared. But the hospital staff talked with him and helped pass the time.

"They're angels," Sam recalled.

Sam was taken in for surgery at 3 p.m., the last procedure of the day. And of course, he was concerned that Dr. Sawyna might be tired by this point.

"Doc, are you okay?" Sam asked as he was wheeled into the operating room on a gurney.

"Yes," the doctor laughed. "I did three of these this morning so they were good practice for you."

The doctor put the mask over Sam's face, and he was out.

* * * *

Sam woke up in pain. The surgery had taken four hours. Five probes were attached to various parts of his rib cage and stomach, and he felt like someone had beaten him for a week with a baseball bat. The doctors wanted him to move as much as possible, but he couldn't even sit up. He called the nurse, and she brought in four people—two in front of Sam pulling and two behind him, pushing—to help turn him over and get him up out of bed. He wound up walking for half an hour, and he felt a little better.

Regularly, the nurses would bring in small medicine cups filled with Crystal Light, soup or Jell-O™. But Sam didn't care about eating.

"I don't know what happens, but your stomach is so small, and I guess from the cutting and touching all the nerves, you don't even care about eating or drinking," Sam said. "So, I figured if I finished one of the medicine cups an hour, that would be good."

He was told to finish one every fifteen minutes. He complied, and the pain began to decrease with each passing day.

Sam went home two days after the surgery, slept on the recliner in his living room for about a week, then was finally able to lie down in his own bed. More importantly, he was losing weight—twenty-four pounds in the first week. He was on a high, and didn't care at all about eating. Ten days later he visited the doctor, and had lost a total of thirty-six pounds.

"Okay, go back to your regular eating," the doctor told him. "Eat whatever you want, but watch out for red meat, because it will be too dry."

He was told that the new 'pouch' in his stomach was very small, and had a very small opening, so it was important to chew everything to the point where it was almost mush before swallowing.

"Eat whatever you want that stays down," the doctor advised. "But try to be smart, stay sugar-free. What will help you the most is eating anything that flies or swims, because it's moister."

Sam left the doctor's office and stopped at a Perkin's Restaurant on Linden Blvd. near the NCC campus and told the waiter at the counter that he'd recently had gastric bypass surgery and could only eat certain things.

"Can you make me just three scrambled eggs and a chicken breast?" Sam asked.

No problem. Sam took the food back to his office, took a forkful of the eggs and a small bite of the chicken, and was full. He took it home for his kids.

Two days passed and Sam hadn't eaten. He began to feel lightheaded.

"You dummy, you've got to eat," his wife, Chris, told him.

Sam told her they needed to purchase some sugar-free products.

"Why?" she asked.

"Because the doctor told me so."

"Sam, your stomach is the size of a golf ball. Do you think two ounces of regular pudding is going to kill you?"

The argument made sense. So Sam began eating regular pudding and ice cream, along with healthy foods like turkey and fish. And the weight kept flying off.

Previously, Ness and Nikki were the only players who knew that Sam was having the procedure. But as spring practice began in mid-January and he continued to shed pounds, he shared the story of his surgery with the entire team. He had a goal, he told them, of losing eighty pounds by March 10, the day the Myrtle Beach Snowbird Softball Tournament began. He wound up at seventy-seven. Close enough.

Eighteen months later, by the spring of 2007, Sam had lost 162 pounds, and weighed in at a svelte 223. But more important than the poundage, he felt differently about himself and his confidence level was up. The stigma was gone.

"Before the surgery, I wore shorts all the time because that's all I could wear," Sam explained. "Now I wear them because I like them. And I can wear pants now. I went from a size sixty-two waist to a size forty, and my sugar and cholesterol levels are down."

Each day, though, is still a battle. Sam explained that his mental capacity is still at the point where he wants to order four cheeseburgers, two orders of fries and a milk shake, and eat everything. He still puts certain foods, and certain portions on his plate, but then he takes two or three bites and he's done.

"Every day I fight it in my head," Sam stressed. "I want to eat a cheeseburger, and I ask myself, 'Why did you do this? Why did you do something you can't reverse?' But then I jump on the scale and I've lost another twelve pounds. There's my answer. That's why I did it."

He still laments the things he missed out on when he was tipping the scales at 386 pounds. He didn't attend the weddings of some of the girls who played softball for him at NCC, and he skipped the funerals of people who were close to him.

"I was too fat and didn't have anything to wear," Sam explained. "You can't wear shorts to a viewing or a wedding. So I would make up an excuse that I had something to do."

Now, there would be no more excuses.

FIFTEEN

The new year was barely two weeks old when Sam, aching stomach muscles and all, began scrutinizing the group of players who were trying out for the 2006 NCC Lady Spartans softball team. The coach was sore, but he was also excited to get spring practices underway.

Part of the reason for that excitement was the new Spartan Center gymnasium, a state-of-the-art facility that easily erased any nostalgic feelings for the old gym that sat in the 'pit' of the College Center building.

"It's beautiful," was Sam's simple assessment. "It's so open. It's brighter, and the ceiling is much higher. You can actually simulate a field in that gym."

Setting up for practice was easier. In the old gym, it could take twenty minutes or more to set up the batting cage. In the Spartan Center, Sam just flipped a switch and the batting cage was efficiently lowered into position from the ceiling. And because the gym was so large, Sam could conduct infield and outfield practice at the same time.

What he liked best, however, was the gym's proximity to the outdoor softball field.

"When the weather turned nice, I could walk out the back door of the gym and be within thirty yards of the softball field," Sam explained. "I could have the team doing fielding drills outside, then walk inside to watch some players hitting in the batting cage. It gave us a lot more freedom to do the things we couldn't do in the old gym."

But nothing's perfect. Softball practice began in mid-January, but the NCC men's and women's basketball teams were in the midst of their winter schedules. If the teams were playing on the road, there was no problem getting court time for softball practice. But if the basketball teams were practicing, the softball team usually couldn't get on a court until eight o'clock in the evening.

"The gym can be divided into three large courts, so you would think it's easier to accommodate everyone, but it's not," Sam explained. "One of the gyms has to be kept open for students to use. And if one of the basketball teams has a home game, the bleachers have to be pulled out and the divider walls have to stay open, so you can't practice."

As a result, Sam would often bring the girls in on Sunday mornings to practice for about three hours starting around 9 a.m.

Scheduling inconveniences aside, Sam quickly noted something different about the team he was assembling for the 2006 season. It wasn't that prior years' teams weren't experienced, but the girls who were now coming out of high school, for the most part, had a deeper level of experience—a result of the time they spent on travel teams and playing in national competitions. The girls from prior years could handle pressure, but many of them learned to do so on the job, so to speak, while playing for NCC. The girls Sam was now bringing into the fold already had that experience.

Despite the vast amount of playing experience possessed by many of the girls, it didn't change the way Sam approached spring practices.

"We start at the beginning, because technique is what wins games," Sam explained. "Technique and reaction. Because if you know what to do in given situations, then, when those situations present themselves, you will react the right way. On the softball field, it's not like a written test where you can write down the answer, then cross it out and fill in the correct one. It's reaction and knowledge, and it has to happen right the first time."

And Sam never assumed that players knew all there was to know. He recalled asking a player to bunt during the 2003 eastern championship game. The girl fouled off the first two bunt attempts, so with two strikes on her, he gave her the sign to swing away. Instead, she again tried to bunt, and bunted the ball foul. Undaunted, she got back in the batter's box and prepared to hit until the umpire told her that she was out. She didn't know that with two strikes, if you bunt the ball foul, it's strike three.

"I still get girls coming in who don't know how to slide," Sam said. "So I bring in an old blanket, throw it on the floor, give the girl a helmet, have her run, and then hit the carpet and slide. Or, I take them to a hill outside, water down the grass, and have them slide down the hill, just to get comfortable with it. You assume they know everything, but they don't. That's why I start at the beginning."

Despite their vast amount of playing experience, they were still different girls with different personalities. Regardless of the larger and more modern practice facilities, as the weeks rolled by, Sam would get reports from his two captains, Ness and Nikki, that one player was fighting with another, or one player wouldn't listen to the captains, or another had a cocky attitude. By mid-February, cabin fever had struck again.

* * * *

Sam saw it brewing. Like a pot of water doing a slow burn, he knew it was coming. And he was intent on keeping it from boiling over.

The coach waited until practice had concluded, then called all the girls together and walked them to the back corner of the gym, in a small area between the gym wall and the end of the bleachers. He told the girls to go sit against the wall, then turned to the assistant coaches and snapped, "Stop, this one is on me." Later, Sam apologized to them in front of the team.

But there were no apologies in his conversation with the girls. He told them that the first thing they needed to under-stand was that they were not last year's team. They were the 2006 Lady Spartans, not 2005, and whatever happened last year was history. He cautioned them against trying to do too much, and against thinking they had to be as good as last year's undefeated team.

"You're different," Sam stressed. "So stop trying to act like last year's team and instead act like yourselves. Don't try to replace anybody, and don't try to fill shoes. If you put so much pressure on yourself, you'll wind up not doing enough. Just be the best team that you can be, and whatever happens, happens."

Then he addressed the bickering. "And if I hear any more bitching at one another, I'll pull you into my office and you can hash it out there. And if you can't resolve it, then we'll have two fewer players on the team. This is not Little League. You're in college now, so I don't want to hear any more screaming and yelling. These are your teammates. And if you can't get along, get out."

It was a message Sam hated to deliver, even though he knew it was necessary. He hated playing the role of the bad guy, but he also knew if he didn't command respect from the girls, they would walk all over him and the assistant coaches. So he emphasized to the girls, "We will give you as much respect, maybe more, than you give us. But we'd better get respect."

Sam also understood the girls' frustrations, to a point. After four or five weeks of practicing indoors, they wanted to get outside and compete. Many of the new girls who were trying out for the team didn't believe they could show their true abilities inside a gym. They also got extremely frustrated having to use rubber-soft IncrediBalls during indoor practices. The balls didn't travel as far when hit, and their rubber consistency would cause them to easily bounce out of a player's glove. That would get the girls upset, because it made them feel like they weren't fielding well. They would get depressed because they were worried they wouldn't make the team.

And then the girls would get their periods.

"Sometimes they'd get bitchy," Sam explained. "But they'd come right out and tell me, 'Look, I'm pissed off, and this is what's going on.' That's too much information, but at least I know. Then I have to try to remember who's on what cycle."

Wanting to compete, however, was not a bad thing. It was a tactic used effectively by head football coach Bob Stem when Sam was an assistant coach at Bethlehem Catholic. Stem used to stop the boys from hitting each other in practice for a few days. The players would get to the point where they wanted to hit someone really bad, and Stem would just walk that attitude right into Friday night's game.

"The man was smart beyond smart," Sam said.

But you can't coach women's softball like high school football. It's just a different animal. So Sam borrowed some training techniques from his football days just to keep workouts interesting. He placed cones around the gym floor just like on a football field and had the girls run football drills—zig-zags, forward and backward runs, and side-shuffles.

Still, he knew that the trip down to Myrtle Beach for the annual Snowbird Softball Tournament was where his teams always came together. Sam called the trip "the greatest bonding experience."

"You drive eleven hours in a van together," the coach explained. "You get to talk. When you get down to Myrtle Beach, you go out together as a team, so the girls get to know each other more."

And in the heat of the games, the girls—and Sam and his assistant coaches—got to see what each player had inside.

Because as often was the case, players played the game with much more intensity than they practiced.

* * * *

The trips to Myrtle Beach didn't just happen. Fundraising was the key. It was a winter activity that, in some respects, helped bring the team closer together. It also caused animosity.

The problem was two-fold. Some girls didn't raise as much funds as others did, but it wasn't necessarily their fault. If the girls didn't live in the area, it was difficult to sell tickets to a Comedy Night. People they might normally sell tickets to, such as family and friends, were not likely to travel an hour or two at night in the winter just to see the show, then have to make the long trip back home the same night. So Sam gave them the option of working to get prizes donated for the auction that would be held the same night as the comedy show.

But then there were girls who just didn't want to do anything. So, Sam clearly spelled out the options up front. The girls could fundraise by selling tickets to the event. They could arrange to have gifts donated if they were unable to sell tickets. They could—in addition to working the night of the event, which everyone on the team did—work the night before to help set up. They could simply pay for the trip out of their own pocket, or they could opt not to make the trip, the latter of which did not have any impact on their chance of making the team.

The money that needed to be raised was significant. The cost for entering the Myrtle Beach Tournament and staying at the hotel for the week was $285 per person. Multiplied by seventeen—four coaches and thirteen players—it came to almost

$4,900. The college supplied the three vans for driving to Myrtle Beach, but the softball team had to supply the gas, which ran approximately $650 for the round-trip. Then, Sam had to feed everyone—two meals a day for seven days, since the hotel supplied breakfast. Sam allotted $3,000 for that, bringing the total needed to a minimum of about $8,500.

But Sam always tried to fundraise over and above what was needed for the Myrtle Beach trip.

"During the season, we receive $100 from the school for each away game we go to, and that's only $6 per kid to eat," Sam explained. "So, we fundraise as much as possible, then put that money in an account that we can pull from throughout the year to take the girls to a Friendly's Restaurant or some place similar for dinner when we have road games, buy them cleats or sweatsuits, or use at the end of the year for gifts and a team dinner."

Comedy Nights were standard fundraising events. But in 2006, Sam and the girls held their first Night at the Races, and it proved very successful.

A Night at the Races is a Jupiter, Florida-based company that rents out a DVD or VHS tape containing twelve up-to-date races, including horses, trotters or dog races. These are actual races that have been videotaped from multiple camera angles to create a sense of being at the race, and include narration from start to finish by many of the country's top-rated announcers. There are usually twelve races on a DVD or tape, with twelve horses in each race.

"You put the tape in, hit play, and it shows the horses walking by with their numbers as they go to the gates," Sam explained. "Then you stop the tape, and people go and place their bets. The odds are calculated based on how many tickets are sold. Jack and I calculate the odds, post them, then hit the play button. It's a lot of fun, and you can make some good money that way."

There are other interesting fundraising wrinkles supplied in the Night at the Races kit. For example, those attending the event could buy a horse for $15—for example, fifth horse in the third race. That would get them into the event, include all the food they could eat, and if the horse they bought won its race, they would win $50. There's no limit to how many horses a person could buy, and they could still bet on any horse they wanted throughout the evening.

In addition, the tenth race of the evening is a corporate race. The girls on the softball team would approach businesses in the area and ask if they wanted to buy a horse in the corporate race for $100. If enough companies wanted to purchase a horse, there would be two corporate races, race 10A and 10B, running at the same time. If the horse the company purchased finished first, the company would win $500. So, twelve horses in a race at $100 per horse is $1,200. After paying out $500 to the winner, the softball team was $700 ahead in fundraising.

"That was our gas money," Sam explained. "And everyone had fun in the process."

The most difficult part of the event was finding a hall in which to hold the event, then getting the food donated. But Sam found that companies in the Lehigh Valley were very giving.

"They just wanted to help out," Sam said. "The people around here are just unbelievable."

In return for the donated food, Sam would put a sign on the table indicating that the food item was donated by a specific company. In the program booklets handed out for the event, companies that donated would be listed and thanked for their participation. If a company made a significant donation, Sam would also put the company's name on the back of a tee-shirt that the girls would wear during pre-game practices all year.

One of the hardest things for Sam was knowing that a girl was not likely to make the team yet seeing her working hard at fundraising. But since final cuts for the team were not made until about three weeks before the Myrtle Beach Tournament, Sam could not tell a girl not to fundraise.

"We asked all the girls up front, do you want this money to go into one big bowl, or do you want to keep a separate tab on what you make, and once you hit your goal, you can stop fundraising?" Sam explained. "The girls always say to put it into one pot. They're a team, so they'll work as a team. But I let them know that if they get cut from the team and don't make the trip to Myrtle Beach, the money stays with the team. Do they want to take that chance? And they all say they understand."

That scenario played out in 2006.

"My toughest day is walking into this office, closing the door and telling a girl that she can't play," Sam explained.

In 2006, that scenario played out with a girl whom Sam had kept on the team the previous season. What made the situation so uncomfortable was that Sam was keeping her college roommate, Lana Good.

Sam called Lana into his office first.

"You've made the team, but, I have to cut your roommate," Sam told her. "I'm telling you first so that you're prepared when you go back to your dorm room. Also, are you going to have a problem with the situation, considering you two have to live the rest of the semester in the same room?"

"No, no problem," Lana said.

Sam called the girl into his office.

"That was rough," Sam recalled. "But when she came back that year, she wasn't the same. She wouldn't run. When we were running, she would stop half way and sit down. She thought she had improved, but she had regressed. Her attitude wasn't the same, and it wasn't a safe environment for her there because she could have gotten hurt."

Sam, as was his custom, checked with all his assistant coaches before making a final decision, and they agreed that she would have to be cut.

"It breaks your heart, because it's not as though we don't like the girl," Sam explained. "She just wasn't good enough to play for the team."

And the 2006 NCC Lady Spartans were about to show just how good a team they were.

SIXTEEN

Does history repeat itself? Does lightning strike twice in the same place? Could the NCC Lady Spartans storm through another Myrtle Beach Snowbird Softball Tournament undefeated?

Those were the questions weighing on the minds of Sam and his coaching staff as they sped southward along I-95 on Saturday morning, March 11, 2006. Well, okay, maybe they weren't thinking too much about the first two questions, but they certainly thought about the third, even if none of them was wondering out loud.

Word travels far and wide within the college softball community; Sam and his players learned as much when they found themselves cruising the highway side by side with the Lady Pioneers of Alfred State, a four-year college in New York State. The two entourages kept pace for several miles, with the girls from each team engaged in an on-the-road conversation by holding up signs in the windows of their respective vans.

Where are you guys from? Where are you going?

It turned out that the Lady Pioneers were also driving to Myrtle Beach. Sam eventually met up with their coach at the pre-tournament meetings on Saturday evening.

"Do you want to play on Sunday?" Sam asked.

"Aren't you the guys who were 40-0 last year?" she responded. Sam nodded. "My girls know that. They would die if we even tried to play you."

The Spartans' reputation was growing.

The NCC vans rolled into Myrtle Beach late Saturday afternoon and, after the unpacking preliminaries, Sam and his assistant coaches attended the pre-tournament meeting where they learned that Northern Iowa Area Community College, whom they already had on their schedule, was looking for a game on Sunday.

Not an exhibition, however. The Trojans and their coaches wanted to play a game that counted. And they wanted to know if the Lady Spartans were interested.

Sam gathered his assistant coaches. They were already scheduled to play Northern Iowa on Tuesday morning as part of the tournament.

"What do you want to do?" he asked.

"I think the girls are ready to play now," Pic offered.

"Yeah, let's not hold them back any longer," Robbie agreed.

Sam walked over to the Northern Iowa coach after the meeting. "Okay, we'll take you on in a real game. Win or lose, it counts. The regular season starts now."

Sam knew he had Nikki ready to go, so there was no need to worry . . . until he got to the field Sunday morning and saw the Trojans warming up. He watched for a few minutes, then turned to Pic.

"Maybe we should have waited another day and had some practice," Sam suggested. "They look like a machine out there."

A machine that needed a tune-up once the game started. Nikki was her usual dominant self, and the Spartan bats came to life early and often. Both Ness and Lex hit home runs, and the Spartans prevailed easily, 13-1.

The only negative to the day was an injury to freshman infielder Kellie Connolly. After singling in her first at bat, she went to third on another hit and slid in hard. When she stood up, she said it felt like there was a stone inside her slider pad. She rolled down the pad, brushed off her knee, and continued playing. Later that inning, ice was being applied to a lump the size of a walnut on her knee. She said she was fine, but Sam insisted she sit the rest of the game.

Kellie was taken to the hospital after the game where they discovered that she had ruptured the bursa sack in her knee. She was on crutches for the rest of the week.

Sam left the field at the end of the game and briefly allowed his mind to wander. *This team looked so good and we pulled them apart*, Sam began thinking. *Maybe we can do this thing all over again.*

Then the veteran coach snapped back. He was getting too far ahead of things, as usual. He told himself to stop being stupid and to just coach one game at a time and relax. There was no need to think that far ahead. Then he smiled as he thought about the team he had assembled for the 2006 season.

"They sure looked good," he said.

Later that night, however, Lana Good took ill and Sam found himself back at the hospital. She had tonsillitis, and her throat was swollen shut. She needed antibiotics, so Nikki's mom, Kim Jenson, accompanied Lana into the examination room. When Lana pulled up her sleeve for the injection, the doctor said, "Oh no, that's not where it's going. We're going to drive a little further south on this one."

Lana got the shot and was fine, but she couldn't play for the next two days. The injury bug had bitten the Lady Spartans.

Sam had to wonder, was it an omen?

* * * *

The tournament officially began on Monday morning, and the Spartans' first opponent were the Lady Lynx of Lincoln Community College in Illinois. With Jenna Turner on the mound, the Spartans broke on top quickly, scoring four runs in the first inning, and held a 5-1 lead after three.

But the Lynx hung tough, adding three runs in the top of the fifth inning to close within 5-4, but could not get over the hump, as the Spartans held on for a 5-4 win.

After the game, Sam expressed some concern.

"Lincoln was a good team, but we just sat and relaxed, and that was the one thing I didn't like," Sam said. "You worry about that every year. Is your team going to have the killer instinct? Are they going to be able to turn it on if they need to shift into a second gear? I was a little worried."

Monday's second game erased those worries. The Massasoit Community College Warriors were a good team, based on

Sam's research, but with Nikki on the mound and the offense in high gear, the game was over early. Ness connected on a two-run homer early, and the Spartans had a 10-0 lead by the third inning in a five-inning, mercy rule-shortened game they won 15-4.

But, there was another casualty, although this one proved more of an irritant than of the disabling variety.

The week before the Myrtle Beach Tournament, Nikki had been in Arizona with her sister, Danielle, who pitched for DeSales University. She and her parents then flew from Arizona to North Carolina where they rented a car and drove to Myrtle Beach. But Nikki needed a new pair of cleats, and she loved Ringor non-metal cleats. So, Sam placed an order, and the cleats were delivered right to the Bermuda Sands Hotel on Monday morning.

"She put them on, and she loved them," Sam recalled.

But with Ringor cleats, the foot has a tendency to slide a bit in the shoe, and over the course of pitching the second game on Monday, Nikki tore the nail on the big toe of her left foot. A blood blister formed under the nail, and swelled to the point where at the back of the nail, toward the cuticle, the nail was pulling away from the skin.

"It was her plant foot when she's pitching," Sam explained. "Can you imagine the force coming down on that foot?"

But Nikki was a warrior, and she kept right on playing.

* * * *

If it's Myrtle Beach and it's time to eat, it must be time for a buffet. And that meant it was time for Sam to bust one of his co-captains.

"I can't wait for the buffet we're going to tonight," Sam would tease Nikki. "It has everything, and it's cheap. Of course, I don't know if the food is any good, but we can eat all we want."

Nikki would roll her eyes, turn and walk away, calling over her shoulder, "Coach, I don't even want to talk about buffets. Get away from me."

So Sam compromised. Instead of going to six buffets during the week in Myrtle Beach, the team dined at only three. On two other nights, Sam cooked meals—spaghetti and meatballs one night, chicken and broccoli fettuccini alfredo another night—in the coaches' suite at the hotel. Robbie and Pic also grilled steaks, hamburgers and hot dogs on the grills adjacent to the hotel on another occasion. In the end, everybody was happy and the team ended up saving money.

"I bought the food in bulk and brought it to Myrtle Beach with us, so there were no other fees involved, so it worked out well for us," Sam said.

But that didn't change the coach's opinion of buffets.

"Sometimes you go to a restaurant and they give you two carrots and a slice of lunch meat and call it a big beef dinner," he explained. "But at the Great American Seafood and Steak Buffet, it's $12.95 for all you can eat. There are four different kinds of steaks, seafood and anything else you can imagine. And if you try something and you don't like it, fine, put it down on the table, they'll clean it up and you can go get something different. You do that at a restaurant, now you have to order a whole different entrée."

On the way out of Great American one night, Roxy decided to put her acrobatic skills on display by hopping over the railing on the walkway leading to the restaurant. She didn't make it, getting stuck midway and wobbling back and forth on the railing, a mixture of screams and laughter coming from her mouth as she assessed the predicament she was in.

Complicating matters, Roxy was wearing a short jeans skirt, and as she tried to balance herself on the railing long enough to extricate herself, she also had to keep her skirt from flying up in the air.

"The other girls were peeing themselves they were laughing so hard," Sam recalled.

The next morning, Roxy had huge black and blue marks on the inside of her thighs from her balancing act on the high wire, but no further damage.

* * * *

On Tuesday morning, the Spartans had their regularly scheduled game against Northern Iowa, the team they had defeated handily just two days earlier. But this was a different day and a different game, and the Trojans more closely resembled the team Sam had watched warming up on Sunday morning.

Prior to the game, Nikki was hitting soft-toss with Roxy, her injured toe throbbing. Roxy tossed the ball, and Nikki hit it, over and over again, until Roxy tossed the ball when Nikki wasn't looking. The ball landed square on Nikki's injured big toe. Nikki jumped and yelled, then realized that the pain and pressure were rapidly subsiding. The force of the ball landing on her toe had caused the blood blister to pop.

"Hey, that actually feels better," Nikki said.

It was a one in a million shot. Now Nikki was able to wrap the toe and pitch in relative comfort.

The Spartans were locked in a 1-1 tie after four innings when the Trojans scored four runs in the top of the fifth to take a 5-1 lead. The Spartans, however, answered with four of their own in the bottom half to again knot the score at 5-5. The Trojans added a single run in the top of the sixth for a 6-5 lead, but the Spartans rallied in the last of the seventh when Ness singled to drive home Lisa with the tieing run. International tie-breaker time.

Knotted at 6-6, the Trojans pushed across two runs in the top of the ninth, and seemed to have the game in hand. But the Spartans wouldn't quit. With Caitlyn McGouldrick on second base to start the inning, Nikki and Ness were leading the cheers.

"This isn't over," they yelled in the dugout.

Lisa singled to put runners on the corners. A sacrifice bunt moved Lisa to second, and Ness singled with two out to bring home both runners and tie the score. On the throw home, Ness moved to second where she scored the winning run on a double by Roxy in the Spartans' come-from-behind 9-8 win.

"The girls went out of character at that point," Sam said. "They went nuts, jumping around, screaming and yelling. And I could see that they were a group that would not let anything stand in their way. They didn't get frazzled when they were down. They had the confidence that, no matter what was going on in the game, they had a chance. They would not allow themselves to quit."

The second game of the day was against the Lady Catamounts of Potomac State College, from West Virginia. It was a team Sam remembered well. During the tournament two years ago, players and coaches waved rebel flags and beat on tambourines in the dugout, while hurling some not-so-kind racial comments in Robbie's direction. Sam pounded that into the girls the night before the game and that morning in the dugout. They were ready.

With Nikki on the mound, the Spartans put a six-spot on the board in the first inning, helped in part by a two-run homer from Ness. The Lady Cats got single runs back in the third and fourth, but the Spartans answered with a run of their own in the fourth and five more in the sixth, the last two on Ness's second home run of the game.

The Spartans prevailed, 12-5. There would be no flag waving this day.

* * * *

Midway through the tournament the Spartans were undefeated, but Sam felt their toughest test so far would come Wednesday morning against the Blue Storm out of Southwestern Illinois College, a very good junior college team.

Sam handed the ball to Nikki, and took her aside before the game.

"I told her to show me what she had," Sam recalled. "I told her that she hadn't really shown me anything yet, and it broke my heart to say that to her. Because you really don't have to light a fire under Nikki. But if you push her pride slightly, she'll dig really deep."

Nikki dug deep. She pitched the Spartans to a 4-0 win, throwing a no-hitter in the process. Ness continued to pound the ball, going 3-for-3 with a single, double and home run.

"We had ten hits off a very good team," Sam said. "I was excited. I realized we had something."

And the Spartans needed everything they had—not once, but twice—over the remaining three games of the tournament.

Wednesday's second game was against the Rochester Community & Technical College Yellow Jackets, out of Rochester, Minnesota. Sam's research had indicated they weren't that good a team, but he found out quickly that his sources of information were a bit erroneous.

Jenna was on the mound, and the Lady Spartans carried a 3-0 lead into the third inning. But a grand slam highlighted a five-run inning and the Yellow Jackets had themselves a 5-3 lead. The Spartans came back with single runs in the third and fifth innings to tie the score, 5-5, and that's the way it remained going into extra innings.

Gimp started the bottom of the eighth on second base, courtesy of the international tie-breaker rules. Gimp moved to third on a sacrifice bunt, bringing Lana to the plate. Sam, coaching at third base, talked to Gimp.

"If she hits the ball to the right side of the field, toward first or second base, you're going home," Sam instructed. "As soon as the ball is hit, find its location, then go."

Lana grounded to shortstop, but Gimp broke for the plate anyway. The shortstop fielded the ball cleanly and fired home, the catcher poised at the plate. Gimp dove head first toward the plate, swung her body out to the right to avoid the tag, but stretched her left arm out and brushed her hand across the plate.

"Safe," the umpire yelled.

The Spartans had earned a hard-fought, 6-5 win.

* * * *

Before dinner, Sam gathered the entire team together for an old-time photo, the kind where everyone dresses up in Wild West costumes and poses for the camera. This year would be a first for Sam who, while he loved to keep the photos of the girls as a memento, disdained appearing in them himself.

"I was never in them because I hated the way I looked," he admitted. "And if I did take an occasional photo, I stood behind everyone so all you could see was my head. But since I had lost the eighty pounds, I was feeling better about myself."

Some of the girls were positioned in a bathtub in front of a saloon bar holding bottles of whiskey; the remainder of the team and coaches gathered around them in various standing and kneeling positions. Sam had to get into a pair of long underwear, then wrap a trench coat around himself, don a cowboy hat and kneel alongside the tub with a shotgun in his hands.

"The long underwear were so tight that my face was turning a deep red," Sam recalled. He turned to Nikki and Ness. "These long underwear are like a cheap hotel."

"What are you talking about, coach?" Ness asked.

"There's no ballroom."

Nikki and Ness laughed so hard they just about fell off their bar stools.

Later that evening, the team met at Hooter's for dinner—surprisingly, at the girls' request. And Sam, ever the practical joker, couldn't resist an opportunity. The entire team, including some parents who had made the trip, sat at a long table, with Sam at one end and Roxy at the other. Sam summoned one of the waitresses.

"There's a girl at the other end of the table," Sam explained, "and I'm sure you can see how well endowed she is."

The waitress smiled and nodded, and Sam outlined his plan. A few minutes later, the waitress reappeared alongside Roxy, a Hooter's tee-shirt in hand.

"The manager would like to know, because we're short-staffed tonight, if you would like to help out by serving tables," the waitress inquired.

Roxy seemed perplexed for a moment. "What? What? Who, me?" Then she caught on. "Give me that shirt. Let's go."

Plenty of photographs were taken, and everyone enjoyed a good laugh.

* * * *

By the time Thursday, the last day of the tournament, rolled around, Sam came to understand that the groundskeepers at the Myrtle Beach athletic complex were betting on the tournament games. One crew in particular was betting on the Spartans to go all the way to the finals.

"You have to win this one," they told Sam before the Thursday morning game against Mercer County Community College, out of New Jersey, "because we have you set up with Ferndale next. And we'll have the field perfect for you."

Ferndale Community College, of New Jersey, was the defending national junior college champion, and Sam figured the Spartans would square off against them in the tournament finale. He knew the Ferndale coach well—Gino Sculabasta, and he didn't particularly like him. Sculabasta did not like to lose, and he despised losing to Sam and the Lady Spartans.

And when the Spartans made short work of Mercer County Community College, ending the game in five innings with an 11-1 win, including a grand slam from Lex, the stage was set. Sam talked to the girls before the game against Ferndale.

"This is the game that will take you from being a very good team to a great team," Sam told them. "This is where you can step into the history books at NCC, by beating this team. We were the first team to come through this tournament undefeated, and no one has done it twice. So go out there and be great."

After that inspiring talk, Ness committed two first-inning errors and Lex added a third as the Spartans fell behind early, 3-0, after one inning.

As was his style, Sculabasta liked being outside his team's dugout. When they were at bat he manned the third base coaching box. When they were in the field, he stood in front of the dugout, paced back and forth, and talked, even though he wasn't supposed to be. He yelled at the home plate umpire, complaining about pitch calls, and was warned twice during the game to curtail the comments.

Now, with his team ahead, he stood in the third base coaching box and talked to Sam.

"So, how is everything going, Sam?" Sculabasta asked, sarcasm dripping from every word.

Sam leaned forward in the dugout, pulled his hat down lower over his forehead, and said nothing. He wouldn't even look at Sculabasta. He knew the Ferndale coach was trying to bait him into an argument. Instead, Sam let assistant coaches Robbie and Pic handle the banter.

"It's the way he treats his players, the way he treats the game, and the way he treats anyone around him when he's coaching," Sam explained. "He's a detriment to his players and his program."

There was also a history between Sam and the opposing coach. Several years earlier, in April 2000, Sam and the Lady Spartans made the ninety-minute drive to Ferndale to play a doubleheader. Sam's father was ill at the time, and in the middle of the first game, Sam got a call on his cell phone from his wife, Chris, that his father was not doing well and had been rushed to the hospital.

"He already has a do not resuscitate," Chris reminded her husband. "So if he goes, he's gone. You have to get home."

Sam ran over to talk to Sculabasta.

"My dad's deathly ill; they took him to the hospital. They don't think he's going to make it, I've got to go . . . I can't stay for the second game. I'm taking my team and we're going home."

But Sculabasta had other thoughts.

"No no no . . . you signed up for two games so you're going to play two games or you're going to take a forfeit," Sculabasta said.

"Fine, you got your forfeit," Sam decided, and he loaded the team into the vans and left. Sam's father lived for another three weeks before passing away, but Sam would never forget the way he and the Spartans were treated by Sculabasta. He did not want to lose to this coach. And the Lady Spartans, knowing the history, were determined not to.

But in the bottom of the third inning, Ferndale was winning, 3-0. Then Nikki walked and Jenna crushed a two-run homer, cutting the Ferndale lead to 3-2. The Spartans' confidence began to build, and Sculabasta began to yell—at his players, and at the umpires.

"He's getting nervous," Sam said in the dugout, to no one in particular.

Ferndale added a run in the top of the fourth to up its lead to 4-2; the Spartans responded with one in the bottom of the sixth, on an RBI single by Ness, to cut the deficit to one run once again, 4-3, heading into the last inning.

Ferndale didn't score in the top of the seventh, giving the Spartans one last shot at the defending national junior college champion. But the first two batters were retired easily, and as Nikki—who had been waiting her turn on deck—strode to the plate with two out, her head down and a frown on her face, Sculabasta started yelling to his team.

"We've got 'em," he announced to his team. "This game is ours girls. One more out and we beat them."

Sam pulled Nikki away from home plate.

"Look at me," Sam said as he took hold of Nikki by the ear holes in her batting helmet. "This game is not about me. Don't try to beat him because of me. This game is about you and the girls in the dugout, and I don't want you to give up. Go out there, have fun, and whatever happens, I still love you."

Sam turned to head back to the coaching box when he heard Sculabasta's voice.

"Time out," he yelled. "Everybody in here."

Sculabasta talked to his team, then sent them back onto the field in a different defensive alignment. He moved the third base-man into the outfield so that he was playing with four outfielders, then positioned another player at third base, but deep—back on the edge of the outfield grass. He was guarding against the extra-base hit.

Nikki seemed confused, then looked toward Sam. She flashed him the bunt sign, and he nodded in approval.

Nikki bunted down the third baseline, easily beating any play at first base. Sculabasta, of course, yelled at his infielders for not coming up with the ball.

Lisa was next. She dragged a bunt up the first baseline for a single to put runners on first and second. That brought up Jenna. The count went to 3-2, and Jenna fouled off the next dozen pitches to stay alive. With every foul ball, Sculabasta stomped his foot as he paced along the first baseline. Then Jenna walked, loading the bases.

Ness, perhaps the Spartans' best clutch hitter, stepped to the plate. The count went to 3-0. Sam was thinking, the pitcher has to throw three strikes in a row or she'll walk in the tying run. He leaned over to Nikki, who was standing on third base.

"She's going to walk Ness and we'll tie the game," Sam told her. "But, if there's a passed ball, run in and slide into home. And as you come back to the dugout, turn and wink at the other coach."

Nikki laughed, then yelled encouragement to her teammate. "Come on, Ness."

Sam waved his arms back and forth, giving Ness the take sign. Ness saw things differently. The next pitch was outside, but Ness swung and rocketed a ball between first and second into right field. Nikki, stunned for a moment, stood at third base until she saw Lisa barreling toward her from second. She took off for home, with Lisa in hot pursuit, and they crossed the plate one right after the other for a 5-4 Spartan win.

The NCC dugout exploded. The girls were screaming and pounding on the fence. Robbie and Pic were jumping up and down and screaming. Nikki and Lisa were jumping and hugging each other at home plate. Ness ran up to Sam and hugged him so hard she almost broke his ribs.

Sculabasta kicked the fence, as his players left the field with their heads down.

The two teams lined up for the customary post-game handshake, coaches at the back of the line. Eventually, Sam and Sculabasta met at home plate.

"Great game, Gino," Sam said, then leaned forward and kissed Sculabasta on the cheek before turning and walking away.

The celebration in the NCC dugout continued as Sam took a long, slow walk down the left field line, almost to the fence at the outer edge of the outfield. He kneeled down and thought, "Oh God, thank you for this. Thank you for these girls."

Then he heard footsteps coming up from behind. He turned to see Nikki and Ness. They were crying. They hugged their coach, and Sam began to cry. Nikki stood on Sam's right, Ness on his left. They put one arm each around his shoulders, and Sam put his arms around their waists as they slowly began walking back to the dugout.

And as they walked, Nikki turned and whispered in Sam's ear, "That one was for you, coach."

SEVENTEEN

After the way the Lady Spartans played—and rallied to win in exhilarating fashion—during the Myrtle Beach Snowbird Softball Tournament, the regular season might seem very hum-drum. But the first two teams on NCC's schedule that spring came out of two of the better softball programs in the area. The games proved to be a good litmus test for the Spartans.

First up was York College's Junior Varsity team. And in one of those rare occurrences where teams share the same nickname, the games were a battle of the Spartans vs. the Spartans. Going into the games, however, Sam wasn't expecting a high level of competition. His rationale was that while York's varsity team was traditionally strong, the girls who don't make varsity end up on what is called the JV team, but in actuality is a school club team. How good could a club team be, Sam thought?

"I was shocked," the coach recalled. "I was thinking that since it's a club team, it's made up of kids who didn't make varsity. And if the school had a JV team, they might not make that squad. But this team was good. This was one of the better teams that we played during the season. They were very disciplined; they knew what they were doing."

In fact, the two games against the York Spartans would wind up being among a small handful of games that went the full seven innings.

"It's not that we took them lightly," Sam explained. "They were just a good team."

Nevertheless, the NCC Spartans prevailed by 8-0 and 7-2 scores.

The Spartans next received a visit from the Titans of the Community College of Morris County in New Jersey, a team Sam thought was even better than the York College Spartans.

He also developed an immediate rapport with the Titans' head coach, Greg Wardlow.

"He's a very good coach," Sam said. "The first time I met him, there was just a mutual respect factor going back and forth."

After the games, won by NCC 11-3 and 12-4, Sam sent an email to coach Wardlow. He thanked him for coming out to NCC for the games, and commented on what a good team he had.

Wardlow wrote back that on the drive home, he told his girls that the way NCC plays the game is the level his team is going to strive to achieve; that he wanted his Titans to become a team like NCC.

"That was one of the nicest things anyone has ever said about any team I've coached," Sam recalled. "Not for me and the coaching staff, but for the girls."

The next two sets of games—home doubleheaders against Montgomery County Community College and Delaware County Community College—gave rise to what Sam liked to call 'the signal.'

Neither team was very good, with NCC beating Montgomery 10-1 and 12-3, then thrashing Delaware 29-1 and 16-0. Sam didn't want to take the bat out of his girls' hands, so he came up with a sign for the runners on base to leave the base early. When they did so, the umpires would call them out. Some innings, it was the only way for opposing teams to record three outs.

"I had to come up with something because we were hitting the ball and it was getting pretty bad," Sam recalled. "I guess I shouldn't have done it. The Montgomery coach was a little upset about it, and I felt bad afterward, but I'm not out here to embarrass anyone."

Sam recalled his early years at NCC and an opposing team that would routinely embarrass everyone they played. The team could be leading 40-0, but the coach would still have his players bunting and stealing bases.

"The coach would say he was having his girls bunt so that they would make outs," Sam said. "But even his athletic director admitted that after five years he was sick and tired of listening to opposing schools complain, so he fired the coach."

Sam didn't want to be remembered that way, so he developed 'the signal.' He also made a move during the second game against Montgomery that would impact the entire season. The Spartans were batting in the bottom of the fourth, leading by a wide margin, and it was beginning to get dark outside. Not only did Sam want to make sure the game reached a regulation five innings, he was worried that someone might get hurt. New dugouts were being built along the first and third baselines, so much of the sidelines on the NCC field were in some stage of construction, with fencing bordering large holes dug into the ground.

Sam had already begun telling the girls to run slow between the bases so that they could be tagged out. Then, as Caitlyn McGouldrick came to bat with two outs, Sam called her over.

"Just swing through the pitches and strike out, so we can get this game over with," Sam instructed. "I won't count it against you. It will be a non at-bat."

She swung and missed three times, walked toward the dugout, then turned and threw her helmet and bat down at Sam's feet.

"Don't you ever do something like that to me again," she said. "You ruined my batting average."

Sam couldn't believe what he was hearing. "What did you just say?"

"Don't ever do that to me again," Caitlyn repeated. "Don't ever make me strike out like that again."

Sam pointed toward the dugout. "Go sit on the bench."

After the game, Sam informed her that she was being suspended for two games, and he told her why.

"You don't talk back to us," he explained. "I told you what you were doing, and why you were doing it. You don't question when we tell you to do something; you just do it. This isn't a personal attack on you, it's for the team."

Two days later, Lex came into Sam's office and handed him a bag.

"What's this?" the coach asked.

"It's Caitlyn's uniform," Lex said. "She quit."

Later, Sam called the team together and informed them that Caitlyn had quit. He wasn't surprised by their reaction.

"They were relieved," he recalled. "They said there was one person on the team who was complaining to everybody about the fact that she wasn't playing enough. And they told me later in the year that it was the turning point in the season. They said they felt relaxed, like one unit, instead of one unit here and one individual over there."

The Delaware game, however, had some much lighter moments. Jenna was pitching the first game, and the Phantoms had a young lady on their team whom Sam recalled as one of the funniest kids he had ever seen. Every time she got into the batter's box it was the same routine.

"Come on, Jenna, see what you can do against me," the player would chatter. "Come on, strike me out. I'm a hitter."

Then, every time she would pass Jenna between innings, she would smile and say, "You know I'm only messing with you, right?" Jenna would laugh. And in the end, Jenna struck her out twice.

In the second game, another blowout, Nikki was pitching a perfect game when she approached Sam between innings.

"Coach, I'm going to walk a couple of people, or let them hit, because I feel sorry for them," Nikki said. "I really like these girls, and I like their coach, and I don't want to break their hearts."

"Nikki, you can't do that," Sam said. "They know what you can do. So out of respect, just throw the ball."

Sam said all this, realizing that at the same time he was telling his players to leave base early so they could be called out, which he admitted was somewhat disrespectful. But he rationalized the strategy.

"You make the arrangements with the other coaches, and most of them will say 'Fine, just do it,'" Sam explained. "Even the umpires tell you to do it."

As the season progressed, it was a strategy Sam would employ on a fairly regular basis. But it would also cause considerable controversy.

* * * *

In baseball, when one team beats another by a lopsided score it's called a laugher. The Spartans took that literally and physically in a home doubleheader against the Lincoln University Lions.

Jenna pitched the first game, and she received enough offensive support to spread out over several games. In a mercy rule-shortened affair, the Spartans banged out twenty-eight hits, including four home runs, on their way to a 20-0 win.

Realizing there was no need to throw his ace in the second game, Sam rested Nikki and gave Katie Sculley—an outfielder and designated hitter who pitched on rare occasions at Bethlehem Catholic—a chance to pitch. That opened the door.

"Coach, let me pitch. Let me pitch," Roxy begged.

"If I can, I'll get you in," Sam answered.

Katie was sailing along, pitching a shutout and receiving the same level of run support that Jenna did in the first game. Roxy kept up her mantra.

"Come on, coach, let me pitch."

Sam relented. He put Roxy in. She faced four batters—hit one, and walked the other three, allowing four runs to score.

"Coach, get me out of here," Roxy pleaded when Sam went to the mound to talk with her. "It's not as much fun as I thought it would be." But it certainly was funny to everyone watching.

Katie returned to the mound, finished with a one-hitter and thirteen strikeouts, and the Spartans prevailed 20-5. Roxy's pitching career was short-lived.

* * * *

In the beginning of the season, coaches and players alike circle games on their schedule; teams that they're looking forward to playing or that represent a certain challenge or high-point in the season. Sam had circled back-to-back doubleheaders against Cedar Crest College and Luzerne County Community College. Both schools had good teams; both doubleheaders were on the road.

Cedar Crest is an NCAA Division III school, and while they didn't traditionally have great teams, the Falcons' coach, Kristy Henritzy, was in the process of turning the softball pro-gram around. The Falcons were on top in their league, thanks to solid pitching from a trio of freshmen players.

Sam approached the doubleheader accordingly. He pitched Nikki in the first game, and she responded with a seven-strikeout perfect game as the Spartans won 8-0. Saving the perfect game was a catch Lisa Klinger made in center field that Sam described as, "One of the greatest catches I've ever seen in my life. Running from center field toward left-center, she dove, was off the ground by several feet, caught the ball before hitting the ground, and saved the perfect game."

Riding the horse one more time, Sam pitched Nikki in the nightcap and she struck out nine batters and tossed a one-hitter in a 12-2, mercy rule-shortened NCC win.

Back to back 7-0 wins followed in a doubleheader sweep of Luzerne. And even though the Spartans were victorious, Sam saw that both Luzerne pitchers were able to keep his hitters in check. He made a mental note, because he knew the Spartans would face those pitchers again later in the season.

Another doubleheader sweep, this one by 12-0 and 15-0 scores on the road at Delaware County Community College, brought about a response from the girls that Sam had heard often the year before.

"When are we going to get teams that can play?" the girls asked, noting that except for Cedar Crest, Morris and York, they hadn't played anyone competitive since Myrtle Beach. "Is this what it's going to be like all the time?"

Sam was blunt. "These are the teams in our league, we have to play them. If coaches don't go out and recruit, you're going to see crap. There's nothing I can do about it."

Inside, of course, Sam was not upset by their outburst. He was glad they wanted to play top competitive teams. It showed confidence and a desire to be, and beat, the best. He also knew it was a long season, and he wanted to have all his players strong at playoff time. Playing some weaker teams gave him an opportunity to rest some players from time to time.

And following a wild affair at Montgomery County Community College, everyone could have used a rest.

* * * *

For the better part of two seasons, when the score in a game got out of hand, Sam would have his base runners leave base early, thereby recording a desperately needed 'out' for the opposing team. In 2005, he instructed runners to leave early; in 2006, he had devised a signal. And in the Spartans' doubleheader against the Montgomery County Community College Mustangs, he had given that signal liberally.

"I knew it got the coach upset," Sam acknowledged, "but he never said anything.

Not yet, anyway.

Nikki pitched the Spartans to an easy win, 14-1, in the first game, striking out nine batters in the process. Early in the second game, however, storm clouds began to roll in, and lightning was seen off in the distance. It was the top of the fifth inning, with NCC comfortably out in front 8-0, but it wouldn't be an official game until the Mustangs batted in the bottom of the inning.

Sam wanted to get the game in, so with his team coming to bat in the top of the fifth, he paid a visit to the home plate umpire.

"What do you think?" Sam asked, gesturing toward the impending storm.

"I want this game over with," the umpire responded.

"Do you want me to do anything to get these kids off base, because I have a signal ..."

"Yes, please do it," the umpire broke in. "Let's get this thing over with."

Sam turned to walk back to the third base coaching box when he was stopped in his tracks by a woman's voice. It was the field umpire, standing out between first and second base. She didn't sound pleased.

"Time out. You," the umpire yelled, pointing at Sam, "home plate, now."

Sam turned and looked at the field umpire, but didn't move.

"You heard me," she yelled, louder still. "Get to home plate right now."

Sam walked back to home plate where he was met by the field umpire.

"You're making a travesty of this game," she began. "You're lucky I don't throw you off this field, and throw your team off this field."

That opened the floodgates, as the Montgomery coach joined in, followed in chorus by his players.

"They pull this stuff on us all the time," the Montgomery coach yelled from the home dugout. "I don't know what his problem is. He's constantly making a fool of my players."

Sam was pissed, but he didn't want to get the home plate umpire in trouble by revealing their conversation. He directed his comments to the Montgomery coach.

"Coach, I'm just trying to help you," Sam explained. "If you want, I can turn the dogs back on and we can play like we always play."

"I don't care what you do," the Montgomery coach responded.

Sam turned to the field umpire. "Okay ma'am, I'm sorry. I apologize. It will never happen again."

Sam walked back to the coaching box amid cries from the Montgomery players.

"You're rotten.

"You're making us look stupid."

"Don't ever schedule us again."

Sam stood in the coaching box watching the Mustangs take infield practice before the start of the inning. A ball thrown around the infield almost hit Sam, but the Montgomery third baseman jumped in front of him to catch it, prompting a loud comment from the team's shortstop.

"You should have let it go and hit his fat ass."

Now the Spartans were incensed, Ness in particular, but Sam calmed them down. Then he gave the girls their marching orders.

"Okay, the hell with them," Sam instructed. "Turn it back on and beat the shit out of them."

The Spartans tacked on another six runs that inning, and when Jenna blew away three consecutive batters in the bottom of the fifth, NCC had a 14-0 win.

By now, however, the fans—including many parents in the stands—were shouting and verbally abusing the NCC players. Knowing they had to walk right past the stands to get to their school vans, Sam gathered the team together.

"Put your stuff in your bags, look straight ahead and follow me," he instructed. "Do not respond to them. Do not say anything to them. We are going to leave the field, and you will never come back here again."

Sam led the way, with Robbie and Pic bringing up the rear. As the jeers rained down, the NCC players and coaches walked quickly to the parking lot, got in the school vans, and left.

* * * *

The next morning, NCC athletic director Bill Bearse called Sam in for a meeting. He'd received a phone call from the Montgomery County Community College athletic director, and was informed of the previous day's incident.

"Sam, what are you doing?" Bill asked.

"Bill, we needed to get the game in," Sam explained. "We were beating them so badly, and they couldn't get our hitters out."

"Well, don't do that anymore," Bill instructed. "I don't care how badly you're beating a team, they don't want you doing that. So, just keep on going until they record some outs. And then if they want to complain about you scoring so many runs, tell them that if they don't want you making out on purpose, they ought to prepare their team better. But for now, just play the game."

That's just what Sam and the Spartans did.

EIGHTEEN

The Lady Spartans were storming through another incredible season. They had won their first eighteen games of the regular season and, counting the nine wins they recorded at the Myrtle Beach Snowbird Softball Tournament, their record stood at 27-0. No one was talking about another undefeated season—not yet, anyway. But accomplishing that feat became more possible as each passing doubleheader was logged onto the victory side of the ledger.

Despite the prowess of the NCC softball team, there were days when Sam's mind was thousands of miles away. Kristy Kroll was still in Iraq, and so were Sam's thoughts. He kept in touch via email, but longed for her tour of duty to be over and for her to arrive home safe. The news reports from Iraq didn't make Sam's letter-writing any easier.

> *We heard on the news that a solider from Beth-*
> *lehem was killed today in a non combat-related*
> *accident, Sam wrote. Then I heard that a suicide*

*bomber killed 21 people. I am very worried
about you, because the solider was from the 228th
reserve, and I think that is your platoon. If you
get time, please write back and let me know
you are okay.*

*I've talked about you to all the girls on the team,
and they are both concerned and proud of you and
can't wait to meet you. Please write back when
you can. God bless you. See you soon.*

The emails from Kristy, and their contents, had Sam's
emotions running high and low. In mid-April, Kristy wrote that
she hoped to be home in June, but added that "the Army changes
decisions so often that we never really know what to expect. But
rumor has it that we will be leaving within the next few months."

That news had Sam feeling upbeat, until he read further in
the email.

*I was in the city of Ramadi on a convoy, as I had
a mission to do dental exams at another camp,
Kristy wrote. Man, the city is just not where
anyone wants to be. I was at Combat Outpost.
That camp is literally in the city. It is a creepy
feeling knowing that snipers live in the buildings
that surround the camp. Mortars and rocket-
propelled grenades always find their way into the
chow hall and other buildings at Combat Outpost.
But the mission went well, and the soldiers were*

*so happy that we came out to see them. Even
though we have it pretty bad at Camp Ramadi,
Combat Outpost has it just a little bit worse.*

*I was talking to many people who have been
deployed before. They say it takes double the
amount of time you have been deployed to become
adjusted to civilian life again. That would make
it about three years for me, but I don't really have
that much time to waste.*

*The military allows for soldiers to take leave for
15 days. However, I am the only one with my
job, so I really cannot afford to take leave. I really
need it, though. I am so tired and stressed, but the
mission must go on.*

Those last words might have been foreshadowing. Two
weeks later, just as Sam was beginning to get his hopes up, he
received another email from Kristy indicating that she and Sean,
her boyfriend, had volunteered to stay an additional two weeks
to help train the next group of soldiers coming in.

"They were so close to coming home," Sam recalled thinking, "but they volunteered to stay and put their lives on the line
just a little bit longer to help others. She wasn't even thinking of
herself; she was thinking of others all the time."

Finally, Kristy sent word that she was coming home—arriving back at the 228th Army Reserve in Allentown around Father's
Day, virtually a year to the day since setting foot in Iraq. She was

concerned, though, and indicated that she didn't think she'd be mentally ready to jump into the school mode in the fall, wanting instead to wait until the following spring semester. She hoped it didn't jeopardize being able to play for the softball team. Sam assured her that it wasn't a problem.

He also called the 228th Army Reserve and asked exactly when Kristy was scheduled to arrive. He was told that, for security reasons, information was not supposed to be given out. However, he was given their day and time of arrival at Lehigh Valley International Airport, and told that if he wanted to see her, to be at the Reserve around 9:30 p.m.

Then he realized it was a time for her to be with her family. He'd see her when she got back.

* * * *

During the 2006 season, construction was ongoing for home and visiting team dugouts along the third and first baselines on NCC's softball field. Previously, the dugouts consisted of metal benches on which the players and coaches could sit. But with the success of the 2005 team, Sam and athletic director Bill Bearse realized the girls needed a better field. The content of the conversation was fairly predictable.

"We need to make this field a good field," Bearse told Sam.

"I know, but we don't have money to do this, right?" Sam asked.

"Right."

"Can I see what I can do about getting the materials donated?"

"Yes, go ahead."

So Sam began making the rounds, contacting various area suppliers for blocks, roofing, metal poles and concrete. Some supplies were simply donated, others were obtained through bartering. Bethlehem Vo-Tech took on the construction of the dugouts as a project for its students; an electronic scoreboard was sponsored. Permanent fencing was installed around the perimeter of the outfield. When finished, just prior to the start of the EPCC playoffs, it was indeed the home of a state championship team.

With the upgrades, made possible through the goodness of many area companies, Sam felt it appropriate to give back; to do something good with the platform the team now had. His attention was drawn to the story of Nicole Sheriff, a local fifteen-year-old girl who just two years earlier had died after a two-year battle with metastatic Ewings Sarcoma, or bone cancer.

Sam contacted Doug Sheriff, Nicole's father, who was the athletic director at Saucon Valley High School. He told Sheriff that he and the team wanted to do something on the new field to honor Nicole. Sheriff said it would be an honor, and invited Sam to meet with him at his office in the high school. There, he heard first-hand Nicole Sheriff's story.

Nicole was a good student and a three-sport athlete, competing for her middle school in softball, basketball and field hockey. Her father, a huge fan of Chicago Bears running back Walter Payton, had an autographed photo of Payton in his study. Nicole would watch video of Payton, who wore uniform No. 34, and asked her father why he didn't dance in the end zone like other players did.

"It's because he realizes it's not about him," Sheriff told his daughter. "It's about everyone who got him there."

From then on, Nicole wore No. 34 on all her uniforms.

In April 2002, Nicole was diagnosed with bone cancer. A two-year battle against the disease began, and so did an amazing relationship with the No. 34.

After being diagnosed with bone cancer in April 2002, Nicole was taken to Children's Hospital of Philadelphia. The hospital is located on 34th Street. While waiting to be admitted, she watched a baseball game with her father, and the pitcher for the Atlanta Braves that day wore uniform No. 34.

The hospital room she was assigned to was Room 34.

One day the family went out to dinner, and the taxi they took was No. 34. The bill for dinner that night came to $34.34.

Finally, while traveling to Gettysburg on vacation, they got lost, then found themselves on highway 34 leading to Gettysburg.

Doug Sheriff asked his daughter, "What's with the number 34?"

Nicole responded, "That's my angel who's with me, and let's me know everything is okay."

Subsequently, during her chemotherapy treatments, Nicole learned that ICEEs, a frozen drink, would help break down the mucousitis that develops with treatments and makes it difficult to swallow. They helped keep her hydrated and relieved pain associated with mouth sores.

Nicole set out to help other children, raising money to purchase ICEE machines for hospitals where she had been treated. In the process, the Angel 34 Foundation was formed, and together with the ICEE Company, began installing ICEE machines in children's cancer hospitals across the country.

Sam left the meeting with Doug Sheriff with tears in his eyes. He walked back to his car where his brother, Pic, was waiting for him, and re-told the entire story.

Just as Sam was about to shift into drive and leave the high school parking lot, he was stopped cold.

"I can't believe this," Sam said.

Pic was confused. "Can't believe what?"

Sam turned and faced his younger brother. "What's our record now for all the years I've been coaching at NCC?"

Pic thought a moment, then his face went white. "Oh my God," was all he could say.

Under Sam as a coach, the Spartans' record was 167 wins and 34 losses.

Returning to the college, Sam gathered the girls at the next team practice and told them the story of Nicole Sheriff. Then he added, "Keep your eyes open, because the number thirty-four is going to show up when you least expect it. And when it does, you'll know that Nicole is with you."

* * * *

A special date circled on Sam's calendar was April 17, a road doubleheader at Lehigh Carbon Community College—the first time the two teams would meet since the Spartans' 2004 playoff loss, and a return to the same field where that loss occurred.

The Lady Cougars were having a good season, too. They were undefeated in division play, and Sam knew it would come down to the Spartans and the Cougars in the battle for the No. 1 seed in the EPCC tournament that was only a few weeks away.

He also remembered what happened the last time an NCC team set foot on the softball field at LCCC, and he reminded the girls of that game in NCC softball history, stoking the fire with his players as the date approached.

"I was feeding them on what happened in the playoffs two years ago," Sam said. "About the way we were treated, and how they wouldn't play us last season. I was pouring fuel on the fire, and I wanted it to spread into a wildfire on that softball field."

The Cougars were no pushover. They had a new coach in Amy Dumbrowski. As an assistant at both Parkland and Whitehall high schools, she'd had an opportunity to learn under two very successful coaches, Glenn Ray at Parkland and Tony cocca at Whitehall.

The Cougars also had Leeann Parliman, a very good pitcher who almost came to NCC two years earlier. But as a resident of Lehigh County, the tuition costs to attend LCCC were considerably lower than those at NCC, so she opted to become a Cougar. And she was a hell of a pitcher.

Sam was counting on the motivation factor to carry the Spartans to victory. They were motivated by having to wait a year to play the Cougars; motivated by the playoff loss in 2004; and motivated to win the division and gain the No. 1 seed.

"We have to separate ourselves from the crowd," Sam told his players before the doubleheader. For a while, though, there was little separating the two teams.

The first game of the doubleheader remained scoreless through three innings. But in the top of the fourth, Roxy tripled and walked home on a home run by Gimp for a 2-0 NCC lead.

Then, holding a 3-0 lead, the Spartans broke the game open with six runs in the top of the seventh inning, highlighted by a two-run double from Lisa and a three-run homer by Gimp, her second of the game. Nikki threw a one-hitter in the 9-0 Spartan win.

Sam started Nikki in the second game, too. "I wanted to push them down hard," he said. Jenna pitched the last two, and that's all that was needed as the Spartan bats exploded 11 runs in the first three innings en route to a 13-0, five-inning win.

The Spartan wins gave the Cougars two division losses for the season. NCC had none, so Sam knew that, mathematically, they just had to defeat Luzerne—their next opponent—at least once and the division title would belong to NCC.

On a personal level, the doubleheader sweep was sweet.

"It was satisfying," Sam acknowledged. "And the fact that they didn't score any runs was a great thing. It was good for me because it provided a little bit of closure. It was good for the girls who were on the team last year when they refused to play us. And the fact that we won on their field, the same field where we had lost in 2004, was great."

But there were still a few more mountains left to climb, and a little more closure to realize.

* * * *

In some games, the Spartans pounced on their opponent from the opening pitch; in others, they slowly, almost methodically, build a small lead and then exploded late in the game to snuff out any hopes the other team might have.

The latter scenario took place at Luzerne. The Spartans traveled up to Nanticoke to battle the Trailblazers and, against Luzerne's best pitcher, broke open a 6-0 game by scoring eight runs in the seventh inning for a 14-0 win in the first game of a doubleheader. Gimp hit her third home run in the last four games.

Jenna pitched the second game, and the Spartans nicked away all afternoon, scoring in virtually every inning of a 9-1 win. The division title belonged to the Spartans, and NCC would host the upcoming EPCC tournament no matter what happened the rest of the season.

But as Sam recalled, what happened next mattered a great deal to the girls.

"They knew we played LCCC again, and they really wanted to finish the season with no losses," said Sam, remembering the girls' post-doubleheader comments.

"Let's do it again. Can we?"

"Wouldn't it be unbelievable to do it two years in a row?"

"All right, let's go for it."

Now the motivation was there for a second consecutive undefeated season. Only doubleheaders against LCCC and York College, against whom the Spartans started the season, remained on the regular schedule. The girls wanted it, and that pleased Sam to no end.

* * * *

Back on familiar soil, the Spartans took the field to host a doubleheader against LCCC, and Sam intended to pitch Nikki in both games.

"I just wanted to shut LCCC down," he admitted.

Nikki did just that, and the offense took over early, scoring three runs in each of the first two innings to take the fight out of the Cougars. The Spartans won the first game, 7-0, in a traditional seven innings, then ended the nightcap early with a 10-0, five-inning, mercy rule-shortened win.

The Cougars pitched Leeann Parliman in both games, so even though Sam maintained a close relationship with Leeann, he felt upbeat that the Spartans had beaten LCCC's best pitcher twice in the same day.

Now the EPCC tournament positioning was set. NCC was 12-0 in the division, had secured the No. 1 seed and would host the tournament on its field. LCCC, with an 8-4 division record, was seeded second and would play Luzerne, the No. 3 seed, in one of the semifinals. Delaware County Community College, seeded fourth, would face NCC in the other semifinal. Sam liked those arrangements, especially since the Spartans had pounded the Phantoms 82-1 while sweeping all four games during the season.

Shortly before the season's final games against York College, however, Sam learned that Delaware didn't have enough players to compete. They had nine, but their pitcher was stung by a bee, experienced an adverse reaction and couldn't pitch. It was a forfeit, or maybe just avoiding an inevitable pounding. Either way, the Spartans had a bye into the EPCC championship game, and Sam was already plotting strategy.

"Now we're able to sit for the first game; get to watch the other two teams play," Sam explained. "Both teams have to use their best pitcher, because they need to advance to the championship game. So, we'll be rested, and they'll have to throw either their number two pitcher or a tired number one."

For the girls, however, it was business as usual, and that meant having to take care of the York College JV team first. Not surprisingly, Sam pitched Nikki in the first game. After York scored a run in the first inning, the Spartans began building an insurmountable lead, scoring two runs in the second inning, six in the third, and two more in the seventh for a dominating 10-2 win.

Only one game to go and, of course, there had to be some concern and controversy. With Jenna on the mound, the York Spartans put a two-spot on the board in the first inning, and Sam began his nervous pacing. But York's lead didn't even last a full inning. NCC responded with four runs in the first, three in the second and a lucky seven in the third, then cruised to a 16-3 win and their second consecutive undefeated regular season.

Along the way, however, Jenna hit four different York batters with pitches. To the York players, it added insult to injury. They were being pummeled on the scoreboard, and pasted in the batter's box.

After the game, the York coach approached Sam.

"Sam, this is not my opinion, and there's no animosity between you and I," the coach began. "But our girls were talking, and they don't want to play you again."

Sam understood, but he also knew his pitcher.

"That's Jenna, she's going to hit people," Sam said. "They got pissed because they were losing, and then they were getting hit. It ended the relationship between us and York on a sour note."

Sam didn't dwell on the negative for long. The playoffs loomed, and the Spartans would face the winner of the semifinal game between LCCC and Luzerne. Sam began scouring the season's scorebooks, breaking down the games against Luzerne and LCCC. He charted which batters hit what pitch, and where did they hit it. He knew that if Nikki was on her game, all the stats in the world wouldn't matter. They wouldn't touch her. But he still wanted to be prepared.

And while he wouldn't admit it before the games, he was secretly rooting for LCCC.

"I wanted LCCC in the finals for three reasons," Sam explained. "First, I wanted Leeann to be there, because it was her last year at LCCC and she deserved it. Second, Amy, their coach, has something to prove because it's her first year there, and I like her. So it would be icing on the cake for her to take the team to the EPCC finals in her first season as head coach."

Then Sam smiled, knowing he was saving the best for last.

"The other thing is, LCCC hadn't scored a run against us all season, and I wanted to end it that way," the coach admitted. "I wanted to play them five times during the year and not have them score a single run against us. And I wanted to beat them in the finals. That was my own motivation internally. It really would bring everything around full circle."

It would heal a gaping wound that still hadn't healed. And, in Sam's mind, would bring complete closure to the LCCC saga.

NINETEEN

It was early Saturday morning, April 29, when Sam assembled the Lady Spartans on the NCC softball field for batting practice. The Spartans would have been playing Delaware County Community College at 10 a.m. in one of the EPCC semifinals had the Phantoms not forfeited the game due to a shortage of players. But Sam still wanted the players out early for batting practice before sitting back and watching the noon semifinal between Luzerne and LCCC to see which team they would play at 2 p.m. for the EPCC championship.

Sam walked the girls through some light fielding drills, then retreated to the batting cages inside the gym. He turned the speed dial up on the pitching machine, just in case LCCC won the semifinal and the girls would be facing Leeann Parliman, a power pitcher. He wanted the girls to be ready.

"Leeann is a warrior," Sam explained, "and she's a leader. She will not accept second place."

Shortly before noon, the Spartans and their coaches positioned themselves behind the backstop, ready to watch the semifinal. Luzerne and LCCC had played each other four times that season, with LCCC winning all four games. But the games had been competitive, the scores close. LCCC's total margin of victory over the four games amounted to only ten runs. Anything was possible in a one-game playoff.

As was expected, and much to Sam's delight, the game was a dogfight. When the dust settled after seven innings, the score was tied, 5-5. Neither team scored in the eighth inning, but LCCC pushed across a run in the bottom of the ninth to win, 6-5. Sam's wish had come true. The Spartans would play the Lady Cougars for the EPCC championship, and they would face a tired pitcher. Leeann had pitched all nine innings of the semifinal. And now, after just a 15-minute break, she would have to handle the Spartans' powerful lineup.

The scenario couldn't have been more to NCC's advantage.

Nikki, whom Sam had begun referring to as his knockout punch, was on the mound for the Spartans. And she took charge. Through five innings and the first fifteen outs recorded in the game, Nikki had a hand in twelve of them, either through strike-outs or ground balls back to the pitcher. She was dominating.

Leeann was tired. The effects of a quick turnaround after pitching nine tough innings showed in the bottom of the first. Consecutive singles by Jenna, Ness and Lex loaded the bases, and Gimp cleared them with a triple, giving the Spartans a quick 3-0 lead. Nikki helped her own cause in the second inning, following a single by Lisa with a home run over the left field fence for a 5-0 NCC advantage. The Spartans wrapped up the scoring in the fourth. Lisa's second hit of the game was followed by run-scoring hits from Nikki, Jenna and Roxy—three more runs and an 8-0 lead for the Spartans after four innings.

Nikki recorded three quick outs in the top of the fifth, and the game was over—a five-inning, mercy rule-shortened 8-0 win for the Spartans, and a return to the PCAA Championship for the second year in a row.

All of Sam's wishes had come true.

"They didn't score a run against us all year," the coach recalled. "Combined, over five games, we outscored them 47-0." It was payback, and it was sweet.

It was also a time to celebrate, and the Lady Spartans enjoyed their victory, but they were still taking a business-as-usual approach. They received their medals and trophies, and Sam was presented with the Coach of the Year award, but there were still two more games to win; still one more barrier to a second consecutive undefeated season and state title. The girls were maintaining their focus.

In the midst of the celebration, Sam was tapped on the shoulder. He turned and looked up to see Leeann, who stood nearly four inches taller than the coach. She was crying, and she spoke through the tears.

"Thank you for giving me the opportunity to play something I love," Leeann said, referring to Sam's readiness to have her pitch for the Spartans before she opted to attend LCCC instead. "Can you help me?"

Sam was taken back. "What do you mean? Of course I can help you. What do you need?"

"Can you help me get into a college from here?" Leeann asked. "Nobody is helping me, and I want to go to a four-year college."

Sam thought for a moment. "I have a great college for you if you're willing to travel. It's about four hours from here."

"Yeah, if you can help me, because financially, we're not well off."

"I'll do whatever I can," Sam promised.

* * * *

The next morning, Sam was on the phone with Ralph Hill, the athletic director at Davis & Elkins College, in Elkins, West Virginia. It's the school that Sam's former catcher, Crystal "Hoppy" Hopping was already attending, and that Alexis Walker would enroll in following graduation from NCC.

Sam didn't mince words on the phone.

"I have a girl who will turn your softball program around," Sam said. "She's a pitcher. She's big and strong, a leader; somebody who can help you immensely." He explained that Leeann also played basketball, and had great movement and agility for a big girl. "She's also a good student. I think you should take a look at this kid."

"Okay," Hill replied. "Let me see what I can do." He also informed Sam that Lex was going to get a full scholarship for two years to attend the school. Sam was pumped, and he had his fingers crossed.

Not long after, Sam was dining with some fellow Bethlehem Catholic alums at Starter's Pub. It was a regular routine the group enjoyed several times a year. During the evening,

Sam's cell phone went off. He didn't recognize the number, but answered the call.

"Hello."

"Hi coach, this is Leeann." She was crying.

"Hi honey. What's wrong? Do you need me to come over?"

"No coach," Leeann answered. "You just don't understand what you did for me."

Sam was confused. "What are you talking about?"

"Davis and Elkins just called. They're giving me $20,000 to go to school there."

Sam couldn't believe what he was hearing. "You've got to be kidding me."

"No coach, I'm not," Leeann explained. "This is one of the greatest things anyone has ever done for me. They're giving me $20,000 each year to go to school there; to play softball and get an education. I can't thank you enough."

"Honey, graduate from college with a degree and make me proud, and that will be thanks enough."

The medals aside, Sam knew this was *really* what coaching women's softball was all about. He hung up the phone and smiled. It was an awesome feeling.

* * * *

The Spartans' opponent for the PCAA Championship was a familiar one—Community College of Beaver County. This year, however, because of the PCAA's alternating site procedure, the Titans of CCBC would travel eastward to Bethlehem, where the best two-of-three championship series would be played on NCC's home field. The newly constructed dugouts had just been finished, and with a scoreboard and new fencing surrounding the outfield, the field was primed to host a championship series.

Sam knew the Titans and their head coach, Steve Ellington, well. The Spartans had defeated the Titans in 2003 and 2005 for the state title, and the Spartans had been well treated during each trip out to Beaver County—with the exception of the medal ceremony snub the previous year. With the Titans making their first trip to the NCC campus, Sam wanted to offer some hospitality.

Sam called Ellington, and the two coaches exchanged congratulations on winning their respective conferences. Sam ran through the litany of questions—When are you coming out? Where are you staying? Do you need anything from us? Are we going to exchange gifts?

This last question had been a sticking point a year ago, and again, Ellington said his athletic director didn't want to exchange gifts. Nevertheless, the two coaches decided they would make the exchange. For Sam, that meant a visit to the NCC bookstore to pick up a host of NCC mugs, pencils, teddy bears and other assorted trinkets for the Spartans to present to their CCBC counterparts.

The next item on Sam's checklist was food, so he asked his athletic director, Bill Bearse, if NCC should host a dinner during the Titans' visit.

"Did they do a dinner for you last year?" Bearse asked.

Sam shook his head. During their visit in 2003, yes, but not last year. Bearse tossed out another question.

"Well, do you think it's right that we should do one for them?"

"Well, it would be nice if we did," Sam answered. "But I understand that we shouldn't spend the money if it's not the right thing to do."

"It's not about being the right thing to do," said Bearse, ever the diplomat. "I want to do it. But I don't think it's fair for our school to pay if their school didn't. I also don't want them to feel they have to do it the following year."

Sam understood, but he still felt a desire to do something.

"Would you mind if I went out and got food donated, or made some of the food?" Sam asked.

"If you want to do that, that's fine," said Bearse.

So, Sam visited the local eateries and wound up getting enough food donated to host a banquet—hot dogs, Buffalo wings, pizza, Rita's Italian Ice, cake and more. The coach may have wanted to beat the Titans' butts and win another PCAA title, but he didn't want to send them home hungry.

* * * *

Sam had the Spartans well prepared, and well rested, for the PCAA Championship. During the week leading up to the games, Sam had the large television and VCR from the school's fitness center brought into the Spartan Center gymnasium. He ordered in pizza, and showed the girls a tape of the 2005 title games, since most of the Titans' players were back for a second year.

At one point, he took all of the girls aside—except for the three seniors, Nikki, Ness and Lex—for a brief talk.

"You do whatever it takes to win these games," Sam said. "You do whatever it takes to put a gold medal around their necks, because they've earned it. And they'll remain undefeated, and carry it with them for the rest of their lives." Fittingly, when the team had tee-shirts made up, the wording on the back read 'Whatever it Takes.' Pic and Jack, with the girls' support but without Sam's knowledge, added the No. 34 to the sleeve of each shirt in honor of Nicole Sheriff. When the coach saw the number on the sleeve, he broke down.

Sam also let the girls see how the CCBC players acted after NCC had won the championship, and how he and the team were snubbed during the medal and trophy ceremony. That got the girls psyched. If nothing else, Sam certainly knew how to push his team's buttons.

But the day before and morning of the games, the Titans added fuel to the fire.

On Friday afternoon, the day before the championship games were to begin, Sam and Pic were making some final field preparations when the bus carrying the CCBC Titans pulled into the NCC parking lot. One by one, the players and coaches stepped off the bus, gathered as a group, then began walking toward the softball field.

Sam could hear Ellington talking to his players as they approached.

"This is the team that threw stuff on our field last year," Ellington began, referencing the bags of grass and dirt the NCC players deposited at their respective positions. "These are the people who desecrated our field, and now they have a new field. What do you think we should do?"

Sam wasn't surprised by Ellington's tactics. In fact, he expected them.

"I love the guy," Sam said. "He's a good coach and a very moral man. But he feeds off emotion. And his team feeds off that emotion. If that emotion stops, they start fighting among each other and they're finished."

Hearing Ellington's comments, Sam and Pic winked at each other. They knew what they had to do.

The following morning, during batting practice inside the gymnasium, Sam gathered the team for a pre-game talk. He made certain to address the issue of emotion.

"We have to jump on them fast," Sam explained. "If we do, they're going to go right into the toilet. We have to get on them, stay on them, and don't let them get any kind of momentum that could swing things."

The girls were ready. They were on a mission. They didn't need a pep talk to get them pumped. And the Titans own actions would be icing on the cake.

* * * *

It was a beautiful Saturday morning when the Spartans left the gymnasium and hit the softball field. More than 200 people were positioned along the foul lines on folding chairs and blankets, most of them NCC fans anxious to celebrate a second-consecutive state championship.

As the Spartans began to stretch and loosen up, Ness was the first to notice that the field looked different. At each of the infield positions, and at home plate and in the pitcher's circle, the CCBC players had carved their names into the dirt with their cleats. The fiery shortstop and team co-captain was incensed.

"What the hell do they think they're doing?" Ness wondered aloud. "Who the hell do they think they are, doing that to our field? It's our field, and they're putting their names on it. Well, this is not going to happen."

The Titans were taking infield practice, standing at their respective positions. Ness didn't care. One by one, she walked to each infield position and, right in front of the Titan players, scratched out their names with her cleat. When she was done, she looked up at the Titan players, nodded her head, then turned and walked back to the NCC dugout.

"Ness has guts, and she has pride," Sam said. "No one is going to do that on her watch."

The theatrics over, it was time to play ball. Sam had Nikki ready to pitch both games. She was his knockout punch, and he was determined to sweep to the championship; he had no intention of returning on Sunday for a tie-breaker game after splitting the first two on Saturday. He was shooting for all the marbles.

Nikki was on her game, but the Spartans were a bit off. Nikki walked in the first inning and scored on a double by Ness for a 1-0 NCC lead. But over the next several innings, the Spartans wasted several scoring opportunities. Sam noticed.

"We were running the bases terribly," the coach recalled. "Nobody was paying attention to me when they were on base."

In the second inning, the Spartans had two hits and a walk, but failed to score. By the fifth inning, with the Spartans still clinging to a 1-0 lead, Sam began verbally driving the team.

"We're better than this, and I don't want to throw the game away playing like we are," Sam said in the dugout. "You're not playing your game. You're thinking too much, trying to do too much. Work as a team, not nine individuals out there."

Not surprisingly, it was the captains, Nikki and Ness, who again teamed up to drive the NCC train. In the bottom of the fifth, Nikki singled and Ness crushed a two-run homer, putting the Spartans up 3-0.

Meanwhile, Nikki was dominant on the mound. She logged nine strikeouts in the game while allowing only two hits, and shut the door on the Titans as the Spartans prevailed, 3-0, in the first game. Halfway home, and Sam could hear the Titan players beginning to squabble.

The Spartans batted first in the second game, and Nikki picked up right where she left off in the first game. She clubbed a first-inning home run for an early 1-0 lead. But in the bottom of the second, the Titans struck back—physically and verbally.

The Titans' catcher led off. Sam remembered her well from the 2005 PCAA Championships.

"She's a psycho," the coach recalled. "Last year, she was growling behind the plate. And she screams every time she comes up to bat."

The catcher had a lot to scream about following her second-inning at-bat. She got hold of a pitch up in the strike zone and drove it over the left field fence for a game-tying home run. Then, as she began rounding the bases, she started screaming. When she reached second base, she slowed down, stared at Ness, raised her arms in the air, and screamed even louder.

The umpire was waiting for her at home plate.

"You don't do that kind of stuff on this side of Pennsylvania," the umpire admonished. "You don't stop and intimidate a player. If you want, I'll take away the home run and give you a double for intimidation."

She was warned, but the Titans were psyched. Their catcher had given them some momentum. And in the bottom of the fourth inning, the score knotted at 1-1, two singles sandwiched around a walk produced another run for a 2-1 Titan lead.

The Spartans were boiling when they returned to their dugout for the top of the fifth inning.

"There's no way this team is going to beat us," Nikki announced.

"I don't care what we have to do, we're going to win this game," said Ness.

"I'm going to kill them," Gimp added, before Sam intervened to channel the girls' emotions.

"Beat them on the scoreboard and that's the worst way you can beat them," Sam advised. "This is the last opportunity for some of the players on their team, and they'll have to carry it with them that they couldn't beat you in two years. It will hurt them more mentally knowing they had a chance to beat you twice, and couldn't do it. So go for it now. Jump on them, and they'll start bitching like they did in the first game. Then it's done."

Then Sam looked in his players' eyes.

"Now, when you go up to bat, put the swagger back in your walk," he said. "Turn the cockiness control way up. Let it out, emotion-wise, and carry us through the rest of this game."

The Lady Spartans wasted little time heeding their coach's advice, standing against the dugout fence, yelling and encouraging their teammates. It worked. Lisa singled, Nikki walked, and consecutive run-scoring hits by Jenna, Ness and Roxy brought home three runs and put the Spartans back on top 4-2. Then, in the top of the sixth, Lisa sparked another rally with a single and scored on Nikki's triple. A single by Jenna plated Nikki for a 6-2 NCC lead.

Bottom of the seventh. Three outs to go. Nikki struck out the first batter and retired the second on a grounder to Gimp at third. The next batter hit a soft line drive back toward the pitcher's mound. Nikki grabbed it for the final out, shot a quick glance at the Titan dugout, then spun around and tossed her glove into the air. She took about three steps toward shortstop and Ness, who was already sprinting toward the mound, jumped into her arms.

The girls in the dugout joined their teammates in celebration on the field. Sam held the coaches back briefly. The girls had just completed a 38-0 season. It was their moment, he thought, let them enjoy it.

* * * *

In the midst of the championship celebration, the girls told Sam they wanted to give each of Nicole Sheriff's parents, Doug and Linda, a medal. The coach, of course, had no qualms with that arrangement. He called the Sheriffs onto the field as the girls huddled up. Then they displayed two state championship medals. "These are for Nicole," they said, and they put one each around Doug and Linda Sheriff's neck.

Tears flowed freely from Linda Sheriff's eyes, and both parents exchanged warm hugs with the players.

Sam then turned to the CCBC players. "We have a big dinner inside the gymnasium. Come on in."

But the Titans wanted no part of a post-game dinner, and several of them let their feelings be heard.

"What are you, crazy?" several girls said in unison. "Why would we want to eat with you? We're going home." Then they turned and walked toward their bus.

Sam was beside himself. "I did all that work to get the food, to be a nice guy, and you're going to spit in our faces," he said, though the Titan players were out of range.

Gimp took her coach by the arm. "Screw them," she said. "It's more food for us. They're disrespectful. Let them get their asses out of here and we'll eat the food ourselves."

They did, and the taste of victory—and of a second consecutive undefeated season and state championship—never tasted so good.

TWENTY

When the Lady Spartans went undefeated and won a state title in 2005, NCC posted billboards in two locations overlooking Rt. 22 to announce the achievement to the entire Lehigh Valley. The same was done in 2006—a second undefeated season, a second billboard looking down over traffic in the Valley.

But now word was spreading, and the college wasn't alone in its desire to acknowledge the Spartans' achievement.

Sam was sitting at his desk one morning in mid-June when the phone rang. The caller was State Senator Lisa Boscola.

"We'd like to do something to honor the girls," the senator said.

"That's great," Sam said, then asked, "Do you think the Governor might want to do something?"

"Let me find out."

It didn't take long. Boscola called back to say that Governor Ed Rendell wanted to meet with the team in Harrisburg.

"Okay," Sam said, "but it can't just be this team. It has to be the team from 2005 too, because they were 40-0 first. We have to include all of them."

"No problem," Boscola said. "Get as many of them as you can, let me know all the names, and we'll set it up."

Sam began making the arrangements. He contacted all the girls from both teams and most were able to attend. School vans were scheduled for the trip, and all the assistant coaches arranged time off from their regular jobs so they could attend. The plan was to meet the Governor at the capital between noon and 1 p.m. on June 23.

"We were going to be brought down onto the floor of the Senate and honored in front of everyone," Sam recalled. "We were psyched about that."

A phone call from the Governor's office the day before the trip altered plans. The Governor had an emergency luncheon to attend—former Governor Tom Ridge was being honored—so the team would instead be meeting him at the Governor's mansion around 11 a.m. And the Senate was not going to be in session that day, so introductions on the Senate floor were cancelled.

Sam and the team rearranged their schedule and arrived at the Governor's house toward the end of the luncheon. They were taken into the house, through the foyer, and out onto the steps of a patio at the back of the house. A photographer was waiting, and he began positioning everyone on the steps for a photograph with the Governor.

"Leave one open space in the back row," the photographer instructed. "The Governor is going to walk through that back door, take the picture, and then leave."

Sam was disappointed. "I couldn't believe it," Sam recalled. "I had always seen him sitting and talking about the Eagles for an hour after their games. Why couldn't he spend some time with us? But then I thought, shut up, Sam. You're getting to meet the Governor, and he's going to say you did a really great job. But inside I felt, it's not about me, it's about the girls. I really didn't care if he didn't talk to me personally, but I wanted him to talk to the girls."

The photographer had everyone standing in position for several minutes, waiting for the Governor's arrival. Finally, Governor Rendell walked through the doorway and into his reserved spot in the back row. The photographer took several photos, as did some of the girls' parents who had made the trip. Then the Governor raised one arm.

"Okay, that's enough," he instructed. But he didn't leave. He stayed and talked with the girls for about fifteen minutes, about everything from their championship season to his golden retriever's recent hip surgery. The girls presented the Governor with a sleeveless vest, and he told them to stop by the capital because he had some gifts set aside for them.

"Nothing major," the Governor said. "Just something from me to you guys."

Then, as the team was leaving, he stood and shook each player's hand, thanked them and offered his congratulations.

As they walked back through the Governor's house and out the front door, Nikki Jenson's mother turned to Sam. "Don't you think that was nice that he stayed and talked to the girls?"

Sam agreed. "Yeah, it was neat."

Mrs. Jenson added, "Don't you think it's funny that it's an election year?"

Sam could not contain his laughter.

* * * *

The drive back to Bethlehem wouldn't be complete—wouldn't be typical of the NCC women's softball team—if it were incident-free. The three vans—driven by Pic, Robbie and Sam, respectively—pulled into a Red Robin Restaurant for a late lunch before the drive home.

"Well, it's good that we had the vans for the trip," Sam said as everyone was being seated.

"Yeah, but on my van, the window is broken and it's shut with masking tape," Pic complained.

"That's nothing," Robbie added. "My van's gas gauge is broken, and it's on E all the time."

"Are you sure it's not empty?" Sam asked.

"I'm sure," Robbie responded. "The gas gauge is just broken. Besides, they wouldn't send us out with an empty tank of gas."

The vans weren't back on the road thirty minutes before Sam received a call from Robbie on his cell phone.

"I ran out of gas," Robbie announced.

"Is there some place nearby where you can get gas?" Sam asked.

"No. You're going to have to get me a can of gas."

Sam called Pic on his cell phone. Both he and Pic were ahead of Robbie, so they would have to turn around and drive back to where Robbie's van had run out of gas. Sam told Pic to buy a can and fill it with gas, and meet him back at Robbie's van.

"And get a receipt so I can be reimbursed," Sam instructed.

An overpass crossed the highway just before the exit where Robbie's van had stalled. As Sam approached, he looked up to see the girls from Robbie's van standing on the overpass and waving to passing tractor trailers; pumping their arms and yelling, "Honk, honk, honk."

"What a great view," Sam recalled, shaking his head. "My girls, standing on top of an overhang, screaming at truck drivers."

Finally, Sam and Pic reach Robbie's van, sitting on the side of the road at the bottom of a hill. At the top of the hill, obscured from view when standing at the bottom on the hill, was a gas station. Sam shook his head as he recalled the scene.

"He didn't even walk up to the top of the hill to see if there was a gas station," Sam said. "And of course, Pic forgot to get a receipt for the can and the gas, so I had to pay for that out of my pocket."

Robbie emptied the gas from the can into the van. Sam gave him $50 and told him to fill up at the station at the top of the hill, and to get a receipt.

Back at NCC, Sam asked Robbie for the receipt for the gas.

"Oh, I forgot to get one," Robbie said.

Meeting the Governor had turned into an expensive proposition.

* * * *

Immediately after the 2006 season, Sam began actively recruiting for the following year. He had already been scouting girls for some time, but the summer months were when the recruiting process was thrown into high gear. Six girls from the 2006 team would not be returning—Nikki Jenson, Janess Lyle, Alexis Walker, Lana Good, Jennifer Kiefer and Tabitha Niceforo. In Nikki, Janess and Alexis, Sam knew he had some big shoes to fill.

Three years earlier, Sam had tried recruiting a shortstop named Kelsey Bee from Warren Hills High School in New Jersey. She didn't come to NCC, but in the process Sam learned that she had a younger sister, Katie, who was also a good player. So, when the Warren Hills coach called to say that Katie, a third baseman, was interested in coming to NCC, Sam went to watch her play.

"First of all, she's drop-dead gorgeous," Sam said of Katie Bee. "She's a big, strong, muscular girl. And when you look at her, she has a fire and intensity in her eyes. She can go from that strikingly beautiful face to one that says 'You're in my way and I don't care what I have to do to get passed you, I'm coming through.'"

Sam had phoned to tell Katie he would be coming to one of her games, but didn't tell her which one for fear of making her nervous. That strategy went by the boards when Katie came to bat in the first inning and her family shouted out, "Sam's here." Unfazed, Katie crushed a home run to right centerfield.

Sam put a check mark next to Katie's name. "Yes, that's who I want." The feeling was mutual.

"My mom encouraged me to go to a community college for my first two years, but I really didn't want to go to Warren County Community College because I didn't want to give up playing softball," Katie recalled. "I was wondering what other community colleges were in the area, and then I remembered seeing the billboard on Rt. 22 and thought, that's a good stepping stone. Not just a community college team that nobody has heard about. I thought it would be a good opportunity to make a name for myself."

One down, five to go.

* * * *

At least once a year, a terrific player just falls into Sam's lap. While recruiting the 2007 team, it happened twice.

Tami Kilousky wasn't your typical college freshman. She was twenty-one-years old, a former pitcher, and she hadn't thrown a softball in almost three years. But it wasn't because she didn't want to.

As a junior at Kutztown Area High School in 2002, Tami pitched the girls' varsity softball team to a state championship. She was poised for a super senior season. Then, just before the season started, Tami was in a car accident and broke her collarbone above her pitching arm. But even after the injury healed, she wasn't the same pitcher.

"My movement was the same, but I wasn't as fast," Tami recalled. "I couldn't keep us in games. It was depressing, because I was going to go to DeSales University, but I switched because I knew I wasn't going to play softball."

Her parents lived in Florida, so Tami enrolled in the University of South Florida.

"It was completely to please them," she explained, and she hated it there. She moved back to Pennsylvania and enrolled at Temple University. She thought about playing softball, but now she was on her own, financially. Between work and school, she just didn't have the time. Eventually, she left Temple for financial reasons, and spent some time at two different community colleges before winding up in the nursing program at NCC.

Tall and slender and an avid fitness enthusiast, Tami was in the NCC Fitness Center regularly at 6 a.m. before class. She would often talk with Gene Smith, the facility assistant who opened the Fitness Center each morning, and when he noticed her Kutztown softball t-shirt, the conversation turned to pitching. He suggested she fill out a Candidate's Interest Form and consider playing for the Spartans. She did, and the next day she met with Sam.

"The way he made everything sound, I said 'Okay, I can do this,'" Tami recalled. "And it got me all excited and made me remember that being on the mound and being in control was the greatest feeling. Because there were points in my life where I didn't think I had control of anything except when I was on the mound."

Sam was excited, too. He called Tami's high school softball coach.

"She single-handedly took us to the state championship in Class AA when she played," the coach said of Tami. "She's coachable, and she'll lead. She'll do whatever it takes. That's a great pick-up."

It was music to Sam's ears.

* * * *

The state of Florida dropped another player in Sam's lap.

Sam was sitting in his office one morning when he received a phone call from Katie Pence. Katie had been a three-sport athlete at Belvidere High School in New Jersey, and was an exceptional student who wanted to major in hospitality management. That academic focus, combined with her familiarity with the Orlando area from many vacation trips her family had taken, had prompted her to enroll in the University of Central Florida.

"I thought it would be a good fit," Katie explained. "And I took into account that my family wasn't going to be there, but I didn't realize how hard it would be without them."

It was also hard moving back home after one semester at Central Florida.

"It was painful for me, and really difficult," Katie said. "In my mind, I felt like I had failed. But it's something I'm dealing with. I wouldn't want to go through the experience again, but having done it, it's made me stronger."

Just as with Katie Bee, Katie Pence had seen the billboards for NCC's championship softball teams. She told Sam she was moving back home. She wanted to know if there were still openings, and if so, could she come try out for the team?

Sam said, "Yes," although he hadn't seen her play. So he called her high school softball coach, and heard what he wanted to hear.

"She played shortstop for us, but she can pretty much play anywhere except catcher and pitcher," the coach explained. "She's the best player I've ever had. She can play the outfield, and she'll run down any ball hit to her. And she almost killed three people last year with her hitting. She hit a pitcher on the leg with a line drive, knocked her out for two weeks."

Of course, not too many coaches will say bad things about a former player. But Sam knew he had the real deal when he attended a tournament about a week later at the HealthQuest Dome in Flemington, New Jersey. Another coach strolled up to Sam and began to chat.

"I hear there's a girl from Jersey coming back to the area," the coach began. "She's a good ball player, probably the best I've ever seen play the game, and I've been around a long time.

But, you're never going to get her because she's too smart. That's nothing against your school, but she can definitely play Division I."

Sam nodded. "That's cool. What's her name?"

"Katie Pence."

Sam smiled. "She's already signed to play for us."

The coach nodded. "That's an unbelievable pickup you just got."

The icing on the cake came several weeks later, after Katie had thoroughly impressed Sam during a tryout. Sitting in his office at lunchtime, she opened her lunch bag and pulled out a roast beef sandwich with lettuce on wheat toast. When she bit into the sandwich, it made a loud crunch.

"What's that sound?" Sam asked.

"Stackers, coach, they're the greatest," Katie said, referring to the pickle slices on her sandwich.

Sam loved Stackers. "Right there, we melded," the coach recalled. "We were one."

* * * *

Yet another surprise recruit was Saucon Valley High School's Anna Stem.

Sam attended a softball game between Saucon Valley and Catasauqua with the intent of scouting Maxine "Max" Szulborski, a junior who played first base for Saucon. He knew there was a good chance she would one day come to NCC, and eventually she did. But the pleasant surprise of the day was watching this feisty little junior catcher crack a double and a game-winning single for Saucon Valley. It was Anna Stem.

"She had a cannon for an arm, and was poised behind the plate," Sam recalled. "But I knew there was no way I was going to get her because she had a 4.3 GPA. I said hello to her anyway."

It turned out that Anna was best friends with Robyn "Dirty" Carey, who played on NCC's 2005 championship team. And Dirty had the skinny on Anna.

"Coach, you might have a shot at Anna," Dirty told Sam. "Her father passed away, and her mother is now divorcing her step-father. They don't have money for her to go to college, so you may have a chance at her."

Shortly thereafter, Sam was watching an all-star softball game among nine- and ten-year-olds in which the niece of one of his assistant coaches was playing. He noticed the umpire at second base looked familiar. It was Anna Stem. And again, Sam stopped to say hello.

Later, he would get a phone call from Anna.

"Coach, do you think it would be possible for me to come and play for you?" Anna asked.

"Heck yeah," Sam answered. "But we have a long time to go before registration for next fall after you graduate."

"No, I mean come play for you now."

"What are you talking about?" Sam asked. "You're only in your first semester as a senior."

"I'm done with all my courses and graduating early. I can come to you in January but there will be a one-week overlap between when I finish high school and the start of the spring semester at NCC. Can I do that?"

Sam said she could, but he doubted he could arrange for financial aid since, technically, she wouldn't receive her diploma until June 2007. "If I can't get you financial aid, will you be okay?"

"I don't know coach," Anna answered, her voice dejected. "I may not be able to go to college then."

"Oh no, not with your brains and talent."

Sam talked to athletic director Bill Bearse. "Bill, we have to help this kid. I want her to play, because she's outstanding. But even if she doesn't, just keeping her in school is important."

"Go up and talk to Sue Kubik and see if there's Foundation money, because she qualifies academically for that," said Bearse.

The funds were available, and Sam was able to phone Anna with the good news.

"Whether you play softball or not, that's up to you," Sam explained. "But school is taken care of. And once you're here, we'll work to get you a scholarship to go on to a four-year college."

On the other end of the line, Anna and her mother were crying tears of joy.

* * * *

Lauren Oswald was a catcher at Northampton Area High School, Jamie Rider was a pitcher at Nazareth Area High School. Both were playing out of position, and playing sporadically, at their respective schools. Part of the reason was that there were already good players entrenched in the positions they played.

But Sam got a good recommendation on Lauren from her coach and from Jenna Turner, who had played with Lauren at Northampton. She was a good athlete who had played basketball during her first two years in high school before focusing solely in softball. He watched her get several hits during a summer league game, and knew she was coming to NCC regardless of whether she played softball or not, so he invited her to try out for the team.

Jamie's problem was her inability to consistently control her emotions. She wasn't pitching at Nazareth, because first Nikki Jenson and then Brooke Hull were ahead of her, and more recently she wasn't playing much second base, either. But she was a good player, as Sam recalled from watching her in summer league games with the Allentown Patriettes.

"Jamie is an emotional girl, she won't hold anything back," Sam explained. "She'll get pissed on the mound, and she'll yell, and I knew that wasn't going to work. But she was a good pitcher."

Sam watched Jamie pitch during a few summer league games and, seeing her get angry on the mound, would yell out, "No emotion, Rider. No emotion." Jamie would look up, see Sam, and laugh.

"Jamie is the kind of girl that if she hates you, she won't even look at you," Sam said. "If you likes you, she'll do anything you ask. She will literally run through a wall for you because she doesn't want to disappoint you."

Sam and Jamie developed a relationship. She looked forward to seeing him at her games, and she would hug him when the games were over.

Emotionally, he knew she could be all over the map. But she was a good kid, and a good pitcher. He took a chance.

* * * *

Recruiting—the active, aggressive and diligent way in which Sam went about recruiting—had its price. More often than not, that price was time spent away from his family, in particular, his twins Nicholas and Devan.

One afternoon, Sam was watching a softball game, scouting two seniors two played for Dieruff High School. As was the custom, Sam had his cell phone turned off during the game.

After the game, Sam spent a few minutes talking with the girls and their parents, then got in his car and turned his cell phone on. There was a voice message from Devan.

"Dad, I don't know how to tell you this, but Nicholas is at the dentist," the message stated. "He got hurt."

Sam quickly called the dentist—a friend of the family Sam had known for a long time. He found out that Nicholas had been riding his scooter down a large hill, going fast, when he hit a bump, flipped over the handle bars and landed face first on the cement. The majority of his two front teeth were snapped off. All that remained were two thin slivers of each tooth.

Sam hit the gas and raced over to the dentist's office. When he got there, Nicholas was sitting in the dentist's chair, smiling, no Novocain, having his front teeth bonded. His chin was scraped, as were the palms of his hands. Otherwise, he was fine.

"There was a huge bump," Nicholas told his father. "I thought I could make it. I yelled, and I guess I opened my mouth too long and got my teeth bashed out."

Sam was relieved, but still troubled. It was yet another time when he was busy doing things for the softball team when his family needed him.

* * * *

Sam's office at NCC was always a welcome place for the young women on the softball team. They could catch up on their homework, eat lunch or just hang out. It wasn't surprising to see several players camped out in the office at various times on any given day.

That was the scene one mid-September afternoon as Sam sat at his desk completing administrative paperwork. He heard a buzz coming from the girls in the room.

"Is that her? Is that her?" they were whispering to each other.

Sam looked up to see Kristy Kroll standing in the doorway to the office. His eyes opened wide, and he jumped up from his desk and moved to the doorway where he embraced Kristy in a hug.

"I just lost it," Sam recalled, his eyes welling up with tears as he remembered the scene. "I went over and hugged her and I didn't want to let go."

Kristy, too, was touched, and was moved to tears as she spoke softly to Sam.

"I'm home. I'm safe. You can stop worrying."

Finally, Sam let go. But it would be a long time, if ever, before Kristy forgot that hug.

"There was something about that hug," Kristy said. "He was like a father to me in so many ways."

And now the man whom former player Jenn Davis had nicknamed The Godfather had his softball family together again.

TWENTY-ONE

When Sam wasn't recruiting, he spent the bulk of the summer and fall putting together the team's schedule of games for the upcoming season, holding clinics for young, aspiring female softball players, and organizing fundraisers. The former—scheduling games—was a more daunting task than one might imagine.

That's because word was spreading about the NCC Spartans. Two consecutive undefeated, state-title seasons will do that. But the Spartans weren't just good, they were very good, and some teams were tired of getting their brains beat in.

"Nobody wants to play us," Sam often lamented. And he had heard every reason/excuse imaginable.

"Sorry, you're too small a school for us to play."

"We know your record, and we don't want to play you."

"The NCAA prohibits us from playing you."

"Our schedule is already full."

Sam had heard it all, and it was frustrating.

"I want legitimacy on this schedule," Sam said prior to the start of the 2007 season, "because the girls coming through now and for the next two and three years are going to be tough to beat. The girls coming in now have been there; they're used to a certain level of play."

On that count, Sam was right. The girls Sam was recruiting were used to playing softball almost year-round. In the spring they played on their high school team. In the summer they played for high-level travel teams, and many played fall softball as well. In the winter, they worked out indoors in batting cages to hone their skills. And in many cases, either because they were coming from the same high school or same summer travel team, they were already used to playing together.

"I'm talking about shortstops and second basemen who know each other's moves," Sam explained. "Pitchers and catchers who are already comfortable with each other. We're way ahead of the game."

That kept Sam scrambling to line up solid competition to keep the girls challenged.

* * * *

January 2007 brought with it a visit to the children's cancer unit at Lehigh Valley Hospital. Sam and several of the Lady Spartans accompanied Doug Sheriff and members of the Angel 34 Foundation board of directors. Donning Santa Claus caps, the players went from room to room handing out NCC t-shirts and spending time talking with the children and their parents. Some girls gave their Santa hats to the children.

"We went into a room where there was this twelve-year-old girl whom had just received a wig from Doug Sheriff and his wife," Sam recalled. "She was trying it on, and was in a very happy mood. We asked if we could take a picture with her, and she said yes. But first she laughed and said she had to take her hair off and comb it so she would look good for the picture."

It was a happy moment in a somber visit.

"I wanted the girls to see that no matter how hard they thought life was, it's nothing compared to what these children and their parents are going through," said Sam. "And it made me realize that I'm damned lucky to have healthy children."

* * * *

One element to the 2007 schedule that Sam grappled with was the question of which spring tournament the team should register for. The past three years, the Spartans had spent spring break in Myrtle Beach competing in the Snowbird Softball Tournament. But there were different issues to wrestle with as the 2007 schedule was being assembled. The biggest issue was that of the team's current winning streak.

With back-to-back undefeated seasons behind them, the Lady Spartans had fashioned a seventy-eight-game unbeaten streak. In the early 1990s, the University of North Carolina women's soccer team, led by the legendary Mia Hamm, set a national collegiate record by winning ninety-three consecutive soccer matches—eclipsing the former record of eighty-eight consecutive wins set by the UCLA men's basketball teams of the early 1970s.

Sam knew that in some people's minds, NCC was just a small community college competing against other small-time schools. But the consecutive win mark was a big-time record, and if the Spartans were setting their sights on toppling North Carolina's 92-win mark, Sam wanted to eliminate any questions. He wanted to make sure the Spartans took on the best competition they could, and erase any doubts about the legitimacy of the record.

An invitation to play in the Walt Disney World Spring Training Tournament in Orlando, Florida, helped clinch the decision.

"It's a more rounded tournament," Sam explained. "It draws teams from a wider area around the country, and I wanted us to face the best."

The decision-making part was easy; funding the trip was another story. Sam took out his calculator—a huge tablet the size of a bathroom scale, it did wonders for those who were farsighted. The four nights and five days in Disney, which included the cost of the hotel room, a three-day hopper pass to the Disney parks, and entry into the tournament came to $468 per person—or nearly double the cost of the Myrtle Beach Tournament.

Then there was the cost of feeding a hungry softball team, which was not a small-ticket item either.

"You're talking $9 just for a hamburger and $4 for fries," Sam said, recalling the prices for food items in and around the Disney All-Star Sports Complex. "That's just for one hamburger. And it's not a Whopper. And when you bite into it, you can almost hear Australian music and kangaroos as the burger bounces along on the table."

Compared to $12.95 for all you could eat at the Great American Steak and Seafood Buffet in Myrtle Beach, it made buffets seem all the more appealing. Even Nikki would have had to agree.

Getting to the tournament was the big challenge. The team could drive in three NCC vans, a trip that would take approximately twenty hours, or they could fly. Sam reserved three vans for the week of the tournament, just in case, but he began impressing on the players and the coaches that they would more than likely be traveling by plane.

Then Sam went online and began researching airfares from Philadelphia to Orlando.

"I kept hearing all the offers of $79 one way, but in actuality, there are only two seats on the plane selling for $79," Sam said. Of course, those two seats were already sold. The first four available seats sold for $226 round trip; after that, the rate went up to $303 round trip. That brought the cost of the trip for fourteen players and six coaches to just over $20,000—$9,500 for the room and tournament, $6,200 for the flight, and $4,500 for food.

"Plus, I had to get the kids shoes and other supplies, so we had to raise around $23,000," Sam said. "And I didn't know if we could do it."

In addition, the airline tickets needed to be paid for when purchased, and Disney wanted the money well in advance of when the tournament started. That was impossible, because the fundraising efforts were still underway. Fortunately, Sam was able to borrow the money from the college and repay it once all fundraising activities were completed. Now he just had to make sure he raised the necessary funds.

Sam scheduled two comedy nights, two Evenings at the Races and a phone-a-thon. But despite the valiant efforts, when the dust settled, the team had raised approximately $15,200—well below what was needed to make the trip by plane. Sam told the team, "We're going to have to drive." He figured they could drive to some place in Georgia, stay the night, and finish the trip the next day rather than drive 20 hours straight. It was still a daunting task, and the girls would be tired before they even started playing. But the fundraising had come up short; there's wasn't much choice.

One afternoon Sam was in his office being interviewed by Katie McDonald, a fellow graduate of Bethlehem Catholic High School and a sportswriter for *The Bethlehem Press*, a local weekly newspaper. Sam talked about the upcoming tournament in Orlando, and said he was looking for sponsors to help fund the trip.

"If you hear anything, let me know," Sam told Katie.

Katie called back a few days later. The newspaper wanted to sponsor the team's trip to the tune of $5,000. What could Sam do in return?

"I can have t-shirts made up with your logo on the back," Sam explained. "We wear the shirts while warming up before every game. And we can put a banner with the newspaper's name on it along the outfield fence."

That sealed the deal. The $5,000 was a big boost in funding the trip, but the team was still about $1,700 short. Then Doug Sheriff called.

"We're going to give you $1,000 of our money for the trip," Sheriff told Sam.

"I don't want it," Sam said. "If we weren't able to raise enough money, then we'll just have to pay for our own food."

"No, I won't hear of it," Sheriff insisted. "Besides, Nicole would want you to have this money."

Sam didn't know what to say. How could he accept money from the Sheriffs? Was eating at Disney World more of a priority than finding a cure for cancer? But Sam also knew he couldn't say no. So he simply said, "Thank you," and took the money.

But the ties to Nicole Sheriff and the Angel 34 Foundation didn't end there.

* * * *

One of the Spartans' fundraising efforts for the Orlando trip came courtesy of Starters Pub in Bethlehem. Sam had 1,200 fundraising tickets made up, gave thirty or so to each girl on the team, and had them pass the tickets around to people they knew. Sam even left a stack of tickets in the college bookstore for students to take. If the ticket was presented to a waiter at Starters after dining, ten percent of the bill—alcohol excluded—would be donated to the team.

The first night Sam received the tickets he told the girls they were going to Starters to eat dinner, and to use the tickets. But there was a caveat. Each girl paid for her own dinner, but there could be only one bill for the entire table. In other words, only one ticket could be used. When the bill arrived, Sam could not believe his eyes. The bill came to $343.41—10 percent of which was $34.34. He was speechless.

Dave Rank, the owner of Starters, also could not believe it. He immediately got on the phone to Doug Sheriff to inform him of the event. Then he went back to Sam.

"That's a one following the four in the total bill, so I'm giving you $1,000 just for that," Dave said. "This shouldn't be happening. This is crazy."

Sam knew it was crazy, and he wanted the occasion preserved. The next day he took the original bill back to the college, told the story to Sue in Central Duplicating, and gave her the bill to be laminated. But when Sue brought the laminated bill back to Sam's office, she was crying.

"I'm so sorry," she said in between sobs.

"What are you talking about?" Sam asked.

"This has never happened before, Sam. Never, and I've done laminations for many years. But, everything disappeared off the receipt. That can't be a magic trick."

Sue thought she had ruined the receipt, but Dave at Starters had given Sam several photocopies, so although the original was blank, the copies were still intact.

And the legend of Nicole Sheriff and the number 34 continued to grow.

* * * *

Practice for the 2007 season began as it always did, on the first day of classes for the spring semester—January 16. It was also when Sam's neatly crafted ball of yarn began to unravel.

After considerable thought, conferring with his assistant coaches and—for the first time—allowing a silent vote among the girls on the team, Sam announced that Roxy and Jenna would be co-captains for the 2007 season. The problem was that there were two other girls, both second-year players, who thought they deserved to be captains: Lisa and Gimp. Both told Sam how they felt.

"I kind of felt like coach Sam made me believe I was going to earn the spot, in the sense of how much leadership I showed in 2006 and in the beginning of 2007," Lisa explained. "But when it came down to picking captains it was like high school all over again. It was about who could make the team laugh rather than who might make the team laugh but still love and think about the game."

Gimp echoed those feelings.

"We voted right in the beginning of the year when the new girls didn't know us six who were returning," she explained. "They just voted based on who they had talked to. I was disappointed, because I've always looked at myself as kind of a leader. Coach had told me that I was going to be a captain, but that never happened, so it was disappointing."

In the team's silent vote, there were two votes for Kristy and one for Lisa—all the others were for Roxy and Jenna. In addition, Sam had his reasons for the choices he made.

"I told Gimp on several occasions that she's a great player and could be a good leader, but that she had to stop saying things without thinking," Sam explained. "I told her that she had to control her temper and change her attitude when she spoke to people; that she ought to put a seven-second delay on her mouth because what she said was hurting people's feelings. The players wouldn't follow her or respect her."

Lisa was a different story. Sam knew that she was an intense and dedicated player who led by example. But he felt that, at the time, she had too much to contend with away from the softball field.

"She was going to school full time and had a job that occupied a lot of her time," Sam said. "Her home life was not good, to the point where she was mentally and physically traumatized. Her parents had split and were living apart for a while, and the financial situation was terrible. I just thought she had way too much on her plate to take on the added responsibility of being captain."

It was the beginning of the friction and the formation of cliques that would eventually pull the team apart. Sam felt that even though some of the second-year players weren't captains in name, they could still act like leaders without the title. That didn't happen. And the first-year players who possessed solid leadership skills remained silent, deferring—as one might expect—to the girls in their second year on the team.

"Gimp was mad because she wasn't chosen as captain, so she would undermine Roxy," Sam recalled. "Roxy would say something, Gimp would say something else, and many of the girls would listen to Gimp, which wasn't right. I don't know if it was a rebel thing or just to get back at Roxy, but they wouldn't listen to her. And that would frustrate Roxy."

The tension was magnified when Sam told Gimp he would be moving her from third base to second base—with good reason. Gimp had injured her right shoulder the previous summer but felt it would come around on its own. It didn't, and in the spring she learned she had a torn labrum in her shoulder. She did therapy to make the muscles in the shoulder stronger, but she still had trouble making the throw from third to first base. When Sam moved her to second base, she wasn't happy.

"Any decision I make affects everyone on the team," Sam said. "Every decision is going to piss somebody off. And being the way I am, trying to please everybody all the time, I don't please myself. I can't make everybody happy, but I don't like to disappoint people, either."

The seventy-eight-game winning streak hanging overhead didn't help. The players sensed that Sam was preoccupied with the streak, and obsessed with raising enough money to make the trip to Orlando. It came to a head during a snowstorm in mid-February. The school closed at 3 p.m. and all evening classes were cancelled. But the softball team had a phone-a-thon scheduled for that evening, and Sam called the girls—even the four who commuted every day from New Jersey—to make sure they were still coming in, despite the weather.

The next day, Roxy cornered Sam following practice.

"You would never put anything above us, and now you're thinking about money first, and the streak," Roxy said. "You made us come in when the school shut down because of the snow. You're way too serious, and you're making everying about the streak. You're losing touch coach, this isn't you."

Sam recalled the incident well. "It was like getting hit in the stomach with a baseball bat." He changed his focus and lightened up. He went back to trying to make practices fun, even if outside pressures were consuming him inside. "You have to have the tears of a clown. You have to put on a happy face and act like nothing is wrong."

But that didn't ease the dissention on the team. For Sam, it felt like it was the 2004 season all over again. He thought about cutting some players. Sam, Robbie and Jack even went to the point of putting together some hypothetical lineups if they decided to cut certain players. In the end, however, Sam's emotions got in the way and he worried that it might hurt some of the girls down the road.

"If I have to tell a recruiter the girl was cut because of her attitude, they won't want her," Sam explained. "If I lie and say she was cut because of an injury, they still won't want her. Or If I say she was cut because she wasn't a good student, they won't take her. So, what the hell do you do? You live with it, because you don't want to hurt the girl's future."

Just before the trip to Orlando, the girls held a party. Everyone got together at the home of one of the players. Afterward, they said it was the greatest thing in the world.

"We all felt like a team," Kristy said. "It felt really cool."

"Everyone let go of everything, and we really bonded well," Katie Bee explained. "That was important before going down to Florida."

But would it last?

* * * *

The worst feeling for a coach is to have girls who you've recruited fail to make the team, especially when the reasons are academic-related rather than due to a lack of skill or ability.

Two girls that fell into that category came to NCC from Dieruff High School. Sam was high on both girls, especially one named Rhonda.

"She could fly," Sam said, recalling her speed in the outfield. "With her initial step she was like lightning to the ball. But I was told she had an attitude—a tough attitude, a street attitude. It was hard to get through to her."

Sam would ask the two girls repeatedly, as he would with all the girls, how school was going? They'd say, "Everything's fine. Don't worry about it coach. Everything's great." And because of privacy rules, there was nothing else Sam could do. But several years earlier, he had tried.

He drafted a letter, a "plain, vanilla letter," as Sam called it, to the girls' teachers. He introduced himself, and wrote that he knew that one of his players was in the teacher's class. He kept it real basic so that he could give the letter to the girls and they could present it to their teachers.

"I wrote that I was aware of the privacy law, and that I didn't want to know the girls' grades," Sam explained. "I asked if the teacher could just inform me if the girls were participating in class, if they were even showing up for class, or if they were failing or had poor grades, so that I could stay on top of them and get them as much help as possible."

Sam took the letter to his athletic director, Bill Bearse, seeking approval. He didn't get it.

"Sam, you can't give this out to the teachers," Bearse said. "It's not a good idea because of the privacy laws. I wouldn't want the teachers to feel they have to overstep their bounds."

The letter never went out, and Sam was left with getting his information from the girls and relying on the trust factor.

"But if they don't trust me enough to tell me what's going on, there's nothing I can do," Sam explained. "If they trust me enough to talk to me, I'll do whatever I can to help them."

For these two girls, however, that trust just wasn't there.

TWENTY-TWO

Sam had reserved the vans, he was sure of it. He knew he'd need them to get the team and all of the equipment down to Philadelphia International Airport for the flight to Orlando. He'd sent an email requesting that the school vans be available.

But the email was never received. So on Saturday afternoon March 10, there were no vans . . . but athletic director Bill Bearse said he would make sure the team got to the airport in good shape. With the help of a friend of Anna Stem's mother who rented a U-Haul trailer for all the equipment, and two assistants from fitness center who drove the team down in vans, they made it in time for their 5:25 p.m. flight on Southwest Air.

The scene at the airport was a mad house. Checking all the luggage and getting through security were major hassles. Sam had his wife, Chris, and children, Nicholas and Devan, with him.

"We almost had to strip down to our underwear to get through security," Sam recalled. And while Chris had to re-dress the kids, Sam was running between the security checkpoints to make sure the girls had gotten through okay.

Ness, who was working as an assistant coach while she completed her studies that semester, was stopped and told she would not be allowed through wearing her hooded sweatshirt; she had to take it off. Fortunately, she was wearing a t-shirt underneath, something she seldom did, or she would have had to walk through security without a shirt.

Making matters worse, several of the girls on the team had never been on a plane, so they were nervous wrecks.

Sam found the best solution to the madness.

"I had three beers in me before I got on the plane, so I was playing handball with God," the coach recalled. "I had no idea what was happening."

* * * *

Stepping off the plane in Orlando, Sam thought the chaos was finally over. The tournament coordinators arranged to have everyone's luggage picked up at the airport and delivered to the hotel. Sam thought that was great. He would soon realize otherwise.

The NCC entourage arrived at the All Star Sports Resort at 9:15 that night, and the girls wanted to walk around the complex. All Star Sports is a sports-themed resort comprised of ten buildings themed around various sports. Athletic icons such as football helmets and basketball hoops decorate the courtyards and public areas. The complex is so large that motorcoach service is available for easy access to all parts of the resort.

Sam wanted the girls in bed early. The team's first game was at 8 a.m. the following morning, and Sam wanted them on the bus by 6:15 a.m.

"You're allowed batting cage time at 7 a.m., and field time at 7:30 a.m., so I wanted to make sure we got there early," Sam recalled.

One problem: the luggage had yet to arrive—and it wouldn't arrive until between midnight and 3 a.m. Everything—from the girls' uniforms to the bats, gloves and cleats—was still in transit to the hotel. Sam, and many of the girls, waited up until 3 a.m. to make sure that everyone's luggage had arrived.

Then, with about three hours of sleep under their belts, the team boarded the bus for the Wide World of Sports All-Star Complex.

* * * *

Finally, something went smooth.

The Spartans' equipment was loaded onto the bus at the resort, then taken off the bus at the sports complex and placed on a cart where it was delivered to the field on which the team would be playing. Each player and coach received a Wide World of Sports identification badge for access to the complex. Sam kept all the badges together, then handed them out as each girl walked through the turnstile. Once inside the complex, Sam collected the badges to make sure nothing got lost.

A long, winding path took the team past several lacrosse fields and tennis courts before arriving at the softball fields. The morning sun was just peaking over the horizon, but it was easy to see that each of the complex's four softball fields was incredibly well maintained. The outfield grass was cut so low and tight to the ground it looked like a golf course putting green. The eight-foot pitching circles had Mickey Mouse ears outlined in lime.

Some of the pitching circles also had a bow outlined at the base of the circle, signifying Minnie Mouse.

The Softball Quadraplex at Disney's Wide World of Sports Complex features four softball diamonds in a giant circular pattern. Outfield fences measure 305 feet in a perfectly symmetrical configuration. Each field accommodates both fast-pitch and slow-pitch softball teams, and features bullpens, spacious dugouts, and helmet and equipment shelves. A large tower stands in the center of the complex, with four windows—one facing out to each of the four softball fields—at the top from where each of the games is announced. Sam rode an elevator to the second floor of the tower where he handed in his lineup card and was given two new game balls.

"It's really neat, and very professionally run," Sam said. "But you only get two balls for each game. So if they're hit out of bounds, you have to chase after them and bring them back."

Sam had requested that the Spartans play their games early in the morning so that the girls would be able to make use of the theme park passes in the afternoons. He also didn't want them to play their games under the heat of a blazing afternoon sun. Other than one game that was scheduled for noon, his request was accommodated. All of the Spartans' games started at 8 and 10 a.m. each morning.

"And the tournament organizers ask you who you want to play," Sam explained. "I really didn't care who we played, I just wanted to play against good competition."

Sam got his wish.

* * * *

The Spartans had a doubleheader scheduled against New York University on the first day of the tournament. NYU is a large, four-year college attended by nearly 40,000 students. The college did not have a varsity level softball team, just a club team. But that meant the girls on the club team were the best the school had to offer.

If that wasn't cause for concern, Sam could not believe what he was watching as the Lady Spartans warmed up.

"Each of them looked like they had an anchor attached to their ass," Sam said. "They were dragging. They were up late, had jet lag from the trip, and lost an extra hour of sleep because of the change to Daylight Saving Time."

Sam also had a decision to make. A transfer student from Cabrini College, named Alice Polson, had come out for the team in preseason and performed well. Sam heard good things about Alice from the Cabrini coach, who said she was capable of playing both third base and second base. She also hit the ball well in practice, so he had to decide between Alice or Katie Bee at third base in the first game.

Ness went to Sam with a recommendation.

"I think you ought to start Alice at third base, coach," Ness said. "She's consistent. Bee is dropping the ball all the time, not getting off good throws, and doesn't seem to be working hard enough."

Sam disagreed. "Bee can play the game. Alice will play, but Bee is the No. 1 right now. Trust me, okay?"

"Okay coach, but I don't know."

It was a decision that set in motion a series of nasty events.

Jamie was on the mound for the first game as the Spartans, the home team by virtue of a coin flip, took the field, and she was in trouble immediately. The first two NYU hitters singled, and Jamie walked the third batter. Bases loaded, no out.

On the first pitch to the next batter, catcher Anna Stem tried to pick off the runner at first base but neglected to signal Roxy, who was playing first, that she would be throwing down. The throw sailed past first and rolled all the way down the right field line as all three runners scored. NYU 3, Spartans 0 in the first inning.

Back in the dugout, Anna began crying hysterically over her throwing error. Sam walked over and sat next to her.

"Anna, you can't sit here and cry," Sam said. "Things happen. We'll get it back. You just need to relax."

But the Spartans weren't hitting. And when Sam looked in their eyes he saw a tired, listless team that was not functioning on all cylinders.

Then, in the top of the third inning, a single, a sacrifice and two passed balls allowed another unearned run to score, giving NYU a 4-0 lead. Sam pulled Anna from the game and put Lauren Oswald behind the plate

In the fifth inning he switched pitchers, bringing in Tami, who held NYU in check. But the Spartans' bats were silent. And as the team came off the field for the bottom of the sixth, Sam turned to Pic on the bench and verbally threw in the towel.

"Buddy, this is over," Sam told his brother.

Maybe the girls overheard their coach talking, maybe not, but with two outs in the bottom of the sixth, trailing 4-0, the lights went on. Roxy and Kristy singled and Bee crushed a triple off the left field fence to close the gap to 4-2.

Tami retired NYU in order in the top of the seventh, and the Spartans went to work in their last at bat. Jamie started things with a double. One out later, Lauren singled to center to score Jamie to cut the deficit to 4-3. On the throw home as Jamie was scoring, Lauren moved to second where she then scored on a single by Jenna. Game tied, 4-4, but not for long. Katie Pence singled to move Jenna to second, and Roxy singled to drive home Jenna with the winning run in the Spartans' come-from-behind 5-4 win.

"I couldn't believe it," Sam recalled. "Everyone was jumping and screaming, and it was only the first game of the season. The emotion was back."

But trouble was just beginning. Sam had inserted Alice at second base midway through the first game, then penciled her in to start at second base in the second game. Robbie had another idea.

"Let's go with Gimp at second and keep our strength," Robbie suggested, aluding to Alice's strikeout and groundout in two at bats in the first game. "Gimp's going to hit."

Sam took Alice out of the lineup.

The Spartans' bats picked up where they left off in the first game. Batting first as the visiting team, the Spartans batted around, scoring 10 first-inning runs for a commanding lead. Five more runs in the second inning made it a 15-0 laugher. Tami didn't give up a hit over the first two innings. Sam brought in Kristy to start the third, and she was just as dominant in the pitching circle. Kristy and Tami combined for a no-hitter as the Spartans left no doubt in a 20-1 blowout of NYU.

* * * *

The schedule was the same the following morning—on the bus and ready to go at 6:15 a.m.—though it was anything but routine.

The night before, Gimp—who was sharing a room with Kellie and Alice—told Sam that Alice was upset because she wasn't playing enough.

"She's pissed off because she said you lied to her about playing time," Gimp explained. "Now she's bitching and moaning. This isn't good."

That next morning, Alice poured fuel on the fire when she was late for the bus.

* * * *

The Spartans' first opponent on day two of the tournament was the Lady Vols of John A. Logan College, a top-notch team out of Illinois. Sam watched them warm up, and they were everything he thought they would be. Every girl was tall, sleek and athletic with a great throwing arm. They moved crisply and cleanly from activity to activity as the coach moved among them much as a drill sergeant in the army.

Sam walked over to the Lady Vols' coach.

"Coach, your team looks great," Sam noted. "How many scholarship players do you have on the team?"

"All sixteen of them are on full scholarship," the coach answered. "How many do you have?"

Sam shook his head. "We don't have any. We don't give athletic scholarships."

"That's what I'd heard," said the Logan coach.

The two coaches stood side by side in silence for a few moments before the Logan coach resumed the conversation.

"Well, if we win this game we're counting it, but we're not counting it if we lose," he announced.

Sam couldn't believe what he was hearing. "What did you say?"

The Logan coach repeated himself, adding, "You're a smaller school than we are, so we don't have to count the game. You can do the same thing."

"No I can't," Sam said. "This is an official game for us."

The Logan coach shrugged his shoulders. "Okay, just as long as you know that if we lose we're not counting it as an official game."

Sam turned and walked back to the Spartans' dugout, clearly angry. As he walked past Ness, Pic and Robbie he announced, "This game is not being counted." But as he found out later, they misinterpreted his comments.

On the field, the Spartans took control. Tami put the Lady Vols down in order in the top of the first, and a two-run single by Bee put the Spartans up 2-0 after one inning.

The turning point in the game came early, in the top of the second inning. The Lady Vols had a runner on second base with two out when a batter lined a single to center field. Katie Pence charged the ball and threw a strike to home plate where Lauren slapped a tag on the runner for the third out of the inning, maintaining NCC's 2-0 advantage.

"Our girls were going nuts, and the Logan players were pissed off because they lost out on a chance to score," Sam recalled.

The Spartans added a third-inning run on a single by Lauren and a double by Roxy for a 3-0 lead. But the Lady Vols broke through in the top of the fourth; a two-run double cut their deficit to one run. But Kristy singled to open the home fourth and eventually came around to score on a passed ball, giving the Spartans some breathing room with a 4-2 lead after four innings.

The Lady Vols added another run in the top of the fifth, but two singles and an error gave the run right back to the Spartans, who carried a 5-3 lead into the sixth, and they held on to win the game by that same score.

After the game, Ness walked up to Sam with Robbie and Pic right behind her.

"Why did you do that?" she asked.

"What are you talking about?" Sam answered.

"Why did you go into this game agreeing not to count it? Why did you let that happen? Why are you so worried about this streak?"

Sam realized that he had miscommunicated. His coaches thought he saw how good the Logan College players looked and, not wanting to put the streak in jeopardy, told the Logan coach that he wouldn't count the game if the Spartans lost.

"No," Sam said, shaking his head, "*They're* not counting it. We're counting it."

Then they understood.

* * * *

The second game of the day, played against the Community College of Rhode Island, was uneventful—at least on the field. The Spartans scored six first-inning runs on their way to a five-inning, mercy rule-shortened 10-2 win. All the drama was played out in the dugout before the start of the game.

Alice didn't play in the game against Logan, and didn't start the game against Rhode Island. Bee started the Rhode Island game at third base, and Sam was going to start Alice at second base. The assistant coaches suggested Sam keep Gimp at second base because she was playing good defense. Sam agreed, and changed the lineup.

In the dugout, Alice had a meltdown. She was crying, then began making calls on her cell phone. Shortly thereafter, she packed her bag and left the dugout.

"What the hell is going on here?" Sam asked when he saw that Alice had left.

Robbie and Pic were visibly angry. "She left the dugout," Robbie said. "She's on her cell phone, crying about everything. You have to get rid of her."

But Sam let his emotions get in the way. Alice soon returned to the dugout, and in the second inning, Sam pulled Bee and inserted Alice at third base in an attempt to calm the waters.

"I was stupid," Sam explained, "and I knew I was wrong after I did it. But I was trying to appease everyone and diffuse the situation.

Instead, it made things worse.

The next day, in between games of a doubleheader against the University of Minnesota – Morris, the Spartan players let Sam know how they felt.

"This is bullshit," Roxy said. "This can't happen. You cannot set a precedent where she's going to get her way because she cries. She shouldn't have been on her cell phone in the dugout, that's a rule. Why are you doing this?"

Gimp, who was sharing a room with Alice, told Sam that she had been on the phone the night before with her father, saying that she was sick of the way things were and was going to get on a plane and come home.

Sam went to Alice and told her that, for her actions on the bench and for leaving the dugout the previous day, she was being suspended for the remainder of the tournament.

"Coach, I was told to leave the bench by Kellie," Alice explained. "She said I should go to the bathroom and compose myself, so that's what I did."

Kellie corroborated the story.

"Yeah coach, that's what I told her," Kellie said. "I didn't want her putting on an act in front of everyone."

Sam reduced the suspension to one game.

* * * *

In sharp contrast, Katie Bee—who was having a sensational tournament both at the plate and in the field—demonstrated a warrior mentality just prior to the doubleheader against the University of Minnesota Cougars. Bee had injured the big toe on her right foot and, similar to Nikki Jenson's injury the year before in Myrtle Beach, a large blood blister formed under the toe nail.

"These were the first games of the season," Bee recalled, "and I couldn't think about anything other than playing and winning. I didn't want to think about how badly it hurt."

But it hurt, and the pain got progressively worse each day, to the point where her toe was throbbing and her eyes were tearing just from trying to run warmups. At times it hurt so badly she could barely stand on it.

"I asked coach if he had anything," Bee explained. "A pin, a knife—anything. I had to do something."

Sam gave Bee his nail clipper, and Ness accompanied her into the rest room. Five minutes later, she came out and asked Sam to wrap her toe for her.

"Bee, that won't do any good," Sam tried to explain. "Until you get that pressure ..."

"The pressure's gone, coach," Bee said, and handed Sam his clippers.

Bee had taken the edge of the pin tool, normally used for filing, inserted it under her toe nail and popped the blister. Then she squeezed her toe until the blister was completely drained.

Sam wrapped her toe, and Bee said it felt great. It must have, because Bee had six hits in the doubleheader and continued her flawless play in the field as the Spartans swept the Cougars, 7-1 and 8-0.

* * * *

Later that evening, the drama continued.

Katie Pence's parents own a condo in Orlando, so they invited the entire team over for a lasagna dinner. They also rented out the movie theatre in the condo development so that all the girls could watch a movie together, in private. It had the potential to be a great evening but, other than Katie, only five other girls showed up. It was the first real sign that there were problems; that the team was breaking off into cliques, and it pissed Sam off.

"I told the girls who didn't go that it was a stupid thing to do," Sam explained. "First, the Pences spent a lot of money and went out of their way to make it a nice evening. Second, I gave each girl $150 for food money for the week at the start of the trip. They could have saved themselves meal money. They used the excuse that there was only one car to transport everyone from the hotel to the condo, but that was bullshit. It could have been a great outing, but they chose not to show up."

Katie, too, was very upset. She had invited the entire team, and thought that everyone was coming. "Then at the last minute, some people called and said they were going shopping. It was supposed to be a team thing. It wasn't mandatory, but it would have been nice if the entire team had come."

Katie speculated that the no-shows were just the early repercussions of the Alice incident.

"I don't think that one situation had much of an impact, but the way the coaches handled it, I think that started to wear on people," Katie explained. "From the beginning, the coaches said that you can't get upset over playing time. And if you do get upset, you'll be reprimanded. Based on that, I don't think the situation was handled properly, and I think people got upset because of that."

The next night, it was more of the same. After completing a sweep of the eight-game tournament with 10-2 and 10-1 wins over Oakton College of Illinois, a team dinner was held in the lodge at the far end of the Magic Kingdom. It was the team's last night in Orlando, and on the heels of running the tournament table, a great start to the season.

Except that Alice didn't show up for the dinner. Sam was upset, as were the girls. But with eight consecutive wins to start the season, the Spartans' undefeated streak stood at eighty-six games. Just seven more game—seven more wins—and they would re-write the history books.

Sam was looking forward to getting back home, and getting down to business. There was much work to be done.

* * * *

The Spartans' Southwest Air flight touched down in Philadelphia International Airport around 11:30 Thursday morning. The players and coaches made their way through the terminal to the baggage claim area where they picked up their belongings and headed outside, greeted by a bitter rain that seemed even colder after five days in Orlando.

Bill Bearse and Carmen, one of the fitness center assistants, drove down in school vans to meet the team. So did Alice's father. He pulled up to the curb, Alice jumped into the car, and they were gone.

Later that day, back at home, Sam received an email from Alice. She wrote that she didn't want to say anything to Sam's face because she felt there would probably be yelling and fighting, and she wanted to avoid a confrontation. She wrote that Sam had made many promises to her, most of which involved playing time in games, and he had not followed through on those promises. She was quitting the team and would turn in her uniform.

That dropped the number of players on the team to 13 and ended the ordeal, and Sam was fine with the outcome.

"I was sad to see her go because I liked her as a person," Sam reflected. "But you can't have that stuff going on. I didn't do a good enough job policing things in Orlando, but now it was over with."

But new drama was waiting just around the corner.

TWENTY-THREE

While storm clouds had begun brewing in Orlando, it was nothing compared to the deluge that Sam and the Lady Spartans faced when they returned home following the Disney Spring Training Tournament.

The Spartans flew back into Philadelphia International Airport on Thursday, March 15, and were scheduled to play back-to-back doubleheaders that weekend, on Saturday and Sunday, against Salem Community College, of Carneys Point, New Jersey. But Sam received word that the college didn't have enough players to field a team, so all four games were canceled. A late winter snowstorm that blanketed the Lehigh Valley with eight to ten inches of snow on Friday buried any chance of filling in the schedule with other games. Since the doubleheaders against Salem were out-of-league games, they were never rescheduled.

Heavy rain cancelled a doubleheader against PSU – Harrisburg on Saturday the 24th, and Lincoln University told Sam they had just hired a new coach and the team wouldn't be ready for the doubleheader scheduled for Sunday the 25th, so four more games were lost. The Lincoln games were eventually made up later in the season, but the PSU games were washed away.

The washouts and cancellations meant that the Spartans, hot following their performance in the Disney Tournament, had plenty of time to cool off. Nearly two weeks passed since their last game in Orlando before the team was able to play a competitive softball game.

"It was hard to keep the girls motivated," Sam recalled. "It was hard to keep going back into the gym and doing the same thing day after day. It was disappointing to me, to the coaches and to the players."

Making matters worse, Sam soon learned that league opponents LCCC, Luzerne, Delaware and Cecil community colleges would not be fielding teams that season, which meant 16 more games—four against each school, two at home and two on the road—were wiped off the schedule. Those canceled games left huge, gaping holes in the Spartans' schedule that would later come back to haunt the team.

Could it get any worse? Absolutely. The first EPCC/WPCC (Western Pennsylvania Collegiate Conference) Challenge was scheduled for the weekend of March 31 and April 1. Four teams from the WPCC—Community College of Beaver, Butler Community College, Westmoreland Community College and the Community College of Allegheny South—were going to take on four teams from the EPCC. The Spartans were going to host the tournament on their field.

After Sam learned that the three EPCC schools would not be fielding teams, he began scrambling to find teams to fill the open spots. However, about one week before the tournament, the four WPCC schools contacted NCC athletic director Bill Bearse and told him that they needed to use the weekend to reschedule games that had been postponed from earlier in the season due to poor weather. They were backing out of the tournament. Bearse relayed the bad news to Sam.

"It was one disappointment after another," recalled Sam, who was spending hours on the phone trying to fill in the open dates with games. "A team would say they would play us, and then change their mind. Or the weather would cancel the game. Every time the girls got pumped up because we'd be playing, they'd get knocked down again. It was terrible."

So, before a pitch was thrown in the Spartans' 2007 regular season, not counting the tournament in Orlando, approximately twenty-six games—or more than half the season—had been canceled.

The problems were compounded because the Spartans were seven wins away from establishing a new collegiate record, and the media demands for time with Sam and the girls were mounting. The coach found himself pulled in different directions, and no one stepped in to pick up the slack.

"What should have happened at that point was the assistant coaches should have taken over and just started to run with the team," Sam explained. "They know how we do things at practices. But there were times when I came back to the gym from doing an interview and everyone was just sitting around. I wanted to flip out."

Many of the girls began to get lazy, saying they had something to do and couldn't stay for practice. Sam became disappointed that, in his absence, the team's captains, Roxy and Jenna, didn't take charge and get the girls motivated to practice. But that was another effect of the cliques that had formed on the team. Other players noticed.

"We had one captain who wasn't outspoken enough, and another captain who spoke a lot, but when it came down to it, couldn't lead the team and tell the girls what they needed to hear," Tami Kilousky said. "And the two of them didn't talk together, which had an effect on everyone else. Because if the captains are separate, then everyone else is separate."

Third baseman Katie Bee echoed those thoughts.

"A lot of the second-year players, I think they were kind of lazy, maybe too comfortable," Bee said. "Especially the captains; they weren't leading the team. They weren't pushing us. When the coaches aren't around, the captains are supposed to take control, but they didn't. We wound up with too many cliques and groups."

"You look toward your captains for discipline and uplifting moments, but that wasn't there," added Lisa Klinger. "It kind of made the rest of us feel like we were fending for ourselves rather than having two people on the team to lead us."

Practices began to unravel. Sometimes, they were canceled outright. For many of the first-year players who were used to practicing on a regular basis in high school, it was an odd and frustrating feeling.

"We weren't practicing every day, which is very abnormal for me, because once you get into the season you should be practicing every day," Katie Pence said. "And even when we were practicing, I felt that the practices weren't challenging. We would hit a little bit, and then people would sit around, and that's not my style."

Things came to a head when the media began requesting interviews with some of the girls on the team. Sam directed them to the two captains, Roxy and Jenna, and would also make some of the second-year players available. When one of the local television stations spoke with Roxy but skipped over Jenna, Jenna became furious. She was soon overheard saying to some of the girls on the team that if she wasn't going to be interviewed and treated like a captain, she was no longer going to act like one.

"If I tell the media to go talk to the captains, but they don't talk to them, it's not my fault," Sam explained when he learned that Jenna was upset. "Why would I keep one of my captains out?"

The reason, according to some of the players, was that Sam favored Roxy.

"Everything was so focused on Roxanne being a captain, and coach always listened to what Roxanne had to say and never told Jenna what was going on," Gimp noted. "Jenna always felt left out."

Whether it was true or not was irrelevant; the point was, that's what many of the players believed. The fact was, however, that Roxy understood not just the softball end of the game but the business and administrative end as well. She knew, and understood, that Sam received $100 from the school per road game for meals for the girls. Any dollars spent above that figure came out of his pocket. Some of the girls on the team didn't understand that, or didn't care.

"There are a lot of girls on this team who have filet mignon tastes, and we have a ground beef budget," Sam explained.

Once, after a road game at PSU – Abington, the girls said they wanted to eat at a Red Robin. Sam said "fine," but they were unable to find a Red Robin along the road so Sam suggested they go to a Friendly's Restaurant. Shortly thereafter, the NCC vans passed an Appleby's, and many of the girls began yelling that they would rather go to Appleby's than Friendly's.

"We're going to Friendly's because that's what we can afford," Sam explained, and Roxy added her support. That caused a scene.

"You always talk coach into going someplace because that's where you want to go," the girls told Roxy. "You're not thinking about everybody else."

"No, this is all the money coach has," she tried to explain. "If we go over the one hundred dollars it comes out of his pocket."

Many of the girls didn't see it that way. Those who did, many of them first-year players, choose not to say anything for fear of stepping on toes. Kristy, who had seen her share of *real* conflict in Iraq, blamed a lot of the problems on immaturity.

"I was the oldest on the team, and I couldn't relax around some of the girls because I thought they were so immature, and it was making me mad," Kristy explained. "There was just too much conflict and too much drama. It seemed that each group was talking about another group. I pretty much stayed to myself for a long time."

Sam could only shake his head. It was 2004 all over again.

* * * *

On Tuesday, March 27, almost two full weeks since their last game in Orlando, the Spartans were again able to take the field. Despite all the drama and controversy that had infiltrated the team off the field, the Spartans still knew what to do when their cleats hit the dirt.

In a doubleheader against PSU – Abington, the Spartans scored early and often in two mercy rule-shortened wins, 10-0 and 17-1. Two days later they followed that doubleheader sweep with another, this one against Penn College by final scores of 10-5 and 13-1.

With the four victories, the Spartans' consecutive game winning streak now stood at ninety. They had surpassed the eighty-eight wins amassed by the UCLA Bruins basketball teams of the early 1970s, and were staring down history and the University of North Carolina women's soccer team's mark of ninety-two wins.

But you can't win games you don't play, and that weekend's scheduled EPCC/WPCC Challenge had been canceled. Sam got on the phone and started making calls.

"I had to find somebody to play," explained Sam, not wanting to leave the streak hanging any longer. The pressure was already affecting everyone on or connected with the team. "I wanted to get the damn thing over."

Several weeks earlier, Sam had been on the phone with Jen Edwards, the women's softball coach at Montgomery-Rockville Community College in Maryland. Jen asked if the two teams could play on the weekend of March 31 and April 1. A tournament they were scheduled to play was canceled. Sam said the Spartans had the EPCC/WPCC Challenge, but would get back to her if anything changed.

Jen was the first person he called.

"Do you want to come up here on Saturday?" Sam asked. "We'll play you two games on Saturday, and I'll get you another team to play on Sunday."

"That sounds great," Jen said.

Sam was going to have PSU – Abington play Montgomery-Rockville on Sunday, and the Spartans were going to play Lincoln University, games that had been postponed earlier in the season. But the new Lincoln coach said his team still wasn't ready. That left Sam in the lurch. If the Spartans won both games on Saturday against Montgomery-Rockville, they would tie the record at ninety-two consecutive wins, but would then have to wait twelve days until their next scheduled game.

Sam didn't want to push things back again, so he called Jen.

"Do you want to play us again on Sunday?" he asked.

"Okay," she said, "but just one game on Sunday."

Then Sam told her about the streak, and about all of the press and commotion that might be going on that weekend; that in fact, her team could have the 'distinction' of being the Spartans' ninety-third consecutive victim.

"Why didn't you tell me that before we signed the contracts?" Jen asked. "I don't know if I would have come up under those circumstances."

"Jen, you know I'm not here to embarrass anyone," Sam explained. "And I don't know who you've got on your team."

Montgomery-Rockville agreed to play two games on Saturday and one on Sunday. The stage was set for the Spartans to break the record on Sunday afternoon on their home field. Now all they needed was for the weather to cooperate . . . and to win.

* * * *

Sam gathered the team together in the gymnasium before Saturday's doubleheader against Montgomery-Rockville. He didn't want to say a lot, because the girls already felt he was too focused on the streak. But he felt he had to say something.

"You're three games away from doing something that no other college team has ever done," he began. "I have no idea what this other team is like. So we need to go into this first game, feel this team out and see what we can and can't do. And then, I want you to take your place in history. And I promise you, if you win these two games today, every player on the team will play in tomorrow's game, and every pitcher will pitch in that game."

But nothing went smoothly for Sam and the NCC Spartans during the 2007 season, and that included the record-setting weekend of games. The weather cooperated on Saturday, but player and coach personalities were even harder to predict.

Before the season had started, Roxy went to Sam and told him about her sister's field hockey team at Phillipsburg High School. The team gave cowbells to the parents in the stands, and they would ring them to help rally the team during the game. Roxy wanted to do the same for the parents during Spartan softball games that year.

Sam approved, and purchased a large, white cowbell with NCC Spartans printed across the base. It hadn't been used during the first portion of the season, but for this special occasion of games, Roxy took it out of Sam's office for it's inaugural ringing.

The girls began to ring and bang on the bell during the warm-up. That didn't sit well with one of the assistant coaches.

"No, you're not going to use this now," said Robbie, taking the cowbell away. "You haven't used it all year, don't use it now. It's stupid."

Roxy flipped out.

Sam came out to the field and the incident blew up in his face.

"What the hell is going on?" Sam asked. He was briefed, then told Robbie, "Let her use it. It's no big deal."

But by then Roxy had copped the attitude of, "Well, I don't want it now."

Later, the Spartans were finishing their warm-up in the field. As a routine, the girls would run off the field by position, starting with the outfield. As they ran off, they would line up along the third baseline, the first player lining up close to home plate. Each succeeding player would 'high-five' the girls already lined up, starting at home and working toward third base, and then take their position in line.

Roxy played catcher or first base, so she was usually one of the last to leave the field. On Saturday, as she approached the string of players standing along the third baseline, she began slapping hands with her teammates in reverse order, starting near third base and working down toward home plate instead of the other way around.

Her teammates began yelling, "No, no," but Roxy just shook her head and said, "It's no big deal."

But to Robbie, it was. "Don't start changing things now," he yelled.

"It's nothing; it's just superstition," Roxy yelled back.

It started a fight, right there on the sidelines in front of players, parents and the visiting Montgomery-Rockville team, minutes before the games were to begin. It didn't last long, because Roxy had had enough.

"I can't take this anymore," she yelled. "I'm quitting."

Sam took Roxy off to the side. "I don't want to hear that out of you again. I understand that Robbie shouldn't have done what he did, but you shouldn't have, either. So, I'm going to call this a wash."

Roxy wasn't benched for any of the weekend games for yelling at the coaches. In Sam's mind it was no harm, no foul. But that's not how other players saw it.

"When you allow a captain to yell at a coach, of course the other players think they can do it, too," Tami said. "Things like that should not happen, especially since we have a coach who isn't exactly a drill sergeant. There was no reason for that, and it got to me. Being a first-year player, I didn't want to say anything. But, it was just one of the many times where things were handled the wrong way."

Sam reflected on the situation. He knew it was mishandled. He also knew that he allowed his emotions to cloud his judgment.

"It happened right in front of the team, and I should have sat Roxy," Sam said. "But these games were important. I didn't want any of the girls to miss these games."

The Spartans clearly had plenty of fight in them. Now Sam was hoping they carried that fight out onto the field and through the weekend.

TWENTY-FOUR

It was not a good day for the Montgomery-Rockville Knights.

When Lisa Klinger slid home with the Spartans' first run in the first game of Saturday's doubleheader, she collided with the Knights' catcher, tearing the girl's ACL and MCL. The catcher, who was considered the Knights' best player, was lost for the weekend. And when she went out, so did whatever fire the Knights may have had.

In the first game, the Spartans did what they usually did—they scored early and often. Lisa set the table, going three-for-three and scoring three runs, while Roxy pushed the runs across with two doubles that plated five runs. Anna Stem also collected three hits, including a triple, and scored three runs.

On the mound, Tami faced only eighteen batters in the five-inning, mercy rule-shortened game, allowing just three hits and no walks, as the Spartans prevailed 21-0. Making matters worse, the umpire disqualified five of the Knights' bats, stating that they were illegal.

"It really wasn't the best of days for them," Sam noted.

The second game wasn't much different, although Sam added some intrigue when he borrowed a page from Major League Baseball manager Billy Martin and went with a jumbled lineup. Katie Sculley was on the mound with Tami at first, Jamie at second, Kristy at short and Gimp at third. Around the outfield, Jenna was in left, Roxy played center and Lauren was in right.

"After the screaming and yelling that took place before the game, I was trying to get some kind of tension relief where everyone could just have fun," Sam recalled. "It was almost like with cabin fever, just trying to release the tension."

It worked, at least as far as the results indicated. Sculley faced just eighteen batters in another five-inning, mercy rule-shortened affair, allowing just one run on three hits. Jamie provided the power, knocking in four runs, including a three-run homer in the third inning, as the Spartans collected their ninety-second win in a row by the score of 14-1. They had now equaled the record set by the University of North Carolina women's soccer team, and were on the verge of making history.

* * * *

The sky was overcast on Sunday morning and a light rain was falling across the Lehigh Valley. It was cold and damp, not surprising for early April, but not ideal conditions for an important softball game.

Sam's phone rang at 7:30 that morning. It was Bill Bearse, the school's athletic director. There was excitement and anticipation in his voice.

"How's the field?" Bearse asked.

Sam laughed. It was a rare, lighthearted moment during an emotionally draining three-week period, and Sam went with it.

"Bill, I'm in bed, so I can't see the field from here," Sam answered. "But I trust our guys will have the field ready by noon."

In Sam's mind, of course, there was no way the game would be postponed.

"If I had to get 900 hair dryers and extension cords out there that field was going to be dry," Sam said. "It was cold, it was damp, but everything was set in motion. And with Rockville staying overnight, there was no way I was going to cancel the game. Even if we had to push it back by an hour or two, we were going to play."

Sam had anticipated a media circus that morning. Local Philadelphia channels 3, 6 and 10 had all said they would be present. Service Electric Sports and 69 News had also scheduled coverage, as did ESPN. But when he arrived at his office, the Spartan Center hallways were empty.

"What the hell," Sam recalled thinking. "We hadn't even gotten our fifteen minutes of fame yet and it was over."

Service Electric and 69 News would eventually show up, but the other stations sent word that they thought the game would be rained out so they didn't want to take the chance of sending out a camera crew in bad weather.

The light rain stopped around 11 a.m., and while the day remained cold and gray, the field was in good shape and the game went off as scheduled—a major relief for Sam.

"I wouldn't have been able to handle one more day of that stuff," the coach recalled. "I'm forty-seven-years old, and I know

I've been through a lot of stuff, but this was the most pressure I think I've ever faced in my entire life. Even the gastric bypass—nothing compared to the pressure of chasing this record."

* * * *

The sidelines were lined with spectators, folding chairs and blankets set out, braving the elements for a chance to be part of a history-making moment.

Tami was in the pitching circle for the Spartans, and she made short work of the Knights in the top of the first inning. Then the Spartans, as is their wont, took over in the home half. Lisa Klinger, ever the spark plug, singled to start the uprising, and scored on a triple to right field by Katie Pence. Later that inning, Katie Bee crushed a solo home run over the fence in right-center field, and Gimp connected on a two-run shot to left.

The score was 6-0 by the time the Spartans took the field in the second inning, and it seemed the only question remaining to be answered was whether the game would go the regulation seven innings or would the eight-run mercy rule be employed by the fifth inning?

The Spartans added a seventh run in the second inning, then tacked on three more in the bottom of the fourth, two scoring on Katie Sculley's booming double to the fence in left field, for a 10-0 advantage.

True to his word, Sam employed each of his four pitchers during the game. Tami threw the first two innings, Jamie the third and Kristy the fourth. And when Jenna took the circle in the top of the fifth, she quickly recorded the three outs necessary to seal the win and the Spartans' place in the record books.

"It was a huge relief," Sam said after the record-setting win. "I have a photograph of myself handing in the lineup card at the start of a game as we got close to the record, and I'm actually hunched over. My body literally took on the weight and the pressure of the streak and made me hunch over. But when that last out was made, I felt that I could finally straighten up again."

Similarly, the Spartans high-fived each other as they walked off the field, but the feeling was more subdued relief than exuberance. That seemed to bother members of the media who descended on the players for interviews and photographs, and prompted an unusual request by one photographer.

"Could you girls go back out to the field, and then come running off, screaming and jumping, so I can get a photo of that?" the photographer asked.

The girls obliged, but their jumps for joy and shouts of enthusiasm looked every bit staged. The photographer was disappointed, but he'd have to live with it.

The girls explained their sentiments.

"It felt great to be pitching in that game, but the excitement really was not there, at least for me, because I wasn't there for the first seventy-eight games," Tami explained. "It felt like the celebration of the entire ninety-three-game streak was on us, but I can't take credit for that, and I didn't want to."

Katie Pence acknowledged the excitement of playing in the record-setting game, but explained that the lack of drama or suspense in the games the team was playing took away from some of the achievement.

"For me it was amazing," Pence said. "But I think we were expecting it. I mean, we didn't know it was going to happen, but we had a good feeling about it because of the team we were playing. And if you're expecting something, it takes away that element of surprise or excitement."

It was a point well taken. Other than a few close games in Orlando, the Spartans had rolled over their opponents. Were the Spartans that good? Was the level of competition that poor? Fair questions, but moot points to several of the second-year players.

"It feels great to capture this type of record," Roxy explained, standing outside the Spartans' dugout following the win. "This is only going to give us more momentum going forward."

Inside the Spartan Center following the press conference, Lisa Klinger let her emotions show.

"I've been playing softball since sixth grade, and I never would have thought that anything this great would happen to me," Lisa explained as she fought back the tears. "Being part of this program . . . it's going to stick with me for a very long time."

It would turn out to be one of the last very good days of her NCC softball career.

* * * *

Any enjoyment Sam derived from Sunday's win was virtually shattered the following afternoon when the coach received a phone call from a local reporter.

"You guys don't have the record," the reporter announced. "There are tennis and squash teams that have won more consecutive matches. Didn't you research it?"

"We researched everything," said Sam, who had phoned the sports information department at North Carolina, had them check the archives, and was told that as far as they knew, they had held the record. Squash and tennis were not recognized as team sports.

"Well, I have to put this in the paper," the reporter said.

Sam was beside himself. "Give me a couple of days to get in touch with my kids, and to research it more."

"You should have done your research already. And you'd better tell your kids because it's going in the paper tomorrow morning."

Sam was frantic. He grabbed his cell phone and began calling everyone connected with the team, explaining the situation and trying to calm them down—all the while, trying to stay calm himself.

At home later that evening, Sam flipped on the television to watch Service Electric's Sports Scene program, and the topic of the controversial winning streak was the first thing the sportscaster spoke about.

The sportscaster noted that there had been some confusion as to whether or not the NCC Spartans now actually held the record. But he noted that the Sports Scene staff did its research and found that the NCAA does not recognize squash and tennis as team sports. So, the sportscaster announced, the Spartans were indeed owners of the new record.

Sam breathed a sigh of relief, but it was only the beginning of an arduous three weeks. The next day the coach learned that the NCAA would not recognize NCC as holding the record because the school was not an NCAA-affiliated college. He was more angry than disappointed.

He wondered, if the school didn't pay NCAA dues, did that mean that the ninety-three-consecutive wins never happened?

If a tree fell in the forest, it wouldn't matter if 1,000 people witnessed it or no one was present, it would still make a loud noise. The softball games were played, and won—Sam knew that much.

Art Wolf, NCC's women's basketball coach, made the best argument.

"When girls play here, whether it's one or two years, the NCAA takes those years of eligibility away from them," Wolf reasoned. "So when they leave here and go on to a four-year college, if they played here for two years, they've only got two years of eligibility left. If the NCAA doesn't recognize the streak because we're not affiliated, then why are these girls getting years of eligibility taken away from them when they play here?"

Sam summed up his feelings succinctly.

"The NCAA can't take it away from these girls," he said point blank. "They can't take it away from this school. We know we did it, and this school knows we did it."

* * * *

If the media attention, team drama, lack of adequate practice time and cancellation of games were an irritant before the ninety-third consecutive win occurred, they became a major disruption after the record was broken.

Heidi Butler, NCC's director of public information and community relations, was leading the charge to get press coverage of the softball team's achievement. She called Sam early in the week following the record-setting win and told him that she had a proposal from the Associated Press for a story on the team. Was he interested in speaking with them?

"Absolutely." Sam couldn't get the words out of his mouth fast enough. "You don't get these opportunities very often."

The AP wanted to do the story that Friday, which just happened to be Good Friday, and the school was closed. But Sam was able to pull almost the entire team in for a 9 a.m. practice—indoors, because it was raining. Lisa and Sculley were unable to attend because they had to work, as did assistant coaches Jack and Pic.

The AP reporter asked Sam to put the team through a full, functional practice, including hitting and fielding, so the photographer could get lots of photos. While the practice was ongoing, the reporter systematically pulled players out from the practice one at a time to be interviewed. Then he interviewed Sam, which left Robbie alone to run the practice.

"He was getting bitter because he wasn't being interviewed," Sam said. "And Pic, even though he wasn't there, was pissed off because these sessions were taking time away from our practices. But if there's an opportunity to promote this college and this team, I have to take it. If you turn it down, you look stupid, because there are people begging for this kind of publicity."

The publicity was widespread. The AP story ran in major daily newspapers across the country, from The Boston Globe to the Los Angeles Times. It also appeared in European newspapers in Ireland, England and Spain.

For the team, it was a mixed bag. There were girls who appreciated the spotlight, and others who felt it was a distraction.

"I thought having all the news cameras around was exciting," Katie Pence said. "It didn't bother me; I just tried to focus on what I was doing. But it did upset some people on the team if they weren't being interviewed. So in that respect it did disrupt the team."

Roxy viewed it as a dream come true.

"It's like a wedding day, something a young girl dreams about and plans out," she explained. "Getting this kind of notoriety was something that I'd been dreaming of and practicing for my whole life. And to be in this position and have one of my dreams come true, it was just unbelievable."

But it didn't end there.

That same week, Sam was contacted by the CBS Evening News. The NCC women's softball team was one of three features being considered for the program's Assignment: America segment. Each Friday evening, viewers are given a choice of three features they'd like to see on the following week's program. Then they vote on the program's web site.

Sam got the word on Thursday, the day before Good Friday, that viewers would be asked to choose between the NCC softball team, a blogging nun, and a 100-year-old substitute English literature teacher. He gave all the details to Heidi Butler, who sent email notices to everyone affiliated with the school alerting them that the softball team could be featured on the CBS Evening News, and included a web site link so they could vote.

But, timing is everything.

"Heidi sent out all the emails late on Thursday, but everyone was off the next day for Good Friday," Sam explained. "They won't see their email if they don't check from home. And it was a holiday weekend."

The softball team lost out to the 100-year-old substitute teacher, but at least their achievement was mentioned on national television.

The following week, Erin Flynn from PBS called and said she wanted to bring a crew out to do a story on the softball team. It became a multi-day project, starting with interview sessions with each of the girls. Erin also wanted to know about any human interest stories involving girls on the team, and Sam told her about Kristy and Lisa.

"At one point I had to ask Kristy, 'Are you getting sick of this? Am I putting too much pressure on you reliving this all the time?'" Sam recalled.

"No coach, it actually is a little better for me to talk about it," Kristy said. "It gets a little easier each time."

So, PBS visited Kristy's house to film and speak with Kristy and her father. Then they went to Lisa's house to profile Lisa with her grandfather and idol, Willie Morales, who played professional baseball with Sandy Koufax. It was a wonderful moment for Kristy and Lisa. But that individual attention only fueled more animosity among their teammates.

The next day, PBS came out to the NCC softball field to get footage at practice. Sam and Pic were the only coaches around, and Pic was already annoyed at all the distractions the winning streak was causing.

After some general filming, Erin wanted to get shots of Kristy and Lisa hitting, to go with the home footage that had been shot a day earlier. That raised some eyebrows.

"Some of the other girls were starting to fume because PBS was concentrating on Kristy and Lisa," Sam said. "You could see it in their faces—their eyes rolling and their heads turning, whispering to each other."

"There were all these group dynamics," Katie Bee recalled. "Girls would look and say, 'Oh, she's getting interviewed but I'm not.' It was a really big distraction."

Gimp echoed those thoughts.

"Only one or two people had the camera on them," she recalled. "It wasn't focusing on the team aspect, it was focusing on individuals. And those individuals weren't any better than the rest of us."

When cameras were set up in the outfield to film Kristy and Lisa, Pic went over the edge.

"This is bullshit," Pic said to Sam, his body language clearly showing his frustration. "They're taking away our time. We have to practice and we can't do it with these people all over the place. When is this going to end?"

Sam calmed his younger brother, and the PBS feature turned out to be a well-done portrait of the team.

Now, if the Spartans could just play a few games.

* * * *

Relief was the operative word following the Spartans' ninety-third consecutive win.

"I remember we were thinking that maybe now Sam would start relaxing," Bee said. "It wasn't that we weren't having fun, but we just wanted to start playing to play, not because of the streak."

But after the Spartans defeated Montgomery-Rockville on April 1, they did not play another game for nearly three weeks thanks to weather postponements and the EPCC schools that had dropped their teams that year. From April 1 through Wednesday, April 18, the Spartans did nothing more than practice and smile for the cameras. And they didn't do very much of the former, as practices were often cancelled due to lack of interest on the part of some of the players.

Finally, on Thursday, April 19, the Spartans boarded the NCC vans for the two-hour drive up to Williamsport and a doubleheader against the Penn College Wildcats.

Would the Spartans be ready?

TWENTY-FIVE

When the Spartans traveled to Williamsport for their double-header against the Penn College Wildcats, they did so without their complete arsenal. They were missing Tami Kilousky, the team's No. 1 pitcher all season and the pitcher Sam referred to as "my knock-out punch."

Tami was enrolled in NCC's nursing program, a highly regarded program that was difficult to gain entry to. The workload was sizeable and challenging and, unfortunately, Tami had done some procrastinating. She had two reports due the following morning, and she had to be at the hospital for work at 7 a.m.

"I talked it over with my aunt," Tami recalled. "It was like, how could I not go? There was a streak on the line, and I needed to be there. But I reasoned that my school work was more important."

Tami's aunt complicated the decision-making process. "Well, if you don't go and they lose, how guilty will you feel?"

Until then, Tami hadn't even considered that factor.

"I went back and forth, but when it came down to it, I needed to do my work," Tami said. "And there was no way I could get back at 11 p.m. and finish two reports by the following morning."

So she stayed home and worked, and waited for a phone call.

* * * *

The field at Penn College is not a standard fast-pitch softball field, it's a slow-pitch softball field. The outfield fence is 295-feet from home plate all the way around the field, as opposed to 200-feet down the left- and right-field lines and then gradually lengthening out as you move toward center field. The fence is also 20-feet high, a deterrent to hitting home runs. A deterrent to power-hitting teams like the Spartans.

Without Tami, Sam wrestled over his pitching match-ups.

"I know Kristy can pitch, and I know Jamie can pitch," the coach reasoned. "But if I throw Kristy for a full game, she's done. Then I have Jamie and Jenna to fall back on, but Jamie hasn't had the best experience when it comes to fielding ground balls and throwing to first base."

Tami, Sam explained, is a warrior who can get into problems but knows how to work her way out of them. "Jamie can do that to a point, but if she self-destructs, all I'll have left is Jenna. And if Jenna doesn't have a good game, we're sunk."

Sam decided to pitch Kristy in the first game. Trailing 1-0 in the third inning, Kristy helped her own cause by connecting on a two-run homer following Lisa's double to put the Spartans on top 2-1.

In the home half of the third, the Wildcats countered with some power of their own when a player named Morrow smacked a two-run homer for a 3-2 Penn College lead.

Like a boxing match, the Spartans came back with two runs in the top of the fourth for a 4-3 lead, but in the bottom of the inning, Morrow doubled to drive in two more runs and put the Wildcats back on top, 5-4. The Spartans tacked on three more runs in the top of the fifth for a 7-5 lead, and Kristy kept the Wildcats at bay entering the bottom of the seventh. But she was tiring, so Sam brought Jamie in to close out the game.

Morrow, however, had other ideas, and led off the home seventh with her second home run of the game, cutting the Spartans' lead to 7-6. The next batter singled, and then on a grounder back to the mound, Jamie threw the ball into right field allowing the tying run to score.

The game moved into the eighth inning with the international tie-breaker rules in effect. That meant the Spartans started the inning with Lisa on second base. Jenna sacrificed her to third, and Katie Pence doubled to bring home the go-ahead run. Jamie registered two strikeouts and a groundout in the bottom of the eighth, leaving the tying run stranded on second as the Spartans prevailed, 8-7. The streak, now at ninety-four consecutive wins, was intact.

During the late innings of the first game, however, members of the Penn College boys' lacrosse team began a disturbance in the stands. Sitting with their lacrosse sticks, they began pounding the sticks against the metal stands, screaming and cursing at some of the Spartan players.

"Roxy, you're a fat pig," the players shouted. "You're a whore."

"Kristy, I'm in your head. I'm going to get you after the game," another yelled.

That didn't sit well with Sean, Kristy's boyfriend, who served in the same battalion with her in Iraq. He left his seat on the sidelines and started to head over to the lacrosse players but was intercepted by Kristy, who calmed him down.

"We can handle this," Kristy told Sean. "We can hold this together."

Kristy, however, underestimated the "we" in her statement, as the verbal abuse and taunting from the Penn College lacrosse players had a visible impact on some of the Spartans, and things snowballed from there.

"When they started yelling at us in the first game, I was laughing on every pitch because they were saying some ridiculous things," Kristy recalled. "But then some people on the team were getting upset, and they were affecting everybody else on the team by being upset because they couldn't keep it to themselves. I just wanted to scream and say, 'Calm down.'"

But some of the players, those to whom the comments were being directed, began shouting back at the lacrosse team, which only made matters worse.

"You can't let people disrupt what you're trying to do," Katie Pence explained. "You have to block them out.. It shouldn't have had an effect on our team, but it blew up into something everyone began focusing on. We didn't focus on hitting or fielding. It disrupted the team because of the way certain people handled the situation."

Sam, who was furious, approached the umpires. He asked them why they were allowing this level of verbal abuse. Their response was not what Sam expected to hear.

"We don't hear anything, coach," the home plate umpire said.

Bullshit, Sam recalled thinking. "They couldn't help but hear it. And the school's athletic director was sitting in the dugout with the team's coach, who is a friend of mine from a coaching standpoint. And for them to just sit there and allow this to happen was bullshit. It was a travesty."

Roxy was in tears. Many of the other girls were visibly upset. And the taunting continued as the second game got underway and through the first few innings.

"In the pros you can scream whatever you want because the players are getting paid," Sam explained. "These are young ladies who aren't getting paid squat, and they're getting verbally abused and hearing threats of physical abuse. If I had any guts I would have pulled the team off the field and left. If they wanted the damn forfeit so bad, they could have it."

But Sam didn't pull the team. Instead, he challenged them. He told them that people could say what they wanted, but the girls should use it as fuel to prove them wrong. In the second game went on with Jamie in the pitching circle. In the second inning, the Spartans were trailing 1-0 when the Wildcats put runners on first and second. The next batter grounded back to the mound, but Jamie threw the ball into right field, allowing two runs to score. Two more hits followed, and the Spartans found themselves in a 5-0 hole.

Standing in the outfield, thoughts were racing through Lisa's mind.

"I kept thinking, is it coming? Is this where we lose?" Lisa recalled. "In the first game we kept fighting back and we won. But in that second game, it felt like we were tired of playing. I don't know if the other team had more spirit than we did, but when I came to the plate I couldn't think of anything other than the harassment we were getting. And if it affected me, I'm pretty sure it affected the rest of the team."

In the top of the sixth, Bee doubled to drive home two runs and cut the deficit to 5-2. But in the home half of the sixth, the Wildcats collected two singles before Jenna allowed a ground ball to roll under her glove at shortstop and two more runs scored.

"Seven unearned runs," Sam moaned. "And we hit at least seven balls in the second game that would have been home runs on a regular field. But they just played us deep and caught them near the fence."

The Spartans were retired in the seventh, and in the blink of an eye, the streak was over with the 7-2 loss. The Spartans were in shock, and while they sat in the dugout in tears, the Wildcat players were jumping and screaming as if they had won the lottery. Roxy, Gimp and Lisa sat in a corner of the Spartans' dugout and cried. They did not want to be the team that ended the streak, and now they were.

But to some of the first-year players, it seemed like the disappointment was isolated.

"I felt like we kind of just gave up toward the end," Bee recalled. "After the game, there were some tears, but I feel like some of the girls were kind of prepared for losing. And when we all went out to eat, it felt like everyone was talking like nothing had happened. That was more upsetting to me than losing. I felt like no one cared."

Echoed Katie Pence, "I'm a competitor, and I was very upset about the way things happened, because I don't think it was right the way we lost. We battled, but I didn't feel like the whole team was up for the fight."

The Penn College athletic director rushed over to the Spartans' dugout after the game.

"Sorry about that first loss girls, but it was a great game," he gushed. "Thanks for coming up and playing. Great run, sorry we had to end it for you."

Then he turned and left.

Sam addressed the team, and told them not to hang their heads.

"You girls have set a record that won't be broken for a long time," he explained. "You have to be proud of what you've done. Don't beat yourselves up over this. And when you go to school tomorrow, keep your heads high. Be proud, be classy. Don't tarnish this record. Stand up for the fact that you lost, but also for what you have accomplished."

It was a long bus ride back to Bethlehem, punctuated by a phone call Sam made to his son, Nicholas. Told that the team had lost, Nicholas shared his youthful viewpoint with his father. Sam then put the cell phone on speaker, held it out for the girls in the van to hear, and asked Nicholas to repeat what he had just said.

"You guys lost because my dad didn't make you practice enough," Nicholas repeated.

No one argued.

* * * *

Tami was busy working on her papers when she received a text message from teammate Lauren Oswald stating that the team had lost the second game.

"My heart stopped," Tami recalled. "That was my worst fear, the team losing and me not being there."

Later, Sam would console Tami, telling her that she shouldn't feel guilty, and that it wasn't necessarily the pitching that brought the team down. He couldn't ease her pain.

"I felt so guilty for the longest time," Tami said. "It was so hard finding out that they had lost. And I'm not trying to say we would definitely have won if I had been there, but we could have. And that's all I think about."

* * * *

Sam was at his desk the following morning when he heard a knock at the door. It was Dr. Arthur Scott, president of the college.

"He came down four floors from his office," Sam explained. "He didn't call and say, 'Sam, could you come up to my office?' He stopped what he was doing and came down to my office."

Dr. Scott has eyes that reveal his emotions, and that morning, his eyes were sad.

"How are the girls?" Scott asked. "Are they okay? How are they handling this?"

"Dr. Scott, they're devastated, but they'll bounce back," Sam answered.

"And how are you?"

Sam let out a deep breath. "I feel terrible because we ended this thing. I wanted to keep it going."

Scott stepped closer to Sam's desk. "Sam, what you have done, and what the team has done the last two-and-a-half years, has done more for this college than a lot of other things have. It has brought a lot of notoriety and students to this school. And your girls should be nothing but proud of what they've accomplished, on the field and in the classroom."

Sam nodded, searching for the right response, knowing there really wasn't any.

"We'll just start again," the coach said.

Scott reached forward and shook Sam's hand. "If there's anything we can do for the girls, just let me know." Then he turned and left the office.

Fifteen minutes later, Sam received a call from Mardi McGuire-Closson, vice president of student affairs and dean of students at NCC.

"I'm so sorry about what happened," Mardi told Sam. "How are the girls?"

They spoke about all the down time the team had between games, and Mardi said she knew that losing to Penn College had a lot to do with missing all those games.

"Could we have put pressure on those schools to make them play?" she asked.

"Nothing could have made them play because they didn't have enough girls," Sam said.

Then Mardi said something that echoed what many at the college told Sam on that somber Friday morning. "We love you as much today as we did throughout the streak. Nothing has changed. All we have for you and the team is pride."

Sam's eyes teared up as he recalled the conversation.

"The school never turned its back on us," Sam said, emotion etched in his voice. "I was very proud of that."

* * * *

The Spartans rebounded in their final games of the regular season, clobbering Lincoln University and PSU – Abington by scores of 37-0, 15-0, 24-2 and 19-0 in two doubleheader sweeps. They finished the regular season 20-1, a far cry from the number of games they should have played were it not for rainouts and teams disbanding, and won the eastern conference not just by record, but because the other schools had not fielded teams.

They were going to the PCAA state tournament, but who would they play?

Community College of Beaver, the school the Spartans had defeated in three of the last four years to win the state title, had lost to Westmoreland Community College in the WPCC playoffs. But Westmoreland said it was opting to compete in the national championships instead of the state tournament, so it appeared the Spartans would once again face the Titans of Beaver. Sam began making arrangements for the bus trip to Beaver County.

Then controversy set in. Westmoreland learned that the national championships were not being held the same weekend as the state championships. Dick Holler, the Westmoreland athletic director, called Bill Bearse; they wanted to play NCC for the PCAA Championship after all.

"But they already gave it up," Sam said when Bill gave him the news. "Beaver made renovations to their field so that they could host the tournament."

It went to a vote by the PCAA committee, and Beaver was voted out. The Spartans would play the Wolfpack. Sam began changing all the bus and hotel arrangements.

* * * *

It was nearly 3:30 p.m. on Friday, May 4, when the Easton Coach bus pulled into the NCC parking lot. The players and coaches loaded their equipment and boarded the bus, along with several of the players' parents who were making the trip.

The bus arrived at NCC more than thirty minutes late, adding to Sam's anxiety. Since the EPCC Championships were not played, the Spartans had not experienced game conditions in almost ten days. They had practiced, but practicing is not the same as playing, and Sam remembered what happened the last time his team had experienced a long layoff. He also received a scouting report on the Westmoreland Wolfpack from other coaches. The team wasn't strong offensively, but they had a dominant freshman pitcher. Sam knew the Spartans hadn't seen a dominant pitcher since the Orlando tournament, and he was worried.

The four-hour bus ride to Westmoreland County took nearly six hours. The bus driver, fatigued from having just come off his regular day job, drove slower than usual and stopped three times along the route. Frequently, the bus swayed onto the shoulder of the highway for extended periods of time, and Sam kept a close watch to make sure the driver hadn't fallen asleep behind the wheel.

The team passed the time watching "A League of Their Own" on DVD—an uplifting film meant to rouse the troops. But it was a quiet bus ride, and that same, somber mood was evident the following morning as the Spartans began warming up on the grass adjacent to the field at Westmoreland Community College. For many, the motivation to play was gone, eroded by a season rife with team controversy and cut virtually in half by weather and other circumstances that were out of their control.

They would play, but it was clear many just wanted the season over with.

On top of that, the coaching staff was not at full strength. Pic had resigned as an assistant coach earlier in the season, and Janess was busy preparing for finals and graduation. Without them, Sam felt naked and vulnerable.

"At the end of the season, when we needed the most help, we were losing people," Sam recalled. "Pic is the guy who, if my head is spinning, will tell me the truth no matter what. He won't tell me what I want to hear, he'll tell me what I *need* to hear. Losing Pic was like losing my right arm."

Janess had been the link to the championship teams of the prior years, and she could talk to and motivate the girls because she has been there, and in turn they looked up to her. "She was the one who could get the girls going," said Sam. "She was intensity and calm at the same time. Now, emotionally, every phase of the team was drying up."

* * * *

Westmoreland's freshman pitcher was everything the scouting report said she was. She was fast, and her pitches had movement. She retired the Spartans in order in the top of the first, and when the Wolfpack scored a run off Tami in the home half on a double and two groundouts, it looked like that was all Lindberg might need.

The Spartans tied the game at 1-1 in the third on a run-scoring double by Lisa Klinger, and for a moment the team was alive. The girls stood at the dugout fence, kicking and screaming and cheering each other on. For that moment, it seemed like 2005 and 2006 all over again.

But the cheering would be short-lived, and Lisa's double would be the Spartans only hit of the game. With two out in the fifth inning, NCC's defense got charitable. A single up the middle was followed by a looping single to right, with the lead runner advancing to third. On right fielder Kristy Kroll's throw to third, the batter raced for second. Third baseman Katie Bee's throw to second sailed into right field, allowing the lead run to score. A double plated another run, and the Wolfpack had a 3-1 lead.

The runs stood up.

"The Wolfpack's pitcher is a good ballplayer," Sam said following the first-game loss. "She's a good pitcher. She was throwing at least in the mid-sixties, and she had control. And I'd rather get beat in a game like that by a pitcher like that than to get blown out."

History would shortly repeat itself.

Jamie Rider started the second game in the pitcher's circle for NCC and gave up an unearned run in the first inning on shortstop Jenna Turner's throwing error.

When the Spartans came in from the field for their turn at bat, the team gathered in a huddle outside the dugout.

"This is our damn state championship game," Roxy shouted, angry at the lack of enthusiasm and looking to spark the team. "Let's start playing like we know that."

But it didn't happen. There was no motivation.

"You would try to get everyone off the bench, get them up and cheering," Lisa reflected. "But even me, I couldn't get up and cheer because I could see the disappointment in the players' faces, in the coaches' faces. It was like, wow, crappy season down the drain."

Jamie had to leave the game in the second inning when she was hit square in the left knee by a line drive back to the pitching circle. Tami relieved and pitched well, giving up only an RBI double in the fourth.

But the Wolfpack's freshman pitcher was even more over-powering than in the first game. She did not surrender a hit until Roxy doubled with two out in the Spartan seventh.

"We tried to bunt on her, but we just couldn't get the bunts down," Sam said, explaining the team's second-game strategy. "And when we did get them down, that pitcher was all over them."

After Roxy's double, Bee bounced to first, and in a race for the bag, dove head first but came up short for the final out in the Wolfpack's 2-0 win, officially ending the Spartan's season.

The girls sat in the dugout, heads hung low, tears flowing freely. Bee, ever the warrior, was more angry than sad.

"I remember in Florida, one of our captains said that she didn't even feel like being there, and it was only our second game," Bee recalled. "That was the attitude, against some of the teams we played. They just took things for granted. And that's how it felt at the state game. I never traveled for softball, so it was all so cool to me. But all I heard from some of the players was that they wanted to go home; that they didn't want to play another game. Why would they give up? Why would they even say that?"

Those questions would go unanswered.

* * * *

The Easton Coach bus pulled out of the Fairfield Inn parking lot in Westmoreland County shortly after 10 a.m. Sunday morning. The Spartans were headed home, but Sam had a small detour in mind, the destination of which he kept secret from the girls.

An hour later, the bus turned off the highway and wove its way along the back roads of western Pennsylvania's Somerset County until it came to Skyline Road. One mile later, the bus pulled into the parking lot of the Flight 93 National Memorial.

A cold wind blew across the open field as the players, coaches and parents toured the memorial. A tour guide chronicled the events that transpired on the morning of September 11, 2001, when Flight 93, a Boeing 757 that left Newark International Airport bound for San Francisco, crashed at 580 miles per hour into the field adjacent to where they were presently standing. There were no survivors.

When the tour guide finished, the Easton Coach bus driver took out a small American flag and asked all the players, coaches and parents to sign their names. Then he and Sam pinned the flag to the forty-foot-long fence that, along with other flags, flowers, handwritten messages and assorted artwork, had become a lasting tribute to the heroes of Flight 93.

It was an emotional visit, but an appropriate one for a women's softball team that had just experienced a disappointing end to a fragmented season. It sent a message that life can be preciously short, and nothing should ever be taken for granted. As the passengers and crew of Flight 93 should be cheered for their bravery rather than mourned for their death, so should the Spartans remember the good that they accomplished.

"We did something wonderful," Sam explained. "These girls can take this and tell their grandchildren about it. They can embellish it if they want, but the fact still remains that we did it. I know that on April 1, on our field, we beat a softball team and won our ninety-third game in a row. And nobody can say we didn't."

EPILOGUE

Sam couldn't sit still. He moved from table to table, talking to each of the girls in between courses at Buca di Beppo Restaurant in Whitehall. It was the end of the season team dinner, and with six of the girls graduating and others moving on to other schools, it was—in all likelihood—the last time the team would be together as a whole.

It was with mixed emotions that Sam spoke. The season had been a historic one, punctuated by a record-setting winning streak that transcended parts of three seasons. It had also been a disappointing season, marred by a fractured schedule and fragmented team spirit. In many respects, it felt like 2004 all over again, and for that Sam felt responsible. But as he walked among his players, Sam chose his words carefully and opted to accentuate the positive wherever possible.

He told them how proud he was of them, handling the pressures and the challenges of the season that began with the first games in Orlando and continued to build with each passing game. He thanked them, and reminded them that they now had stories to tell their children and their grandchildren.

Then he apologized. He apologized for getting so caught up in the streak that he forgot about being a coach; forgot about the importance of having his team fully prepared for each and every game. He apologized for losing sight of the bigger picture—winning a third consecutive state title—for the truncated season and a schedule that had more holes in it than an old, moth-eaten sweater.

And he apologized to the girls who were moving on.

"I can't go back and change anything; I can't make it right for those of you second-year players who won't be here next year," Sam said. "All I can do is promise those of you who will be coming back that it will be different. And that I will be a better coach."

Then he handed out special gifts to the six second-year players. New uniforms were being ordered for next season, so Sam took each girl's old uniform jersey, mounted it to foam core backing with the girl's name and position pasted below in large, sans serif typeface, and had it framed. Memories encased in class that would last a lifetime.

Outside the restaurant, the girls, Sam and his assistant coaches gathered for one last team photograph. He hugged each of the girls, then watched as they got in their cars and went their separate ways. It was a familiar scene, replayed around the same time each year. But it was never easy saying good-bye.

* * * *

Tami sat on a bar stool, sipping a drink and talking with friends. Mostly, it was Tami doing the talking; mulling the decision of whether or not to play softball for another season. It helped to think things out loud rather than keep them bottled up inside; it was therapeutic.

"I had this agreement with myself that if we had won states, I wasn't going to come back," Tami said for her friends' ears as well as her own. "These players are a lot younger, and all that drama, it was too much for me. So if we won, I was not coming back. I would have proven to myself that I could still do it, and I would have been satisfied."

"But, you didn't win," one of her friends offered.

Slowly, Tami shook her head from side to side. "No, we didn't win. But I'm still going back and forth. Can I do this? Can I juggle school and softball?"

No one answered Tami's question. Her friends allowed the words to hang there in mid air for a few moments; allowed some time to pass for Tami to soak in those words and answer the questions herself.

Finally, one friend broke the silence.

"So, are you playing next year?" he asked.

Right then, as if a light bulb had just gone on, a clear realization came over Tami's face.

"Who am I kidding?" she asked no one in particular. "I'm playing. It's my last chance. Everyone else may be advancing to other schools, but I'll be working after next year. And I guess I still need to prove it to myself."

She lifted her glass and took a long, hard swallow, then emphatically placed it down on the bar.

"I'm going for states," she announced.

It would be music to Sam's ears, and would result in a fairy tale ending to Tami's college softball career. The following spring, Tami hurt her shoulder in the first inning of the first game the Spartans played in Myrtle Beach, but she refused to stop playing. She rested her shoulder by playing first or second base, then slowly worked her pitching arm back into shape from mid-season on. She would end up pitching a solid eight innings in the Spartans' 5-4 win over Westmoreland Community College in the state championship series, exacting revenge for the previous year's defeat. With an 8-0 win in the second game, the Spartans had another title, and Tami had her state championship.

* * * *

If there was a darker day to the season than having the consecutive win streak halted, it came in June when Sam learned that athletic director Bill Bearse planned to retire in December. Bill had diabetes, and after thirty-five years at the college, he was tired and his health had begun to decline. It was time to move on.

"Bill's the person who hired me, and he has always been in my corner," Sam explained. "Now, hearing that he's retiring, I don't know what it's going to be like coming in each morning and not seeing him at his desk."

Sam, a notorious creature of habit, was also very uncomfortable with change.

"He knows me and I know him," Sam said of Bearse, "and we've worked very well together. I don't know who's coming in, but I hope the person taking the position is the same understanding, workable kind of person that Bill has always been."

Bearse's retirement would leave more than a void at the athletic director position. He was also sports management director, bowling and golf coach, and president of the EPCC.

"He is going to be missed around here more than he understands," Sam explained. "Bill has been a pillar in this school. He is the reason for the success of our softball team. If it wasn't for his guidance and presence, most of what we accomplished would not have happened."

Bearse's retirement was still six months away, but Sam missed him already.

* * * *

It was mid June, and the halls of the Spartan Center were so quiet they echoed from the slightest sound. Sam sat in his office talking to a local reporter for a wrap-up story on the team and the season. It was an easy interview; few questions needed to be asked. Sam had a lot on his mind.

"I should have taken Gimp as captain," Sam said, reflecting on what may have been an error in judgment early in preseason. "She had that little chip on her shoulder, but she was driven. She would have gotten people to do things; she would have driven the team. But then I heard the backlash from the coaches. 'No, she has too much of an attitude.' This is where I have to make decisions on my own and live or die with them."

Sam had also considered naming Kristy as a captain, but was told, "No first-year girls as captains." He should have trusted his instincts, he said. The discipline she learned in the military would have made her an excellent captain.

"She's quiet," Sam admitted, "but you put her in a position of leadership and she will run with that ball and never drop it. You don't have to be loud to be a captain, just perform and lead by example."

Sam felt badly that, compared with prior seasons, the team played so few games in 2007—just 23, to be exact. He felt badly for the girls.

"There were girls I wanted to see enjoy the season, because it was their last," Sam continued. "I feel bad for Rox, because I know she cared, and I wanted this to be a great season for her. And Pence," who had informed Sam she would be transferring to nearby Lehigh University to continue her academic and athletic career, "that girl is so driven and so motivated ..."

His voice trailed off, lost in mid thought.

The reporter was about to ask a question when Sam pointed to the bulletin board on the wall alongside his desk. Pinned to the board were the lineup cards from the state championship games against Westmoreland Community College. Across the cards were the phrases, "Be a better coach," "Don't lose focus," and "Always have your team prepared." They were motivational words that Sam had written, a reminder of the different course he would take as coach next season.

"I know from my coaching perspective it's going to be different, because I'm going to drive them the whole time," Sam promised. "I'm not going to be a bastard, I'm not going to yell and scream, but I'm going to push the girls more and we're going to do more. We're just going to keep working. I've already sent out for several DVDs so I can learn more about being a coach. More drills during practices . . . we'll have cardio days where all we do is run or throw or pitch, then batting days, then defensive days . . . but we're going to do cardio every day. We're going to run every day. It may be that one day the bulk of the time is running, and other days just a piece of it will be running, but I'm going to work them a lot harder than we did last year."

Then Sam's softer side caught up with him, and he remembered that NCC is an academic institution first.

"What worries me is the class load that these kids have, and the fact that many of them are also working," the coach explained, back-peddling just a bit. "I don't want to put too much on them. So once the season starts, if we play every Tuesday, Thursday, Saturday and Sunday, I'll just have one practice during the week. Otherwise, they won't have time for their classwork."

Sam said he also learned a lot from the drama and controversy that was an undercurrent with the 2007 team, and he would carry those lessons through in the way he recruited for future teams.

"I now am looking for girls who are disciplined," the coach explained. "I'm not just looking for the athletes. I now watch them when they go on the benches, and how they deal with their teammates. When something goes wrong in a game, how do they come off the field and treat their teammates? How do they treat their coaches? Do they motivate all the time, or get pissed off and sit down? And I've seen a few who were great athletes, and I just turned and went to the next game. I'm not going to have that anymore, where they go to the bench and they yell at their coaches or teammates, or they're sitting down at one end of the bench and pouting while their teammates are at the other end yelling and screaming. I don't want that. I've got enough girls on this team, athletic-wise and discipline-wise, that if one of they has a problem and can't fit in, goodbye. And if I have to cut this team down to fourteen, they'll be the fourteen best players you've ever seen on the softball field. That's what I'm looking for now—disciplined young ladies who know how to play the game, want to play the game, and have a passion. I want a team player, not an individual player. I won't settle for anything else anymore."

Sam reflected on the season—on a lot of what took place off the field. His two older sons, Tony and Sammy, had begun coming to games on a regular basis. The same way Sam used to drive one-and-a-half hours to watch Tony as a youngster, his son was now doing the same. Everything had come full circle.

And when the Lady Spartans broke the record for consecutive collegiate wins, both Tony and Sammy told their father that they were proud of him.

"It made me feel complete," Sam recalled.

But back on the field, there were still a lot of what-if questions running through his mind. What if the team had played a regular, consistent schedule, would they have lost to Penn College? Would they have lost to Westmoreland? Might they still be undefeated with about 120-plus consecutive wins to their credit?

It was Monday morning quarterbacking, and Sam knew better. He shook his head.

"That's what life is all about," Sam said, waxing philosophically. "It's not about how many times you get knocked down, it matters that you get up one more time and keep fighting. That's what we've done, and that's what we'll continue to do."

ACKNOWLEDGMENTS

ABOUT THE AUTHORS

 **SAM CARRODO** was the head softball coach at Northampton Community College from 1998 until 2010. During his 13-year tenure, the softball team compiled a record of 307-63, won five Eastern Pennsylvania titles (2003, 2005, 2006, 2007 and 2008) and four State Championship titles (2003, 2005, 2006 and 2008). Sam has been named EPCC Coach of the Year five times (2003, 2005, 2006, 2007 and 2008), and PCAA State Coach of the Year four times (2003, 2005, 2006 and 2008). He is currently head coach at Liberty High School, a position he has held since 2015, where he was named Coach of the Year in 2015, 2017 and 2024. A graduate of Bethlehem Catholic High School, Sam has also served as assistant football coach at Bethlehem Catholic from 1994 – 2004, and JV softball coach, also at his alma mater. Sam was recently inducted into the Patriot's Park Hall of Fame. He lost his wife Chris in 2022 to brain cancer.

 **ED RABINOWITZ** is a communications professional with more than 45 years of writing experience under his belt. He has served as Publications Manager, and Eastern Public Relations Manager for Volkswagen of America, and Director of Marketing Communications for Continental Insurance. In addition to extensive freelance writing in the healthcare, and personal finance and investing fields, Ed is an award-winning journalist who has covered high school and college sports in Pennsylvania's Lehigh Valley. He has also published two books: *One More Dance*, a nonfiction memoir; and *Bloodline*, based on his experience as an adoptee discovering his biologic family. He recently retired from Lehigh Carbon Community College where he taught communication courses for 15 years.

Printed in the USA
CPSIA information can be obtained
at www.ICGtesting.com
JSHW021737180824
68297JS00003B/93